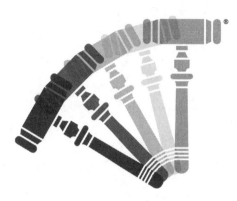

## *Casenote®* *Legal Briefs*

# LABOR LAW

Keyed to Courses Using

**Cox, Bok, Gorman, and Finkin's**
**Labor Law**

Fifteenth Edition

Wolters Kluwer

Law & Business

Copyright © 2011 CCH Incorporated. All Rights Reserved.
*www.wolterskluwerlb.com*

Published by Wolters Kluwer Law & Business in New York.

Wolters Kluwer Law & Business serves customers worldwide with CCH, Aspen Publishers, and Kluwer Law International products.

To contact Customer Service, e-mail customer.service@wolterskluwer.com, call 1-800-234-1660, fax 1-800-901-9075, or mail correspondence to:

Wolters Kluwer Law & Business
Attn: Order Department
P.O. Box 990
Frederick, MD 21705

Printed in the United States of America.

1 2 3 4 5 6 7 8 9 0

ISBN 978-1-4548-0787-2

SUSTAINABLE FORESTRY INITIATIVE
Certified Chain of Custody
Promoting Sustainable Forestry
www.sfiprogram.org
SFI-00756

## About Wolters Kluwer Law & Business

Wolters Kluwer Law & Business is a leading global provider of intelligent information and digital solutions for legal and business professionals in key specialty areas, and respected educational resources for professors and law students. Wolters Kluwer Law & Business connects legal and business professionals as well as those in the education market with timely, specialized authoritative content and information-enabled solutions to support success through productivity, accuracy and mobility.

Serving customers worldwide, Wolters Kluwer Law & Business products include those under the Aspen Publishers, CCH, Kluwer Law International, Loislaw, Best Case, ftwilliam.com and MediRegs family of products.

**CCH** products have been a trusted resource since 1913, and are highly regarded resources for legal, securities, antitrust and trade regulation, government contracting, banking, pension, payroll, employment and labor, and healthcare reimbursement and compliance professionals.

**Aspen Publishers** products provide essential information to attorneys, business professionals and law students. Written by preeminent authorities, the product line offers analytical and practical information in a range of specialty practice areas from securities law and intellectual property to mergers and acquisitions and pension/benefits. Aspen's trusted legal education resources provide professors and students with high-quality, up-to-date and effective resources for successful instruction and study in all areas of the law.

**Kluwer Law International** products provide the global business community with reliable international legal information in English. Legal practitioners, corporate counsel and business executives around the world rely on Kluwer Law journals, looseleafs, books, and electronic products for comprehensive information in many areas of international legal practice.

**Loislaw** is a comprehensive online legal research product providing legal content to law firm practitioners of various specializations. Loislaw provides attorneys with the ability to quickly and efficiently find the necessary legal information they need, when and where they need it, by facilitating access to primary law as well as state-specific law, records, forms and treatises.

**Best Case Solutions** is the leading bankruptcy software product to the bankruptcy industry. It provides software and workflow tools to flawlessly streamline petition preparation and the electronic filing process, while timely incorporating ever-changing court requirements.

**ftwilliam.com** offers employee benefits professionals the highest quality plan documents (retirement, welfare and non-qualified) and government forms (5500/PBGC, 1099 and IRS) software at highly competitive prices.

**MediRegs** products provide integrated health care compliance content and software solutions for professionals in healthcare, higher education and life sciences, including professionals in accounting, law and consulting.

Wolters Kluwer Law & Business, a division of Wolters Kluwer, is head-quartered in New York. Wolters Kluwer is a market-leading global information services company focused on professionals.

# Format for the Casenote® Legal Brief

**Nature of Case:** This section identifies the form of action (e.g., breach of contract, negligence, battery), the type of proceeding (e.g., demurrer, appeal from trial court's jury instructions), or the relief sought (e.g., damages, injunction, criminal sanctions).

**Fact Summary:** This is included to refresh your memory and can be used as a quick reminder of the facts.

**Rule of Law:** Summarizes the general principle of law that the case illustrates. It may be used for instant recall of the court's holding and for classroom discussion or home review.

**Facts:** This section contains all relevant facts of the case, including the contentions of the parties and the lower court holdings. It is written in a logical order to give the student a clear understanding of the case. The plaintiff and defendant are identified by their proper names throughout and are always labeled with a (P) or (D).

## Palsgraf v. Long Island R.R. Co.

Injured bystander (P) v. Railroad company (D)

N.Y. Ct. App., 248 N.Y. 339, 162 N.E. 99 (1928).

**NATURE OF CASE:** Appeal from judgment affirming verdict for plaintiff seeking damages for personal injury.

**FACT SUMMARY:** Helen Palsgraf (P) was injured on R.R.'s (D) train platform when R.R.'s (D) guard helped a passenger aboard a moving train, causing his package to fall on the tracks. The package contained fireworks which exploded, creating a shock that tipped a scale onto Palsgraf (P).

 **RULE OF LAW**
The risk reasonably to be perceived defines the duty to be obeyed.

**FACTS:** Helen Palsgraf (P) purchased a ticket to Rockaway Beach from R.R. (D) and was waiting on the train platform. As she waited, two men ran to catch a train that was pulling out from the platform. The first man jumped aboard, but the second man, who appeared as if he might fall, was helped aboard by the guard on the train who had kept the door open so they could jump aboard. A guard on the platform also helped by pushing him onto the train. The man was carrying a package wrapped in newspaper. In the process, the man dropped his package, which fell on the tracks. The package contained fireworks and exploded. The shock of the explosion was apparently of great enough strength to tip over some scales at the other end of the platform, which fell on Palsgraf (P) and injured her. A jury awarded her damages, and R.R. (D) appealed.

**ISSUE:** Does the risk reasonably to be perceived define the duty to be obeyed?

**HOLDING AND DECISION:** (Cardozo, C.J.) Yes. The risk reasonably to be perceived defines the duty to be obeyed. If there is no foreseeable hazard to the injured party as the result of a seemingly innocent act, the act does not become a tort because it happened to be a wrong as to another. If the wrong was not willful, the plaintiff must show that the act as to her had such great and apparent possibilities of danger as to entitle her to protection. Negligence in the abstract is not enough upon which to base liability. Negligence is a relative concept, evolving out of the common law doctrine of trespass on the case. To establish liability, the defendant must owe a legal duty of reasonable care to the injured party. A cause of action in tort will lie where harm,

though unintended, could have been averted or avoided by observance of such a duty. The scope of the duty is limited by the range of danger that a reasonable person could foresee. In this case, there was nothing to suggest from the appearance of the parcel or otherwise that the parcel contained fireworks. The guard could not reasonably have had any warning of a threat to Palsgraf (P), and R.R. (D) therefore cannot be held liable. Judgment is reversed in favor of R.R. (D).

**DISSENT:** (Andrews, J.) The concept that there is no negligence unless R.R. (D) owes a legal duty to take care as to Palsgraf (P) herself is too narrow. Everyone owes to the world at large the duty of refraining from those acts that may unreasonably threaten the safety of others. If the guard's action was negligent as to those nearby, it was also negligent as to those outside what might be termed the "danger zone." For Palsgraf (P) to recover, R.R.'s (D) negligence must have been the proximate cause of her injury, a question of fact for the jury.

> **ANALYSIS**
The majority defined the limit of the defendant's liability in terms of the danger that a reasonable person in defendant's situation would have perceived. The dissent argued that the limitation should not be placed on liability, but rather on damages. Judge Andrews suggested that only injuries that would not have happened but for R.R.'s (D) negligence should be compensable. Both the majority and dissent recognized the policy-driven need to limit liability for negligent acts, seeking, in the words of Judge Andrews, to define a framework "that will be practical and in keeping with the general understanding of mankind." The Restatement (Second) of Torts has accepted Judge Cardozo's view.

### Quicknotes

**FORESEEABILITY** A reasonable expectation that change is the probable result of certain acts or omissions.

**NEGLIGENCE** Conduct falling below the standard of care that a reasonable person would demonstrate under similar conditions.

**PROXIMATE CAUSE** The natural sequence of events without which an injury would not have been sustained.

---

**Party ID:** Quick identification of the relationship between the parties.

**Concurrence/Dissent:** All concurrences and dissents are briefed whenever they are included by the casebook editor.

**Analysis:** This last paragraph gives you a broad understanding of where the case "fits in" with other cases in the section of the book and with the entire course. It is a hornbook-style discussion indicating whether the case is a majority or minority opinion and comparing the principal case with other cases in the casebook. It may also provide analysis from restatements, uniform codes, and law review articles. The analysis will prove to be invaluable to classroom discussion.

**Issue:** The issue is a concise question that brings out the essence of the opinion as it relates to the section of the casebook in which the case appears. Both substantive and procedural issues are included if relevant to the decision.

**Holding and Decision:** This section offers a clear and in-depth discussion of the rule of the case and the court's rationale. It is written in easy-to-understand language and answers the issue presented by applying the law to the facts of the case. When relevant, it includes a thorough discussion of the exceptions to the case as listed by the court, any major cites to the other cases on point, and the names of the judges who wrote the decisions.

**Quicknotes:** Conveniently defines legal terms found in the case and summarizes the nature of any statutes, codes, or rules referred to in the text.

Wolters Kluwer Law & Business is proud to offer *Casenote*® *Legal Briefs*—continuing thirty years of publishing America's best-selling legal briefs.

*Casenote*® *Legal Briefs* are designed to help you save time when briefing assigned cases. Organized under convenient headings, they show you how to abstract the basic facts and holdings from the text of the actual opinions handed down by the courts. Used as part of a rigorous study regimen, they can help you spend more time analyzing and critiquing points of law than on copying bits and pieces of judicial opinions into your notebook or outline.

*Casenote*® *Legal Briefs* should never be used as a substitute for assigned casebook readings. They work best when read as a follow-up to reviewing the underlying opinions themselves. Students who try to avoid reading and digesting the judicial opinions in their casebooks or online sources will end up shortchanging themselves in the long run. The ability to absorb, critique, and restate the dynamic and complex elements of case law decisions is crucial to your success in law school and beyond. It cannot be developed vicariously.

*Casenote*® *Legal Briefs* represents but one of the many offerings in Legal Education's Study Aid Timeline, which includes:

- *Casenote*® *Legal Briefs*
- *Emanuel Law Outlines*
- *Examples & Explanations* Series
- *Introduction to Law* Series
- Emanuel *Law in a Flash* Flash Cards
- Emanuel *CrunchTime* Series

Each of these series is designed to provide you with easy-to-understand explanations of complex points of law. Each volume offers guidance on the principles of legal analysis and, consulted regularly, will hone your ability to spot relevant issues. We have titles that will help you prepare for class, prepare for your exams, and enhance your general comprehension of the law along the way.

To find out more about Wolters Kluwer Law & Business' study aid publications, visit us online at *www.wolterskluwerlb.com* or email us at *legaledu@wolterskluwer.com*. We'll be happy to assist you.

# Get this Casenote® Legal Brief as an AspenLaw Studydesk eBook today!

By returning this form to Wolters Kluwer Law & Business, you will receive a complimentary eBook download of this Casenote® Legal Brief and AspenLaw Studydesk productivity software.* Learn more about AspenLaw Studydesk today at *www.wolterskluwerlb.com*.

| Name | Phone ( ) |
|---|---|
| Address | Apt. No. |
| City | State | ZIP Code |
| Law School | Graduation Date  Month _____ Year _____ |

Cut out the UPC found on the lower left corner of the back cover of this book. Staple the UPC inside this box. Only the original UPC from the book cover will be accepted. (No photocopies or store stickers are allowed.)

**Attach UPC inside this box.**

**Email** (Print legibly or you may not get access!)

**Title of this book** (course subject)

**ISBN of this book** (10- or 13-digit number on the UPC)

**Used with which casebook** (provide author's name)

**Mail the completed form to:**       Wolters Kluwer Law & Business
Legal Education Division
130 Turner Street, Bldg 3, 4th Floor
Waltham, MA 02453-8901

* Upon receipt of this completed form, you will be emailed a code for the digital download of this book in AspenLaw Studydesk eBook format and a free copy of the software application, which is required to read the eBook.

**For a full list of eBook study aids available for AspenLaw Studydesk software and other resources that will help you with your law school studies, visit *www.wolterskluwerlb.com*.**

Make a photocopy of this form and your UPC for your records.

For detailed information on the use of the information you provide on this form, please see the PRIVACY POLICY at *www.wolterskluwerlb.com*.

# How to Brief a Case

## A. Decide on a Format and Stick to It

Structure is essential to a good brief. It enables you to arrange systematically the related parts that are scattered throughout most cases, thus making manageable and understandable what might otherwise seem to be an endless and unfathomable sea of information. There are, of course, an unlimited number of formats that can be utilized. However, it is best to find one that suits your needs and stick to it. Consistency breeds both efficiency and the security that when called upon you will know where to look in your brief for the information you are asked to give.

Any format, as long as it presents the essential elements of a case in an organized fashion, can be used. Experience, however, has led *Casenote*® *Legal Briefs* to develop and utilize the following format because of its logical flow and universal applicability.

**NATURE OF CASE:** This is a brief statement of the legal character and procedural status of the case (e.g., "Appeal of a burglary conviction").

There are many different alternatives open to a litigant dissatisfied with a court ruling. The key to determining which one has been used is to discover *who is asking this court for what.*

This first entry in the brief should be kept as *short as possible.* Use the court's terminology if you understand it. But since jurisdictions vary as to the titles of pleadings, the best entry is the one that addresses who wants what in this proceeding, not the one that sounds most like the court's language.

**RULE OF LAW:** A statement of the general principle of law that the case illustrates (e.g., "An acceptance that varies any term of the offer is considered a rejection and counteroffer").

Determining the rule of law of a case is a procedure similar to determining the issue of the case. Avoid being fooled by red herrings; there may be a few rules of law mentioned in the case excerpt, but usually only one is *the* rule with which the casebook editor is concerned. The techniques used to locate the issue, described below, may also be utilized to find the rule of law. Generally, your best guide is simply the chapter heading. It is a clue to the point the casebook editor seeks to make and should be kept in mind when reading every case in the respective section.

**FACTS:** A synopsis of only the essential facts of the case, i.e., those bearing upon or leading up to the issue.

The facts entry should be a short statement of the events and transactions that led one party to initiate legal proceedings against another in the first place. While some cases conveniently state the salient facts at the beginning of the decision, in other instances they will have to be culled from hiding places throughout the text, even from concurring and dissenting opinions. Some of the "facts" will often be in dispute and should be so noted. Conflicting evidence may be briefly pointed up. "Hard" facts must be included. Both must be *relevant* in order to be listed in the facts entry. It is impossible to tell what is relevant until the entire case is read, as the ultimate determination of the rights and liabilities of the parties may turn on something buried deep in the opinion.

Generally, the facts entry should not be longer than three to five *short* sentences.

It is often helpful to identify the role played by a party in a given context. For example, in a construction contract case the identification of a party as the "contractor" or "builder" alleviates the need to tell that that party was the one who was supposed to have built the house.

It is always helpful, and a good general practice, to identify the "plaintiff" and the "defendant." This may seem elementary and uncomplicated, but, especially in view of the creative editing practiced by some casebook editors, it is sometimes a difficult or even impossible task. Bear in mind that the *party presently* seeking something from this court may not be the plaintiff, and that sometimes only the cross-claim of a defendant is treated in the excerpt. Confusing or misaligning the parties can ruin your analysis and understanding of the case.

**ISSUE:** A statement of the general legal question answered by or illustrated in the case. For clarity, the issue is best put in the form of a question capable of a "yes" or "no" answer. In reality, the issue is simply the Rule of Law put in the form of a question (e.g., "May an offer be accepted by performance?").

The major problem presented in discerning what is *the* issue in the case is that an opinion usually purports to raise and answer several questions. However, except for rare cases, only one such question is really the issue in the case. Collateral issues not necessary to the resolution of the matter in controversy are handled by the court by language known as *"obiter dictum"* or merely *"dictum."* While dicta may be included later in the brief, they have no place under the issue heading.

To find the issue, ask *who wants what* and then go on to ask *why did that party succeed or fail in getting it.* Once this is determined, the "why" should be turned into a question.

The complexity of the issues in the cases will vary, but in all cases a single-sentence question should sum up the issue. *In a few cases,* there will be two, or even more rarely, three issues of equal importance to the resolution of the case. Each should be expressed in a single-sentence question.

Since many issues are resolved by a court in coming to a final disposition of a case, the casebook editor will reproduce the portion of the opinion containing the issue or issues most relevant to the area of law under scrutiny. A noted law professor gave this advice: "Close the book; look at the title on the cover." Chances are, if it is Property, you need not concern yourself with whether, for example, the federal government's treatment of the plaintiff's land really raises a federal question sufficient to support jurisdiction on this ground in federal court.

The same rule applies to chapter headings designating sub-areas within the subjects. They tip you off as to what the text is designed to teach. The cases are arranged in a casebook to show a progression or development of the law, so that the preceding cases may also help.

It is also most important to remember to *read the notes and questions* at the end of a case to determine what the editors wanted you to have gleaned from it.

**HOLDING AND DECISION:** This section should succinctly explain the rationale of the court in arriving at its decision. In capsulizing the "reasoning" of the court, it should always include an application of the general rule or rules of law to the specific facts of the case. Hidden justifications come to light in this entry: the reasons for the state of the law, the public policies, the biases and prejudices, those considerations that influence the justices' thinking and, ultimately, the outcome of the case. At the end, there should be a short indication of the disposition or procedural resolution of the case (e.g., "Decision of the trial court for Mr. Smith (P) reversed").

The foregoing format is designed to help you "digest" the reams of case material with which you will be faced in your law school career. Once mastered by practice, it will place at your fingertips the information the authors of your casebooks have sought to impart to you in case-by-case illustration and analysis.

## B. Be as Economical as Possible in Briefing Cases

Once armed with a format that encourages succinctness, it is as important to be economical with regard to the time spent on the actual reading of the case as it is to be economical in the writing of the brief itself. This does not mean "skimming" a case. Rather, it means reading the case with an "eye" trained to recognize into which "section" of your brief a particular passage or line fits and having a system for quickly and precisely marking the case so that the passages fitting any one particular part of

the brief can be easily identified and brought together in a concise and accurate manner when the brief is actually written.

It is of no use to simply repeat everything in the opinion of the court; record only enough information to trigger your recollection of what the court said. Nevertheless, an accurate statement of the "law of the case," i.e., the legal principle applied to the facts, is absolutely essential to class preparation and to learning the law under the case method.

To that end, it is important to develop a "shorthand" that you can use to make marginal notations. These notations will tell you at a glance in which section of the brief you will be placing that particular passage or portion of the opinion.

Some students prefer to underline all the salient portions of the opinion (with a pencil or colored underliner marker), making marginal notations as they go along. Others prefer the color-coded method of underlining, utilizing different colors of markers to underline the salient portions of the case, each separate color being used to represent a different section of the brief. For example, blue underlining could be used for passages relating to the rule of law, yellow for those relating to the issue, and green for those relating to the holding and decision, etc. While it has its advocates, the color-coded method can be confusing and time-consuming (all that time spent on changing colored markers). Furthermore, it can interfere with the continuity and concentration many students deem essential to the reading of a case for maximum comprehension. In the end, however, it is a matter of personal preference and style. Just remember, whatever method you use, underlining must be used sparingly or its value is lost.

If you take the marginal notation route, an efficient and easy method is to go along underlining the key portions of the case and placing in the margin alongside them the following "markers" to indicate where a particular passage or line "belongs" in the brief you will write:

N (NATURE OF CASE)
RL (RULE OF LAW)
I (ISSUE)
HL (HOLDING AND DECISION, relates to the RULE OF LAW behind the decision)
HR (HOLDING AND DECISION, gives the RATIONALE or reasoning behind the decision)
HA (HOLDING AND DECISION, APPLIES the general principle(s) of law to the facts of the case to arrive at the decision)

Remember that a particular passage may well contain information necessary to more than one part of your brief, in which case you simply note that in the margin. If you are using the color-coded underlining method instead of marginal notation, simply make asterisks or checks in the margin next to the passage in question in the colors that indicate the additional sections of the brief where it might be utilized.

The economy of utilizing "shorthand" in marking cases for briefing can be maintained in the actual brief writing process itself by utilizing "law student shorthand" within the brief. There are many commonly used words and phrases for which abbreviations can be substituted in your briefs (and in your class notes also). You can develop abbreviations that are personal to you and which will save you a lot of time. A reference list of briefing abbreviations can be found on page xii of this book.

## C. Use Both the Briefing Process and the Brief as a Learning Tool

Now that you have a format and the tools for briefing cases efficiently, the most important thing is to make the time spent in briefing profitable to you and to make the most advantageous use of the briefs you create. Of course, the briefs are invaluable for classroom reference when you are called upon to explain or analyze a particular case. However, they are also useful in reviewing for exams. A quick glance at the fact summary should bring the case to mind, and a rereading of the rule of law should enable you to go over the underlying legal concept in your mind, how it was applied in that particular case, and how it might apply in other factual settings.

As to the value to be derived from engaging in the briefing process itself, there is an immediate benefit that arises from being forced to sift through the essential facts and reasoning from the court's opinion and to succinctly express them in your own words in your brief. The process ensures that you understand the case and the point that it illustrates, and that means you will be ready to absorb further analysis and information brought forth in class. It also ensures you will have something to say when called upon in class. The briefing process helps develop a mental agility for getting to the *gist* of a case and for identifying, expounding on, and applying the legal concepts and issues found there. The briefing process is the mental process on which you must rely in taking law school examinations; it is also the mental process upon which a lawyer relies in serving his clients and in making his living.

# Abbreviations for Briefs

# Table of Cases

# CHAPTER 1

# The Evolution of Labor Relations Laws

## *Quick Reference Rules of Law*

# Vegelahn v. Guntner

## Employer (P) v. Workers (D)

Mass. Sup. Jud. Ct., 167 Mass. 92, 44 N.E. 1077 (1896).

**NATURE OF CASE:** Action for an injunction to restrain peaceful picketing.

**FACT SUMMARY:** An employer (P) sought a permanent injunction against picketing workers (D) who employed both peaceful persuasion and threats of violence against employees entering the premises.

## 🏛 RULE OF LAW
The maintenance of a picket in front of an employer's premises for the purpose of preventing persons in his employ from continuing therein, regardless of the picketers' conduct, is unlawful, and may be enjoined.

**FACTS:** Workers (D) established a patrol in front of Vegelahn's (P) business, which was situated on a busy street during the daytime. The patrol usually numbered two men, although at times it was greater. The workers (D), who were on strike, sought by means of the patrol to prevent Vegelahn (P) from getting workmen, and thereby to prevent him from carrying on his business unless and until he agreed to a schedule of prices. In the course of this picketing, the workers (D) employed persuasion and social pressure and, to some extent, threats of personal injury or unlawful harm against persons entering Vegelahn's (P) premises. Vegelahn (P) petitioned for an injunction to enjoin the strike. Justice Holmes issued an injunction pendente lite (preliminary) which enjoined the workers from resorting to threats, express or implied, of violence or physical harm to body or person, from physically or otherwise obstructing entry to the premises, and from inducing employees to break their lawful contracts. However, in all other respects, Justice Holmes ruled that the patrol, so far as it confined itself to persuasion and giving notice of the strike, was lawful, and limited his injunction accordingly. The matter was then submitted to the full court for consideration of whether Holmes's preliminary injunction should be made permanent or modified.

**ISSUE:** May a permanent injunction issue against peaceful picketing?

**HOLDING AND DECISION:** (Allen, J.) Yes. A patrol, regardless of whether it is used in combination with social pressure, threats of personal injury or unlawful harm, or persuasion to break existing or nonexisting contracts, unlawfully interferes with the rights of both employer and employee. An employer has the constitutional right to secure in his employ all those with whom he can mutually agree upon a price; the employees have a corresponding right to enter into, and remain in, the employment of any

person or corporation willing to hire them. Intimidation, regardless of its nature, interferes with these rights. Patrolling, or picketing, inherently has elements of intimidation. While a combination among persons merely to regulate their own conduct is within allowable competition and is lawful, the combination involved here, designed as it is to do injurious acts expressly directed at another, is outside of allowable competition and is unlawful. Although a court of equity will, as a rule, decline to restrain the commission of a crime, as involved here, a continuing injury to property or business may be enjoined. Finally, since an unlawful conspiracy is presented, an injunction should not be limited to relate only to persons who are bound by existing contracts. Accordingly, a permanent injunction enjoining the picketing will issue.

**DISSENT:** (Holmes, J.) The permanent injunction, including as it does a refusal of social intercourse, and even organized persuasion or argument which is free from any threat of violence, sweeps too broad. The court assumes that a patrol of two men necessarily carries with it a threat of bodily harm. This assumption is unwarranted, since there is no suggestion that the workers (D), presumably law-abiding men, would violate an injunction against picketline violence. The court has previously held that the policy of allowing free competition justifies the intentional infliction of temporary damage, including the damage of interference with a man's business, by some means, when the damage is done, not for its own sake, but as an instrumentality in reaching the end of victory in the battle of trade. This policy should apply to all conflicts of temporal interests, and not just those between rival businessmen. A combination of employers to get the most services from employees for the least cost must be offset by a combination of employees to protect their own best interest.

## ▶ ANALYSIS

Further justification for the issuance of injunctions against peaceful concerted activities by employees was furnished by the Sherman Antitrust Act of 1890, which the courts construed as authorizing injunctive action against not only corporations but unions as well. In response, Congress enacted the Clayton Act of 1914, which declared "that the labor of human beings is not a commodity or article of commerce." Nonetheless, the courts, through a series of narrow decisions interpreting the Act, continued to resort to the Sherman Act and the federal court injunction to curb labor organizing. Not until the Norris-LaGuardia Act

*Continued on next page.*

of 1932 was the federal court's broad use of the injunction effectively restricted.

■■■■

## Quicknotes

**CLAYTON ACT** Legislation passed by the U.S. Congress in 1914 as an amendment to clarify and supplement the Sherman Antitrust Act of 1890.

**CONSPIRACY** Concerted action by two or more persons to accomplish some unlawful purpose.

**PERMANENT INJUNCTION** A remedy imposed by the court ordering a party to cease the conduct of a specific activity until the final disposition of the cause of action.

**SHERMAN ACT** Makes every contract or conspiracy in unreasonable restraint of commerce illegal.

■■■■

# Loewe v. Lawlor

Employer (P) v. Union members (D)

208 U.S. 274 (1908).

**NATURE OF CASE:** Appeal from an order sustaining a demurrer to an action brought under § 7 of the Sherman Act of 1890.

**FACT SUMMARY:** Loewe (P), a hat manufacturer, sought to enjoin Lawlor (D) and other members of the United Hatters of North America from combining with other AFL members to compel Loewe (P) to recognize the union under pressure of boycott of his interstate trade.

## RULE OF LAW
The Sherman Act prohibits any combination whatever to secure action which essentially obstructs the free flow of commerce between the states, or restricts the liberty of a trader to engage in business.

**FACTS:** Loewe (P) and other hat manufacturers doing business in Danbury, Connecticut, the bulk of whose business was through wholesalers and retailers in other states, sought to enjoin under § 7 of the Sherman Act Lawlor (D) and some other 9,000 members of the United Hatters of North America and the 1,400,000 other members of the AFL with whom they were combined. Allegedly, Lawlor (D) and the others sought to compel Loewe (P) to recognize the union through restraint and destruction of Loewe's (P) interstate trade by intimidation, threats, and boycott of customers. Loewe (P) alleged damages of $80,000. The district court sustained Lawlor's (D) demurrer on the ground that the demurrer was not within the Sherman Act. The Second Circuit Court of Appeals certified the question to the Supreme Court.

**ISSUE:** Does the Sherman Act prohibit any combination whatever to secure action which essentially obstructs the free flow of commerce between the states, or restricts the liberty of a trader to engage in business?

**HOLDING AND DECISION:** (Fuller, C.J.) Yes. The Sherman Act prohibits any combination whatever to secure action which essentially obstructs the free flow of commerce between the states, or restricts the liberty of a trader to engage in business. Even though Lawlor's (D) acts interfered with intrastate as well as interstate commerce and he was not involved in interstate trade, the acts sought to be enjoined had to be considered as a whole and were open to condemnation, notwithstanding that a negligible amount of intrastate business might have been affected in carrying it out. Nor could the Sherman Act be held inapplicable on the ground that Lawlor (D) was not engaged in interstate commerce because the Act makes no distinction between classes. Loewe (P), by alleging that Lawlor (D) formed a combination to directly restrain Loewe's (P)

interstate trade, and that certain means were contrived to achieve that end and were employed by Lawlor (D), stated a cause of action within the Act. Reversed and remanded.

## ▶ ANALYSIS

The Sherman Act was passed in 1890, and in it Congress declared unlawful "every contract, combination in the form of trust or otherwise, or conspiracy, in restraint of trade or commerce among the several states, or with foreign nations." The Act's obvious objective was the elimination of price-fixing agreements between manufacturers or suppliers or any other agreement regulating the supply of goods or allocating customers or excluding competitors. However, the Act was soon more often used against unions than corporations. The case above, commonly known as the Danbury Hatters case, was the Supreme Court's first direct decision condoning application of the Act to combinations of workers.

■■■

## Quicknotes

**BOYCOTT** A concerted effort to refrain from doing business with a particular person or entity.

**SHERMAN ACT** Makes every contract or conspiracy in unreasonable restraint of commerce illegal.

■■■

# Thornhill v. Alabama

## Picketer (D) v. State (P)

310 U.S. 88 (1940).

**NATURE OF CASE:** Appeal from a conviction for loitering and picketing.

**FACT SUMMARY:** Thornhill (D) was convicted of violating an Alabama (P) statute that prohibited loitering or picketing about another's business premises without just cause for the purpose of influencing persons not to deal with or be employed by that business.

## 🏛 RULE OF LAW

The dissemination of information concerning the facts of a labor dispute is within the area of free discussion guaranteed by the Constitution's First Amendment.

**FACTS:** Thornhill (D) was convicted of violating an Alabama (P) statute that prohibited picketing or loitering without just cause or legal excuse about the place of business of any other person, firm, corporation, or association of people engaged in lawful business, for the purpose of inducing others not to trade or deal in any manner with or be employed by the business in question, or for the purpose of interfering with or injuring the business. Thornhill (D) was one of six to eight men engaged in picketing the Brown Wood Preserving Company (Brown) for the purpose of discouraging anyone from working at Brown because the union was on strike. This appeal was brought on First Amendment, free-speech grounds.

**ISSUE:** Is the dissemination of information concerning the facts of a labor dispute within the area of free discussion guaranteed under the First Amendment?

**HOLDING AND DECISION:** (Murphy, J.) Yes. The dissemination of information concerning the facts of a labor dispute is within the area of free discussion guaranteed by the First Amendment of the Constitution. The freedoms of speech and press are fundamental. Here, the statute outlaws every method by which a labor dispute can be publicized. The phrase, "without a just cause or legal excuse," failed to restrict effectively in any manner the breadth of the statute; "the words themselves have no ascertainable meaning either inherent or historical." The statute was vague and overbroad and invalid on its face. The First Amendment guarantees the liberty to discuss publicly and truthfully all matters of public concern without previous restraint or fear of subsequent punishment. The activities prohibited by the statute are essential to the securing of an educated and informed public with respect to a matter of public concern. "[T]he danger of injury to an industrial concern is neither so serious nor so imminent as to justify the sweeping proscription of freedom of discussion embodied" in the statute. Reversed.

## ▶ ANALYSIS

In *Senn v. Tile Layers Union*, 301 U.S. 468, 478 (1937), Justice Brandeis wrote that "members of a union might, without special statutory authorization by a state, make known the facts of a labor dispute, for freedom of speech is guaranteed by the federal constitution." The Court in *Thornhill* commented generally. "Every expression of opinion on matters that are important has the potentiality of inducing action in the interests of one rather than another group in society. But the group in power at any moment may not impose penal sanctions on peaceful and truthful discussion of matters of public interest merely on a showing that others may thereby be persuaded to take action inconsistent with its interests."

■=■

## Quicknotes

**FIRST AMENDMENT** Prohibits Congress from enacting any law respecting an establishment of religion, prohibiting the free exercise of religion, abridging freedom of speech or the press, the right of peaceful assembly and the right to petition for a redress of grievances.

**OVERBROAD** Refers to a statute that proscribes lawful as well as unlawful conduct.

**VAGUENESS** Doctrine that a statute that does not clearly or definitely inform an individual as to what conduct is unlawful is unconstitutional in violation of the Due Process Clause.

■=■

# The Establishment of the Collective Bargaining Relationship

## *Quick Reference Rules of Law*

# Republic Aviation Corp. v. NLRB

## Employer (D) v. Labor board (P)

### 324 U.S. 793 (1945).

**NATURE OF CASE:** Appeal from a finding of violation of NLRA §§ 8(1), 8(3).

**FACT SUMMARY:** Republic Aviation Corp. (D) fired four employees, one for violating the soliciting rule by distributing union membership application cards and three others for wearing shop steward buttons before any union had been recognized.

## RULE OF LAW

NLRB orders on complaints of unfair labor practices must be based upon evidence that is placed before the Board by witnesses who are subject to cross-examination by opposing parties.

**FACTS:** Republic Aviation Corp. (D), an aircraft manufacturer, maintained a policy forbidding solicitation of any type in its factory or offices. An employee persisted in distributing union membership application cards during lunch hour after being warned and was fired. Three other employees were fired for wearing UAW-CIO union steward buttons in the plant after being requested to remove them. Republic (D) claimed that the wearing of such buttons would indicate its acknowledgment of the union when one had not been recognized. The NLRB (P) found that the "no solicitation" rule violated § 8(1) of the NLRA as it restrained, coerced, and interfered with employees' § 7 rights. Also, it discriminated against the discharged employee under § 8(3). The discharge of the stewards was found to have violated the same sections. Republic (D) appealed claiming that the NLRB (P) orders rested on policy formulated without due administrative procedure.

**ISSUE:** Must NLRB orders on complaints of unfair labor practices be based upon evidence that is placed before the Board by witnesses who are subject to cross-examination by opposing parties?

**HOLDING AND DECISION:** (Reed, J.) Yes. NLRB orders on complaints of unfair labor practices must be based upon evidence that is placed before the Board by witnesses who are subject to cross-examination by opposing parties. The board cannot substitute its knowledge of industrial relations for substantive evidence. Here, the NLRB (P) sufficiently expressed the theory by which it concluded that rules against solicitation or prohibitions against wearing union buttons must fall as interferences with union organization. As for Republic's (D) contention that regardless of the validity of the rule against solicitation, its application did not violate § 8(3) on the ground that the rule was not discriminatorily applied against union

solicitation, but was impartially enforced against all solicitors, it seems clear that if a rule against union solicitation is invalid as to union solicitation during the employee's own time, a discharge for violation of the rule must violate § 8(3) because such action discourages union membership. Affirmed.

## ⟩ ANALYSIS

The Board set forth the procedure governing the *Republic* case in *Peyton Packing Company*, 49 NLRB 828, at 844. The Board decided that an employer can prohibit union solicitation during work hours, and such a rule must be presumed valid in the absence of evidence that it was adopted for a discriminatory purpose. However, outside of working hours, whether before or after work or during lunch or breaks, an employee can use his time as he wants without unreasonable restraint.

■=■

## Quicknotes

**DUE PROCESS CLAUSE** Clauses found in the Fifth and Fourteenth Amendments to the United States Constitution providing that no person shall be deprived of "life, liberty, or property, without due process of law."

**NLRA (NATIONAL LABOR RELATIONS ACT)** Guarantees employees the right to engage in collective bargaining, and regulates labor unions.

**NLRB (NATIONAL LABOR RELATIONS BOARD)** An agency established pursuant to the National Labor Relations Act for the purpose of prohibiting unfair labor practices by employers and unions.

■=■

# Cintas Corp. v. NLRB

## Corporation (D) v. Union (P)

482 F.3d 463 (D.C. Cir. 2007).

**NATURE OF CASE:** Appeal of decision by the NLRB.

**FACT SUMMARY:** Cintas Corporation (D) had a confidentiality clause in the employee handbook. A union, UNITE HERE (P), claimed that the confidentiality clause interfered with the employee's right to organize and join the union.

> 🏛 **RULE OF LAW**
> A confidentiality clause that does not expressly forbid employee discussions that are protected under the NLRA may still violate the NLRA if employees would reasonably construe the clause to forbid such discussions.

**FACTS:** Cintas Corporation (D) employs approximately 27,000 workers and supplies workplace uniforms to customers throughout North America. The company distributed a handbook to all employees describing a "Cintas Culture" and the company's "principles and values." Under a heading "We honor confidentiality," the handbook provided that "we recognize and protect the confidentiality of any information concerning the company, its business plans, its partners, new business efforts, customers, accounting and financial matters." A separate disciplinary rule warned employees that they could be punished for violating a "confidence" or releasing confidential information without authorization. "Partners" was a term Cintas (D) used to refer to all employees, and the question raised about the Cintas (D) rule was whether it violated the NLRA rights of employees. Section 7 of the NLRA, 29 U.S.C. § 157, guarantees employees the right to form, join, or assist unions, and to engage in other concerted activities for their mutual aid or protection. Section 8(a)(1) of the statute, 29 U.S.C. § 158(a)(1), prohibits employers from interfering with, restraining, or coercing employees in the exercise of their Section 7 rights. UNITE HERE (P) filed an unfair labor practice charge with the NLRB alleging that the Cintas (D) policy violated Section 8(a)(1) of the act, and both an NLRB administrative law judge and the board agreed that the policy was unlawful. Cintas (D) petitioned for review of the NLRB decision, but the court denied the company's petition and enforced the NLRB's unfair labor practice finding.

**ISSUE:** Can a confidentiality clause that does not expressly forbid employee discussions that are protected under the NLRA still violate the NLRA if employees would reasonably construe the clause to forbid such discussions?

**HOLDING AND DECISION:** (Griffith, J.) Yes. A confidentiality clause that does not expressly forbid employee discussions that are protected under the NLRA

may still violate the NLRA if employees would reasonably construe the clause to forbid such discussions. Cintas's (D) argument that the facts before the NLRB did not support an unfair labor practice finding is rejected. The company argued that none of the language in its employee handbook explicitly prohibited employees from engaging in legally protected activity. But the court of appeals previously held in *Guardsmark v. NLRB*, 475 F.3d 369 (D.C. Cir. 2007), that even in the absence of an express limitation on employee rights, a company policy statement would still violate Section 8(a)(1) of the NLRA if an employee could reasonably construe the policy to prohibit activity protected by the act. Cintas (D) argued that there was no evidence in the NLRB record showing that any Cintas (D) employee actually interpreted the confidentiality rule to prohibit protected activity, but the board was required to determine only whether employees would reasonably read the rule to interfere with their rights, not whether any employee actually did reach that conclusion. Additionally, the company argued that it never applied the confidentiality rule in the coercive manner feared by the union. But the NLRB and the District of Columbia Circuit both have ruled that mere maintenance of an overbroad rule that chilled the exercise of Section 7 rights would violate the NLRA. The board was under no obligation to consider whether the disputed restriction has ever been enforced. Cintas (D) also argued that the NLRB misconstrued the confidentiality rule. The company argued that a company rule that mandated confidentiality concerning "partners" should not have been interpreted literally by the board, since a literal reading of the rule would seemingly preclude employees from even discussing their favorite television programs. The argument is not persuasive, because the NLRA does not protect an employee's right to discuss his favorite television show. It does protect employee discussions about the terms and condition of their employment, however. Additionally, the NLRB's unfair labor practice finding was not inconsistent with prior board or court decisions. The language of the Cintas (D) policy that prohibited sharing "any" information about employees was more sweeping than one the court found unlawful in *Brockton Hospital v. NLRB*, 294 F.3d 100 (D.C. Cir. 2002).

> ▎**ANALYSIS**
>
> The key to application of Section 8(a)(1) is that any language that could reasonably be interpreted by an employee as restricting speech or behavior that is otherwise protected

*Continued on next page.*

by the NLRA would violate the NLRA. That standard asks what an average employee might reasonably think about the language.

∎≡∎

## Quicknotes

**NLRA (NATIONAL LABOR RELATIONS ACT)** Guarantees employees the right to engage in collective bargaining, and regulates labor unions.

**NLRB (NATIONAL LABOR RELATIONS BOARD)** An agency established pursuant to the National Labor Relations Act for the purpose of prohibiting unfair labor practices by employers and unions.

**UNFAIR LABOR PRACTICE** Conduct by labor unions and employers, which is proscribed by the National Labor Relations Act.

∎≡∎

# Lechmere, Inc. v. NLRB

Employer (D) v. Labor board (P)

502 U.S. 527 (1992).

**NATURE OF CASE:** Appeal of order allowing union access to employer property.

**FACT SUMMARY:** The United Food and Commercial Workers Union claimed that Lechmere, Inc. (D) illegally barred it from distributing literature on Lechmere's (D) property.

## 🏛 RULE OF LAW
Nonemployee union organizers have the right of access to an employer's property only when the inaccessibility of the employees makes reasonable attempts to communicate with the employees ineffective.

**FACTS:** Local 919 of the United Food and Commercial Workers Union attempted to organize the employees of Lechmere, Inc. (D), a retail store in Connecticut. The store was located in a shopping plaza that contained a parking lot owned by Lechmere (D). Members of Local 919 who were not employees of Lechmere (D) placed handbills on the windshields of cars parked in the lot in front of Lechmere (D). Lechmere (D) removed the handbills and requested that the organizers leave its property. Local 919 then attempted to contact Lechmere (D) employees by picketing on a grassy strip adjacent to the parking lot. Local 919 then filed an unfair labor practice charge with the NLRB (P), alleging that Lechmere (D) had violated § 7 of the NLRA. The NLRB (P) ruled for Local 919 and ordered Lechmere (D) to allow the distribution of literature in the parking lot in front of the store. The court of appeals affirmed the NLRB's (P) order. Lechmere (D) appealed, and certiorari was granted.

**ISSUE:** Do nonemployee union organizers have the right of access to an employer's property under § 7 of the NLRA?

**HOLDING AND DECISION:** (Thomas, J.) No. Nonemployee union organizers have the right of access to an employer's property only when the inaccessibility of the employees makes reasonable attempts to communicate with the employees ineffective. The NLRA grants rights only to employees and not to nonemployee union organizers. However, in *NLRB v. Babcock & Wilcox Co.*, 351 U.S. 105 (1956), the Court recognized that an employer's right to restrict nonemployee union organizers from company property is limited. The *Babcock* decision required employers to yield access to their property when the employees are beyond the reach of reasonable efforts to communicate with them. This exception only applies when nonemployee union organizers do not have any reasonable access to employees outside the employees property. The employees

of Lechmere (D) did not live on Lechmere's (D) property and were not inaccessible to Local 919's reasonable communication efforts. Therefore, the exception to the general rule that *Babcock* allowed did not apply to Lechmere (D), and the NLRB's (P) order was erroneous. Thus, Lechmere (D) could restrict access to their property from nonemployee union organizers. Reversed.

**DISSENT:** (White, J.) The *Babcock* decision did not establish a general rule with narrow exceptions. Rather, a flexible rule of accommodation was established which balanced property rights against the right granted under the NLRA to organize employees. The NLRB's (P) decision that Lechmere (D) should yield access to its property because Local 919 was not able to actually communicate effectively with Lechmere (D) employees should be deferred to.

## ▶ ANALYSIS

Courts have applied the decision in *Lechmere* to deny union agents access to public areas controlled by the employer, such as cafeterias. See *Oakwood Hospital v. NLRB*, 983 F.2d 698 (6th Cir. 1993). The decision makes it unlikely that employers will have to yield property access except where their employers actually live on company property.

■══■

### Quicknotes

**AGENT** An individual who has the authority to act on behalf of another.

**NLRA (NATIONAL LABOR RELATIONS ACT)** Guarantees employees the right to engage in collective bargaining, and regulates labor unions.

**NLRB (NATIONAL LABOR RELATIONS BOARD)** An agency established pursuant to the National Labor Relations Act for the purpose of prohibiting unfair labor practices by employers and unions.

■══■

# The Register-Guard

## Newspaper (D) v. Union (P)

351 N.L.R.B. 1110 (2007), *pet. den. in part sub nom.* Guard Pub. Co. v. NLRB, 571 F.3d 53 (D.C. Cir. 2009).

**NATURE OF CASE:** Ruling by the NLRB.

**FACT SUMMARY:** The Register-Guard (D), a newspaper, prohibited solicitation using company email systems. It disciplined a union member when she used the system for solicitation purposes.

## RULE OF LAW

A nondiscriminatory company communications policy that prohibits employees from using the company email system for any non-job-related solicitations is not overbroad.

**FACTS:** Guard Publishing Company publishes a daily newspaper called the Register-Guard (D) in Eugene, Oregon. The Register-Guard (D) adopted a communications policy stating that email and phone systems owned by the company were not to be used for a variety of non-job-related communication. The Register-Guard (D) was aware that employees used the email system for non-work related communication on occasion, and looked the other way. The Eugene Newspaper Guild (P) represents many of the paper's employees. In May and August of 2000, the company (D) sent the union president, Suzi Prozanski, who was a copy editor in the newspaper's features department, written warnings for alleged violations of the communications policy. She had sent one email during a break from her workstation, and two others from the union office. All three were sent to employees represented by the union at their work email addresses. The first email sent by Prozanski was to clear up confusion about a union rally. The managing editor sent an email to all employees to leave early on the day of the rally because local police warned of possible anarchists attending. Another newspaper employee and member of the union immediately sent an email indicating that it was the company that had called the police. Prozanski sent an email detailing the full story—that although the company had called the police the day before the rally, the police had originated the communication the day before that. The rally took place without incident. The managing editor sent Prozanski a disciplinary warning for using the company's email system to conduct union business. Later that year, Prozanski sent two more emails, the first to remind employees to wear green on a particular day to show unity about the union's position in contract negotiations, and the second to ask for volunteers to help with the union's participation in a parade. The human resources department then sent Prozanski another disciplinary warning for violating the communications policy. The union (P) then filed a charge with the National Labor Relations Board

claiming that the company (D) committed an unfair labor practice by sending the second warning.

**ISSUE:** Is a nondiscriminatory company communications policy that prohibits employees from using the company email system for any non-job-related solicitations overbroad?

**HOLDING AND DECISION:** (Battista, Chairman) No. A nondiscriminatory company communications policy that prohibits employees from using the company email system for any non-job-related solicitations is not overbroad. Employers have a basic property right to regulate employee use of company property, and the communications system in this case is the company's (D) property. Precedent has held that employees do not have the right to use employer-owned property including bulletin boards, telephones, and televisions for Section 7 communications, as long as the restrictions are not discriminatory, and while the board has never before ruled on the specific question of email systems, it is not different from other modes of communication owned by the employer. The dissents' argument that the rule should not apply to emails systems, because under *Republic Aviation v. NLRB*, 324 U.S. 793 (1945), the employees' Section 7 rights and the employer's interest in maintaining discipline have to be balanced against each other, and a broad ban on employee non-work-related email should be presumptively unlawful absent a showing of special circumstances. But that case doesn't apply here, because in that case, the employer rule entirely deprived employees of their right to communication in the workplace on their own time, and that clearly violates Section 8 because it would deprive employees of any time in the workplace at all to engage in Section 7 communications. In this case, Register-Guard (D) does not regulate traditional, face-to-face solicitation, which is protected under *Republic Aviation*. Instead, this case involves the additional method of communication of email. *Republic Aviation* requires the employer to give over its property interests to the extent necessary to ensure that employees will not be entirely deprived of their ability to engage in Section 7 communications in the workplace on their own time, but it does not require that the company give over the most convenient or most effective means of conducting those communications, or hold that employees have a statutory right to use an employer's equipment for Section 7 communications. Being rightfully on the premises confers no additional right on employees to use the employer's equipment for Section 7

*Continued on next page.*

purposes, regardless of whether the employees are allowed to use that equipment for work purposes. And while email has had a substantial impact on how people communicate, email messages are similar to telephone calls in many ways because of their immediacy, and the board has never found that employees have a general right to use their employer's telephone system for Section 7 communications. The email system has not eliminated face-to-face communication or reduced it to a significant level, and the use of email has not changed the pattern of industrial life to the extent that forms of workplace communications sanctioned by *Republic Aviation* have been rendered useless, thus requiring use of the email system. Register-Guard (D) may bar use of the email system for Section 7 activity provided it does not discriminate against Section 7 activity. [The board also upheld Register-Guard's (D) enforcement of its email policy against Prozanski because there was no evidence that the company (D) had permitted solicitation on behalf of other non-union groups (even though it had permitted various other personal uses of the email system, including personal solicitations for sports tickets and the like). As long as it prohibits solicitations of all forms, and not only solicitations having to do with Section 7 communications, there is no discriminatory enforcement.]

**DISSENT:** (Liebman, Member) The issue in any Section 8(a)(1) case is whether the employer's conduct interferes with Section 7 rights, in which case the employer must show a legitimate business reason that outweighs the interference. *Republic Aviation* is the seminal case balancing the interests of the employees and employer with respect to oral solicitation in the workplace. In that case, the board adopted a presumption that restricting oral solicitation on nonworking time is unlawful absent special circumstances. Special circumstances do not exist here. Email is not just another piece of employer equipment, and the employer does not own cyberspace. Where an employer gives employees access to email in the workplace for their regular use, banning all non-work-related solicitations is presumptively unlawful absent special circumstances. The Register Guard (D) has shown no special circumstances for its ban on non-job-related solicitations. The decision of the administrative law judge should be reversed. As to the issue of discriminatory application of the policy, focusing on what types of activities are equal to Section 7 activities misses the point. A Section 8(a)(1) case is not about discrimination, but about interference with employees' Section 7 rights. Discrimination is relevant because it weakens or exposes as pretext the employer's business justification. [The casebook excerpt also contains an excerpt from the court of appeals decision, which enforced the board's order with respect to the first email sent by Prozanski, but not the other emails. The excerpt is difficult to understand because of the editing, but essentially, the court held that the company's (D) discipline of Prozanski for using the email system to solicit employees to wear green in support of the union and to seek volunteers to help with the union's entry

in a city parade violated Section 8(a)(3). The court referred to the distinction between organizational and personal solicitation a "post-hoc invention" that did not actually exist in the company's email policy, and found that the company policy prohibiting non-work-related solicitations made no distinction between solicitations for groups and for individuals.]

## ▶ ANALYSIS

This case is fact-specific, and the email policy at issue, which prohibited use of the company's communications systems "to solicit or proselytize for commercial ventures, religious or political causes, outside organizations, or other non-job-related solicitations," would seem to be equally applicable to personal solicitations of a non-work nature as it is to organizational solicitations. The court's decision does not change the underlying premise that employers may prohibit union access to its email system so long as it does so in a nondiscriminatory manner.

■≡■

## Quicknotes

**NLRA (NATIONAL LABOR RELATIONS ACT)** Guarantees employees the right to engage in collective bargaining, and regulates labor unions.

**NLRB (NATIONAL LABOR RELATIONS BOARD)** An agency established pursuant to the National Labor Relations Act for the purpose of prohibiting unfair labor practices by employers and unions.

**UNFAIR LABOR PRACTICE** Conduct by labor unions and employers, which is proscribed by the National Labor Relations Act.

■≡■

# Excelsior Underwear Inc.

## Union (P) v. Employer (D)

156 NLRB 1236 (1966).

**NATURE OF CASE:** Appeal by union to NLRB of regional director's dismissal of charge.

**FACT SUMMARY:** A union (P) sought the name and address list of employees that was kept by the employer (D) in order to campaign for organization. The employer (D) denied access.

## 🏛 RULE OF LAW
An employer is required to disclose promptly to the union employees' names and addresses in all representation elections.

**FACTS:** Excelsior Underwear Inc. (D) wrote to all employees during a union election campaign. The union (P) asked the employer for a list of employees' names and addresses in order to respond to the employer's (D) communications. The employer (D) refused. The NLRB decided that the significance of the issues required a hearing and invited groups to file amicus curiae briefs and to participate in oral argument. Among the interested parties were the U.S. Chamber of Commerce, the AFL-CIO, the International Union of Electrical Workers, the United Auto Workers, the Textile Workers Union, and the Teamsters.

**ISSUE:** Should an employer be required to disclose promptly to the union employees' names and addresses in all representation elections?

**HOLDING AND DECISION:** [Member not stated in casebook excerpt.] Yes. An employer is required to disclose promptly to the union employees' names and addresses in all representation elections. Prompt disclosure of employees' names and addresses is necessary to insure an informed electorate. The requirement circumvents a situation in which the union is forced either to challenge all those voters who appear at the polls whom it does not know or risk having ineligible employees vote. Prompt disclosure of names and addresses will eliminate the necessity for challenges based solely on lack of knowledge as to voter's identity. In addition, no substantial infringement of the employer's interest flows from such a requirement. And the existence of alternative channels of communication do not prevent the NLRB from requiring the employer to disclose names and addresses, unless the opportunity to communicate made available by the NLRB would interfere with a significant employer interest. The requirement is not limited to situations in which the employer has mailed anti-union literature to employees' homes, or to disclosure to a mailing service. In all election cases, within 7 days after the regional director has approved a consent-election agreement entered into by the parties, or after the regional director or the NLRB has directed an election, or after the regional director or the NLRB has directed an election pursuant to the NLRB Rules and Regulations, the employer must file with the regional director an election eligibility list containing the names and addresses of all eligible voters. The regional director will then make the information available to all parties in the case. Failure to comply will result in setting aside the election. Employees must have the opportunity to vote for or against representation in circumstances free from interference, restraint, or coercion violative of the NLRA, but also from other elements that prevent free or reasoned choice, and a lack of information with respect to one of the choices is such an impediment. Reversed.

## ▶ ANALYSIS

The NLRB rejected the arguments by the employers and supporting amici curiae that the involuntary disclosure of employees' names and addresses violated the employees' right under § 7 to refrain from forming and joining labor organizations and also their right to have their privacy protected against harassment and coercion by the union in employees' homes.

■=■

## Quicknotes

**AMICUS CURIAE** A third party, not implicated in the suit, which seeks to file a brief containing information for the court's consideration in conformity with its position.

**NLRB (NATIONAL LABOR RELATIONS BOARD)** An agency established pursuant to the National Labor Relations Act for the purpose of prohibiting unfair labor practices by employers and unions.

■=■

# NLRB v. Gissel Packing Co.

## Labor board (P) v. Employer (D)

395 U.S. 575 (1969).

**NATURE OF CASE:** Appeal from NLRB finding of an unfair labor practice on the part of an employer.

**FACT SUMMARY:** Shortly before a representation election, an employer (D), who had no objective basis to rely upon, predicted that unionization would force the company to go out of business.

### 🏛 RULE OF LAW
An employer is free to make a prediction to his employees as to the precise effects he believes unionization will have on his company only when such prediction is carefully phrased on the basis of objective fact as to demonstrably probable consequences beyond his control or to convey a management decision already arrived at to close the plant in case of unionization.

**FACTS:** When the president of Sinclair (D) first learned of an organizational campaign by the union with which he had refused to bargain, he talked with all of his employees in an attempt to dissuade them from joining a union. The president (D) emphasized the results of a strike 13 years earlier which had caused a three-month plant shutdown, warned that Sinclair (D) was on "thin ice" financially, and that a strike "could lead to closing the plant" since the parent company had ample manufacturing facilities elsewhere, and that because of the employees' age and limited skills they might not be able to find re-employment elsewhere. Finally, he also warned those who did not believe that the plant could go out of business to "look around Holyoke and see a lot of them out of business." During a period immediately prior to a scheduled representation election, the president (D) sent out pamphlets which called the union a "strike happy outfit" controlled by hoodlums and listed those local businesses which, because of union demands, had gone out of business, eliminating some 3,500 jobs. These contentions were reiterated the day before the election which the union narrowly lost 7-6. The NLRB (P), concluding that the president's (D) statements and communications were not cast as a prediction of "demonstrable economic consequences," but rather as a threat of retaliatory action (in fact, Sinclair [D] admitted at the hearing that it had no basis for attributing other local plant closings to unionization), found Sinclair (D) guilty of violating § 8(a)(1) of the NLRA. The court of appeals enforced the Board's (P) findings and order for a new election. Sinclair (D) appealed.

**ISSUE:** Is an employer completely free under the NLRA to communicate to his employees his beliefs as to the effects of unionization?

**HOLDING AND DECISION:** [Judge not stated in casebook excerpt.] No. The contention that an employer's free speech right, as guaranteed by § 8(c), is firmly established and cannot be infringed by a union or the Board (P), must be rejected. This right must be balanced against the fact that employees are economically dependent on their employers, and, as a result, are more likely than disinterested persons to interpret pronouncements by the employers as threats. Thus, the right of an employer to freely communicate to his employees his general views about unionism or any of his specific views about a particular union is subject to the qualification that such communications do not contain a threat of reprisal or force or promise of benefit. He may make a prediction as to the precise effects he believes unionization will have on his company, but the prediction must be carefully phrased on the basis of objective fact to convey his belief as to demonstrably provable consequences beyond his control or to convey a management decision already arrived at to close the plant in case of unionization. Otherwise, any statement is beyond the protection of the First Amendment. A sincere belief that unionization will or may result in a plant closing is not enough; there must be objective proof. In the present case, the Board (P) could reasonably conclude that the intended and understood import of the message was not to predict that unionization would inevitably cause the plant to close, but to threaten to throw employees out of work regardless of the economic realities. The standards announced in this decision are not unconstitutionally vague. All an employer need do to comply is to avoid conscious overstatements he has reason to believe will mislead his employees. Affirmed.

### ▸ ANALYSIS

The instant decision has been criticized as creating an imbalance between the employer and the union in their appeals to the employees before an election. Some commentators point out that while the union is left unfettered to make any extravagant claims as to benefits the employees will receive if they vote for unionization, the employer can only offset these statements by objective proof. An employer's communications will be found coercive even when his statements on their face include no threat of retaliation or promise of benefit if, by previous actions, the employer has created a coercive atmosphere.

■=■

*Continued on next page.*

## *Quicknotes*

**FIRST AMENDMENT** Prohibits Congress from enacting any law respecting an establishment of religion, prohibiting the free exercise of religion, abridging freedom of speech or the press, the right of peaceful assembly and the right to petition for a redress of grievances.

**NLRA (NATIONAL LABOR RELATIONS ACT)** Guarantees employees the right to engage in collective bargaining, and regulates labor unions.

**NLRB (NATIONAL LABOR RELATIONS BOARD)** An agency established pursuant to the National Labor Relations Act for the purpose of prohibiting unfair labor practices by employers and unions.

**RIGHT OF FREE SPEECH** Right guaranteed by the First Amendment to the United States Constitution prohibiting Congress from enacting any law abridging freedom of speech or the press.

# Midland National Life Insurance Co. v. Local 304A, United Food & Commercial Workers

Employer (D) v. Union (P)

263 NLRB 127 (1982).

**NATURE OF CASE:** Review by NLRB of hearing officer's recommendation that a new union representation election be held.

**FACT SUMMARY:** Local 304A (P) objected to the distribution of highly misleading, antiunion literature distributed by Midland National Life Insurance Co. (D) on the morning of the representation election.

🏛 **RULE OF LAW**
Except in circumstances where a party engages in extremely deceptive campaign practices, union representation campaign statements are not reviewable by the NLRB.

**FACTS:** On October 15, 1980, the day before a union representation election, Midland National Life Insurance Co. (Midland) (D) distributed campaign literature with employee paychecks. The literature included a photo depicting an abandoned facility accompanied by text suggesting that the plant closed permanently due to violence surrounding a labor strike. Testimony from the union indicated that the plant had been open for nearly two years after the strike. Other misleading information allegedly showing Local 304A's (P) failure to keep its promise of securing contracts and wage increases for employees was distributed. The Union had less than four hours to respond to most of the literature, and the Local 304A (P) lost the election, with 107 in favor and 107 against. The Union (P) filed a complaint against Midland (D). The Hearing Officer concluded that the literature contained numerous misrepresentations of fact, without time to respond, and recommended that a third election be directed. The NLRB then examined the Hearing Officer's recommendations.

**ISSUE:** Are union campaign statements reviewable by the NLRB?

**HOLDING AND DECISION:** [Member not stated in casebook excerpt.] No. Except in circumstances where a party engages in extremely deceptive campaign practices, the truth or falsity of union representation campaign statements is not reviewable. During the years under the Wagner Act, the NLRB made no attempt to control campaign literature content. After the Taft-Hartley amendments, in which Congress expressed no disapproval of the NLRB's prior decisions, the NLRB continued to rely on the ability of voters to find propaganda when they saw it. In 1962, the NLRB departed from the refusal to review campaign propaganda, defining the rule that any statement which involved a substantial departure from the truth, whether intended or not, would cause the election to be set aside if other parties did not have time to respond properly to the propaganda. Since then, the NLRB has reversed itself twice. In any event, Congress has clearly given the NLRB substantial discretion to accomplish its mandate. Statements that are clearly propaganda of one party are read in that context. However, if fraud is used to conceal the identity of the writer, the reader can be deceived. Accordingly, only deceptive practices are reviewable by the NLRB. This rule treats employers and unions on an even footing. Here, since that the materials distributed by Midland (D) were clearly employer propaganda, the NLRB will not overturn the election. The NLRB certifies the election results. Decision overruled.

**DISSENT:** (Fanning, Member) For the second time in five years the Board has abandoned the flexible rule for analyzing misrepresentation. The Board now abandons a rule designed to allow accurate information to flow in a free election, with the hope of reducing litigation and speeding the review process. In this particular case, there are many instances of objectionable and fraudulent behavior. Thus, this behavior may have altered the balance of a close (107 to 107) vote.

▶ **ANALYSIS**

This decision offers unusual incentives to unions and employers. Given that the NLRB will not review literature for its truth, so long as it is discernibly propaganda, the incentive is to distribute wildly exaggerated or false information on the day before the election. This would leave almost no time for the other party to respond in a complete manner to the statements.

▪■▪

**Quicknotes**

**FRAUD** A false representation of facts with the intent that another will rely on the misrepresentation to his detriment.

**MISREPRESENTATION** A statement or conduct by one party to another that constitutes a false representation of fact.

**NLRB (NATIONAL LABOR RELATIONS BOARD)** An agency established pursuant to the National Labor Relations Act for the purpose of prohibiting unfair labor practices by employers and unions.

▪■▪

# NLRB v. Lorben Corp.

## Labor board (P) v. Employer (D)

345 F.2d 346 (2d Cir. 1965).

**NATURE OF CASE:** Action to enforce an NLRB order upon finding of a NLRA § 8(a)(1) violation.

**FACT SUMMARY:** Lorben Corp. (D), an employer, subsequent to a strike being called, distributed a paper to its employees asking whether or not they wanted union representation.

## 🏛 RULE OF LAW
Employer interrogation of employees as to their desire to be represented by a particular union is not coercive or intimidating on its face.

**FACTS:** After one employee was allegedly discharged for union activities during an attempt to organize Lorben Corp. (D), an employer, a strike was called. After two days of picketing, the discharged employee asked Lorben's (D) president if he desired to talk with the union. He did not so desire, but on the advice of counsel he circulated among the employees a paper stating the following question: "Do you wish Local 1922 of the Electrical Workers to represent you?" followed by two columns, "yes" and "no". The employees were free to sign or not. All signed "no" . There was no sign of any hostility by Lorben (D) to the union. The NLRB (P) found that Lorben (D), by failing to advise the employees about the purpose of the interrogation and to assure them that no reprisals would follow, violated NLRA § 8(a)(1). The NLRB (P) sought enforcement of its order by the court of appeals.

**ISSUE:** Is employer interrogation of employees as to their desire to be represented by a particular union coercive or intimidating on its face?

**HOLDING AND DECISION:** (Marshall, J.) No. Employer interrogation of employees as to their desire to be represented by a particular union is not coercive or intimidating on its face. Whether particular interrogation interferes with, restrains, and coerces employees must be found in the record as a whole. In the absence of evidence regarding the failure to explain and reassure against reprisal, without more, coercion cannot be found within the meaning of § 8(a)(1). Not only was there no showing of employer hostility, there was no showing of other unfair labor practices. Enforcement denied.

**DISSENT:** (Friendly, J.) The NLRB (P) should be allowed to set standards of conduct that are readily understandable by employers, regional directors, and administrative law judges. Here, the NLRB (P) developed, in light of experience, standards of employee interrogation which should be upheld.

## ▶ ANALYSIS

In *Bourne v. NLRB*, 332 F.2d 47, 48 (2d Cir. 1964), the court suggested factors to be considered in determining whether a particular interrogation of employees is coercive. First, it suggested that the Board consider the employer's background, i.e., whether the employer has a history of hostility and discrimination. Second, the nature of the information sought should be examined, i.e., whether it could be used for reprisals. Third, the ranking in the company hierarchy of the questioner should be considered. And last, the place and method of interrogation is important, i.e., whether the employee was called to the boss's office, or whether the employee was placed in an atmosphere of "unnatural formality."

## Quicknotes

**NLRA (NATIONAL LABOR RELATIONS ACT)** Guarantees employees the right to engage in collective bargaining, and regulates labor unions.

**NLRB (NATIONAL LABOR RELATIONS BOARD)** An agency established pursuant to the National Labor Relations Act for the purpose of prohibiting unfair labor practices by employers and unions.

# International Union of Operating Engineers, Local 49 v. NLRB (Struksnes Construction Co.)

## Union (P) v. Board (P)

353 F.2d 852 (D.C. Cir.1965), *on remand*, 165 NLRB 1062 (1967).

**NATURE OF CASE:** Remand, from court of appeals to NLRB, to reconsider certification of election procedures by NLRB.

**FACT SUMMARY:** An employer issued, with no prior discussions, a ballot sheet to employees which asked them to indicate whether they supported the union as a bargaining entity.

## 🏛 RULE OF LAW
Employer polling of employees regarding desire for union representation violates Section 8(a)(1) of the Act unless: (1) the poll's purpose is to verify a union's claim of majority, (2) this purpose is explained, (3) assurances against reprisals are given, (4) polling is by secret ballot, and (5) the employer has not created a coercive atmosphere or used unfair practices.

**FACTS:** Struksnes Construction Co. (Struksnes) (D) performed highway construction work. A union began work to organize at one job site. The union's agent requested recognition as a bargaining agent by the employers asserting that twenty of the twenty-six employees supported their efforts. Struksnes (D) denied that the union had such support and proceeded to circulate a petition amongst the employees. The petition asked whether or not each employee wanted the employer to bargain with, and sign contracts with, Operating Engineers Local 49 (P). No meetings were called to discuss union representation, and no guarantees that the employees would be free of reprisals were offered. The poll showed that nine men voted for union representation and fifteen voted against. There was no evidence of bias or reprisals against the minority voting for union representation. The union filed a complaint with the NLRB (D). The NLRB found the poll did not violate Section 8(a)(1). The court of appeals found the Board acquiesced in the way the employer polled the men without questioning whether they succumbed to coercion when they voted in the negative as to whether or not they wanted their employer to enter into a contract with their union. The Board, the court ruled, should develop appropriate policy considerations and outline minimal standards to govern the ascertainment of union status or the desire of the employees with respect to a union contract. The court therefore reversed and remanded the Board's (D) order.

**ISSUE:** Are there methods of polling by an employer regarding employees' desire for union representation that violate Section 8(a)(1)?

**HOLDING AND DECISION:** [Member not identified in casebook excerpt.] Yes. Employer polling of employees regarding desire for union representation violates Section 8(a)(1) of the Act unless: (1) the poll's purpose is to verify a union's claim of majority, (2) this purpose is explained, (3) assurances against reprisals are given, (4) polling is by secret ballot, and (5) the employer has not created a coercive atmosphere or used unfair practices. First, employees must be confident that any poll is what it appears to be and not an attempt to find out who supports union representation. Secret ballots further this protection. Secondly, the employees must be confident that an honest vote will not bring reprisals. Finally, the vote can only be relied upon if employees were not subject to unfair, coercive efforts before voting. This meets the dual requirements of assuring fair treatment of employees and protecting the legitimate interest of employers in preventing a minority group of employees from forcing unionization. Here, Struksnes (D) did not explain the purpose of the poll to the employees. The polling was not discreet, given that the employer himself polled several employees and required their signature to accompany their vote. If this case were decided under the new rule promulgated herein, the poll would certainly be struck down. However, given that the job was set to last a mere three months and ended roughly three years ago, no remedial order is necessary or appropriate. The new rule is issued in accordance with the court of appeals order, and the complaint is dismissed.

## ▌ ANALYSIS

This new rule apparently prohibits such polling techniques as the ubiquitous show of hands. Since polling must be by secret ballot under the rule, any in-person polling measures are per se violations of this rule. The question then arises as to whether the rule would withstand judicial scrutiny. If challenged, courts may likely find this element in particular excessively restrictive.

■■■

## Quicknotes

**BARGAINING UNIT** A community of interest, usually a labor union, that is authorized to carry out collective bargaining for workplace benefits on behalf of employees.

*Continued on next page.*

**NLRB (NATIONAL LABOR RELATIONS BOARD)** An agency established pursuant to the National Labor Relations Act for the purpose of prohibiting unfair labor practices by employers and unions.

**REMAND** To send back for additional scrutiny or deliberation.

■══■

# NLRB v. Exchange Parts Co.

Labor board (P) v. Employer (D)

375 U.S. 405 (1964).

**NATURE OF CASE:** Appeal from refusal of court of appeals to grant petition for enforcement of NLRB order against employer.

**FACT SUMMARY:** Exchange Parts Co. (D), an employer, announced the bestowal of new benefits on employees shortly before union representation election was to be held; the union subsequently lost the election.

## 🏛 RULE OF LAW
Section 8(a)(1) of the NLRA prohibits an employer from conferring economic benefits on his employees shortly before a representation election, where the employer's purpose is to affect the outcome of that election.

**FACTS:** Six days after the NLRB (P) ordered a representation election, McDonald, the vice-president of Exchange Parts Co. (D), held a dinner for employees. At that time, McDonald permitted the employees to choose for themselves at what time they wished to have a "floating holiday." McDonald also attacked the union, and pointed out the benefits obtained by the employees without a union. Later, Exchange Parts (D) sent its employees a letter urging them to vote against the union in the forthcoming election and, after listing a number of benefits, stated, "the union can't put any of those things in your envelope—only the company can do that." Accompanying the letter was an announcement of new benefits: the floating holiday and a grant of overtime and vacation benefits. The union lost the ensuing election. The NLRB (P) found that the announcement of the new benefits was timed to induce the employees to vote against the union, and held that this conduct violated § 8(a)(1) of the NLRA. A court of appeals refused to enforce the Board's (P) cease and desist order, noting that the new benefits were put into effect unconditionally on a permanent basis, and that there was no showing the benefits would have been withdrawn if the workers had voted for the union. The NLRB (P) appealed this ruling to the Supreme Court.

**ISSUE:** Does the conferral of employee benefits while a representation election is pending, for the purpose of inducing employees to vote against the union, interfere with the protected right to organize?

**HOLDING AND DECISION:** (Harlan, J.) Yes. The conferral of new benefits, without more, when made by an employer to induce his employees to vote against the union in a forthcoming representation election, is a violation of § 8(a)(1). The contention that a distinction is made for benefits which are permanently conferred must be rejected because the beneficence of an employer is likely to be ephemeral if prompted by a threat of unionization which is subsequently removed. The danger inherent in well-timed increases in benefits is that employees are not likely to miss the inference that the source of benefits now conferred is also the source from which future benefits must flow and which may dry up if it is not obliged. It cannot be assumed that the question of additional benefits or renegotiation of existing benefits would arise in the future. The Board (P) properly concluded here that the conferral of new benefits by Exchange Parts (D) constituted a violation of § 8(a)(1) of the NLRA. Reversed.

## ▶ ANALYSIS

"The giving of things of value to individual employees for their own use, or for the use in urging other employees to vote a certain way in the election, in circumstances which reasonably would lead the donees to believe that it was given to influence their vote, is conduct which interferes with the employees' free choice; and an election was also set aside where the employer made available to employees immediately before the election campaign badges bearing the legend 'Vote on the right side - Vote No.'" Forkosch, A Treatise on Labor Law (2d ed. 1965), § 362, p. 614.

■═■

## Quicknotes

**CEASE AND DESIST ORDER** An order from a court or administrative agency prohibiting a person or business from continuing a particular course of conduct.

**NLRA (NATIONAL LABOR RELATIONS ACT)** Guarantees employees the right to engage in collective bargaining, and regulates labor unions.

**NLRB (NATIONAL LABOR RELATIONS BOARD)** An agency established pursuant to the National Labor Relations Act for the purpose of prohibiting unfair labor practices by employers and unions.

■═■

# Electromation, Inc.

## Union (P) v. Employer (D)

309 NLRB 990 (1992), *enf'd*, 35 F.3d 1148 (7th Cir. 1994).

**NATURE OF CASE:** Enforcement of NLRB finding that employer violated § 8 of the NLRA.

**FACT SUMMARY:** Electromation, Inc. (D) created "action committees" composed of employees and managers to provide employees with mechanism to contribute to discussions about economic issues facing the company. The company was not unionized when the action committees were formed, but was unionized subsequently, and the union (P) brought this action.

## 🏛 RULE OF LAW
The employer-created action committees were labor organizations, as defined by the NLRA, and the employer violated § 8(a)(2) of the NLRA by unlawfully dominating or interfering with the committees.

**FACTS:** Electromation, Inc. (D) employed approximately 200 non-unionized employees. To involve employees in discussions about economic issues that were adversely affecting the company and its employees, Electromation (D) created "action committees" which were composed of six employees and one or two managers. Each action committee was dedicated to a particular corporate issue. The action committees were designated as (1) absenteeism/infractions, (2) no smoking policy, (3) communication network, (4) pay progression for premium positions, and (5) attendance bonus program. An administrative law judge held that the action committees were labor organizations under NLRA's definition, and that the company dominated and impermissibly assisted them.

**ISSUE:** Were the employer-created action committees labor organizations, as defined by the NLRA, and if they were, did the employer violate § 8(a)(2) of the NLRA by unlawfully dominating or interfering with the committees?

**HOLDING AND DECISION:** [Member not stated in casebook excerpt.] Yes. The employer-created action committees were labor organizations, as defined by the NLRA, and the employer violated § 8(a)(2) of the NLRA by unlawfully dominating or interfering with the committees. The statutory definition in § 2(5) of the NLRA provides that an organization is a labor organization if (1) the employees participate, (2) the organization exists, at least in part, for the purpose of dealing with employers, and (3) these dealings concern "conditions of work" or grievances. Under § 8(a)(2), domination is established if the employer creates the organization and determines its structure and function. Here, the employees participated in the committees in order to deal with employers about conditions of work. The employer unlawfully created the committees and determined their structure and function.

## ▶ ANALYSIS

*Electromation* involved a non-unionized employer, but the NLRB also has invalidated employee participation committees in organized plants where the committees dealt with safety and benefits and made recommendations to the employer through managers also on the committees. See *E.I. duPont deNemours & Co.*, 311 NLRB 893 (1988).

◼▬◼

## *Quicknotes*

**NLRA (NATIONAL LABOR RELATIONS ACT)** Guarantees employees the right to engage in collective bargaining, and regulates labor unions.

**NLRB (NATIONAL LABOR RELATIONS BOARD)** An agency established pursuant to the National Labor Relations Act for the purpose of prohibiting unfair labor practices by employers and unions.

◼▬◼

# International Ladies' Garment Workers v. NLRB
# (Bernhard-Altmann Texas Corp.)

Union (D) v. Labor board (P)

366 U.S. 731 (1961).

**NATURE OF CASE:** Appeal from finding of unfair labor practices by both employer and union.

**FACT SUMMARY:** Bernhard-Altmann Texas Corp. (D) granted recognition to the International Ladies Garment Workers' Union (ILGWU) (D) at a time when the union represented only a minority of the corporation's employees, although both parties held a good-faith belief that the union represented a majority of the workers.

---

### 🏛 RULE OF LAW
A showing that an employer granted recognition to a minority union as an exclusive bargaining agent is sufficient to support a finding of violations of § 8(a)1 by the employer and § 8(b)(1)(A) by the union, notwithstanding the good-faith belief by both sides in the union's majority status.

---

**FACTS:** The International Ladies Garment Workers' Union (ILGWU) (D) began an organizational drive among employees of Bernhard-Altmann Texas Corp. (D), whose employees were not represented by any union. During the drive, a group of employees independently went out on strike to protest wage cuts. The ILGWU (D), representing that it had signed up a majority of Bernhard-Altmann's (D) employees, entered into a representation agreement with Bernhard-Altmann (D) and signed a memorandum of understanding settling the strike. About five weeks later, a formal collective bargaining agreement was signed by both sides. The NLRB (P) thereafter brought unfair labor practice charges against both Bernard-Altmann (D) and the ILGWU (D) on the basis that at the time the employer and the union reached their initial agreement, the union in fact represented only a minority of the employees. The charges were sustained by the board (P) and affirmed by the court of appeals. Both the Union (D) and Bernhard-Altmann (D) contended that the charges should not lie since they both held a good-faith belief in the majority position of the union despite the fact that neither side had made an actual check of representation cards against the employer's payroll. Further, at the time the formal agreement was signed, the union did actually represent a majority of the employees.

**ISSUE:** Will a showing that an employer granted recognition to a minority union as an exclusive bargaining unit be sufficient to support a find of violations of § 8(a)1 by the employer and § 8(b)(1)(A) by the union where both sides held a good-faith belief in the union's majority status?

**HOLDING AND DECISION:** (Clark, J.) Yes. Section 7 of the Wagner Act assures employees the right "to bargain collectively through representatives of their own choosing" or "to refrain from" such activity. Section 8(a)(1) prohibits an employer from interfering with an employee's exercise of his § 7 rights and § 8(a)(2) prohibits an employer from contributing support to a labor organization. Similarly, § 8(b)(1)(A) prohibits a union from interfering with an employee's exercise of his § 7 rights. Where an employer grants exclusive bargaining rights to a union that represents only a minority of the employees, the employer has infringed on the § 7 rights of the majority and has impermissibly contributed support to that union. When a union purports to represent a majority of the workers in a unit when it does not actually have such support, it is likewise an infringement of the majority's § 7 rights. The good-faith belief of one or both sides has no relevance to the factual nonexistence of majority representation. The initial memorandum of understanding between the ILGWU (D) and Bernhard-Altmann (D) was void since the union had no standing to enter into such an agreement. The coercive effect of the premature recognition on the union's organizing efforts cannot be ignored. The fact that the union represented a majority of the workers at the time of the formal agreement is negated by that effect. No hardship is imposed on either side by this decision, since no penalties are imposed. If the union now represents a legitimate majority of the employees, a new agreement can be entered into. This remedial order is the only proper result in this instance.

---

### ▌ ANALYSIS

Prior to the principal case, the NLRB had sanctioned the practice of a minority union entering into an agreement with an employer so long as the agreement was conditional on the union actually obtaining majority status. Using the same rationale of coercive influence cited in the principal case, the NLRB reversed its position on such conditional agreements in 1964. While Bernhard-Altmann (D) was named as a defendant in this case, the ILGWU (D) was the only active participant since it was the party on whom the greatest impact would fall.

■■▬■

*Continued on next page.*

## Quicknotes

**BARGAINING UNIT**   A community of interest, usually a labor union, that is authorized to carry out collective bargaining for workplace benefits on behalf of employees.

**NLRB (NATIONAL LABOR RELATIONS BOARD)**   An agency established pursuant to the National Labor Relations Act for the purpose of prohibiting unfair labor practices by employers and unions.

■■■

# Edward G. Budd Mfg. Co. v. NLRB

Employer (D) v. Labor board (P)

138 F.2d 86 (3d Cir. 1943).

**NATURE OF CASE:** Appeal from an NLRB decision ordering reinstatement of two discharged employees.

**FACT SUMMARY:** Edward G. Budd Mfg. Co. (D) argued that two employees who were discharged should not be reinstated, but the NLRB (P) found that they were fired for union activities and should be rehired.

---

**RULE OF LAW**

An employer may discharge an employee for a good reason, a poor reason, or no reason at all, so long as the provisions of the NLRA are not violated.

---

**FACTS:** In 1933, at the suggestion of the management of Edward G. Budd Mfg. Co. (Edward) (D), its employees formed an association and elected representatives to confer with management. Edward (D) cooperated fully with the association and treated the representatives with "extraordinary leniency." In 1941, the U.A.W. was unsuccessful in its attempt to organize Edward (D). The U.A.W. charged that Edward (D) unlawfully supported and dominated the employees' association and that it had discharged two employees, Davis and Wiegand (who was an association representative), for activities in support of the U.A.W. The NLRB (P) ordered the association disestablished and the two employees reinstated. (The court of appeals upheld the NLRB (P) on the issue of disestablishment and the reinstatement of Davis. The discussion below concerns only Weigand, a particularly slovenly worker.)

**ISSUE:** May an employer discharge an employee for a good reason, a poor reason, or no reason at all, as long as the provisions of the NLRA are not violated?

**HOLDING AND DECISION:** [Judge not stated in casebook excerpt.] Yes. An employer may discharge an employee for a good reason, a poor reason, or no reason at all, so long as the provisions of the NLRA are not violated. While Weigand had continually slacked off on the job, was often intoxicated, and brought a woman known as "Duchess" to the rear of the plant to meet workers, he still received five raises. While his firing was often demanded, Edward (D) kept him on because of his position as an association representative. It was not until his union activity was discovered that he was suddenly discharged. "If ever a workman deserved summary discharge (for his work habits), it was he." However, the evidence clearly supported a finding that he was discharged for his union activities and not his poor work quality. Reinstatement was properly ordered. Affirmed.

---

▶ **ANALYSIS**

Section 8(a)(3) violations concern discrimination against an individual or a group involved in union activities. In determining whether there was antiunion discrimination, one should look at the employee's work record, time and quality. Also, the extent, if any, of his union activity must be examined. If there was no union activity, it is difficult to prove a § 8(a)(3) violation. If there was union activity, it must be learned whether the employer had knowledge of it. As for the employer, its feelings toward the union should be determined, as well as its pretext for discharging the employee. The timing of the discharge is not, in itself, proof of discrimination, but it is evidence of the reason for the damage.

---

## Quicknotes

**DISCRIMINATION** Unequal treatment of a class of persons.

**NLRA (NATIONAL LABOR RELATIONS ACT)** Guarantees employees the right to engage in collective bargaining, and regulates labor unions.

**NLRB (NATIONAL LABOR RELATIONS BOARD)** An agency established pursuant to the National Labor Relations Act for the purpose of prohibiting unfair labor practices by employers and unions.

# Mueller Brass Co. v. NLRB

Employer (P) v. Labor board (D)

544 F.2d 815 (5th Cir. 1977).

**NATURE OF CASE:** Appeal from order of reinstatement of an employee.

**FACT SUMMARY:** Mueller Brass Co. (Mueller) (P) fired Stone for absenteeism and Rogers for vulgar conduct and the NLRB (D) ordered reinstatement on the ground that the discharges were motivated by these employees' pro-union activities.

## 🏛 RULE OF LAW
The fact that an employee evinces a pro-union sentiment is not alone sufficient to destroy the just cause for his discharge based upon his breaking of a company rule.

**FACTS:** Mueller Brass Co. (Mueller) (P) employed Stone and Rogers. Stone was fired after failing to report for work when he was first able after a brief period of hospitalization. Rogers was fired for displaying a mechanical penis to female employees and for propositioning certain of them on a dare. Both Stone and Rogers were involved with pro-union activities. The NLRB (D) found that the dismissals were motivated by Mueller's (P) anti-union stance and opposition to pro-union activities of Stone and Rogers. The court of appeals refused to enforce the order of the NLRB (D), and the NLRB (D) appealed.

**ISSUE:** Is the fact that an employee evinces a pro-union sentiment alone sufficient to destroy the just cause for his discharge based upon his breaking of a company rule?

**HOLDING AND DECISION:** (Hill, J.) No. The fact that an employee evinces a pro-union stance is not alone sufficient to destroy the just cause for his discharge based upon his breaking of a company rule. There was no substantial evidence adduced at the trial of this matter that Rogers or Stone were treated any differently by Mueller (P) than any other employee in similar circumstances was treated. Stone was first certified by his physician as being fit for work on May 6, 1974, but did not return until May 14th. He obtained another note from the physician extending the period, but this was simply an attempt to justify his absenteeism. Rogers's conduct was clearly vulgar and offensive and the treatment of both cases was not improper on Mueller's (P) part. The fact that these employees were active in the union and that Mueller (P) has taken an antiunion stance is not enough to require reinstatement. Enforcement of NLRB's (D) order is denied.

**DISSENT:** (Godbold, J.) The majority opinion goes beyond the proper role of a reviewing body. It is a retrial of the case. Stone obtained a letter from his doctor explaining his lateness in reporting back to work after his hospitalization. Rogers's conduct was not out of keeping with the commonplace bawdy sexual horseplay in Mueller's (P) place of business where pornographic pictures and literature were freely passed around. Neither offense would have been sufficient to warrant a dismissal of any employee unless some earlier consideration was factored in. The NLRB (D) found the other consideration was the pro-union sentiments of Rogers and Stone. Their order issued accordingly should be enforced.

## ▶ ANALYSIS

The conduct of neither Stone nor Rogers was so extreme and outrageous as to be clearly grounds for immediate dismissal. However, the conduct of each does warrant some notice with an eye toward discharge. The question is whether the pro-union stance taken by both was considered, and no direct evidence of this was proffered. While the inference that improper considerations were used is permissible, it is equally permissible to infer that Mueller (P) acted in good faith. This case saves companies from fear of firing employees just because they are involved in pro-union activities.

■■■

## Quicknotes

**GOOD FAITH** An honest intention to abstain from any unconscientious advantage of another.

**NLRB (NATIONAL LABOR RELATIONS BOARD)** An agency established pursuant to the National Labor Relations Act for the purpose of prohibiting unfair labor practices by employers and unions.

■■■

# NLRB v. Adkins Transfer Co.

Labor board (P) v. Employer (D)

226 F.2d 324 (6th Cir. 1955).

**NATURE OF CASE:** Petition for enforcement of an NLRB order for violation of NLRA § 8(a)(3).

**FACT SUMMARY:** Adkins Transfer Co. (D), whose employees were teamsters, began a maintenance department with two new employees, but later closed the department and fired the two employees when it determined that it could not operate the department profitably if it had to pay union wages.

## 🏛 RULE OF LAW
In order to establish a § 8(a)(3) violation, there must be evidence that the employer's act encouraged or discouraged union membership.

**FACTS:** Adkins Transfer Co. (Adkins) (D) was a small trucking company which was friendly to and cooperative with its employees' union, the Teamsters. Adkins (D) opened a two-man maintenance shop to keep its trucks in repair and hired two new employees to do the work. The two new men joined the Teamsters. The Teamsters' representative then sought to negotiate a contract bringing the new employees' salaries up to the industry-wide level for maintenance workers. Adkins (D) could not afford to operate the maintenance shop profitably at union pay scales and wanted to avoid a strike. Adkins (D) accordingly closed the maintenance shop, discharged the two new men, and had maintenance work done by outside auto dealers-repair shops at even less cost. Adkins (D) never replaced the two fired workers and did not intend to. The NLRB (P) trial examiner found no § 8(a)(3) violation for union discrimination because the discharges were not intended to discourage or encourage union membership. The NLRB (P) reversed for the reason that the employees would not have been summarily discharged had they not joined the union, and had not sought, through the union, to exercise their rights.

**ISSUE:** In order to establish a § 8(a)(3) violation, must there be evidence that the employer's act encouraged or discouraged union membership?

**HOLDING AND DECISION:** (McAllister, J.) Yes. In order to establish a § 8(a)(3) violation, there must be evidence that the employer's act encouraged or discouraged union membership. Here, there was no union discrimination. A company may suspend or change its business operations as long as the change is not motivated by an illegal intention to avoid its obligations under the Act. "It is true that what might be termed the secondary reason for the discharge of the two employees was because they were members of the union, but the fact that they were members of the union was only incidental, and was not the real reason behind their discharge." Union wage scales were too high to allow Adkins (D) to operate the new shop profitably, and that appeared to be the only motivation for the firings. Enforcement of the NLRB (P) order was denied.

## ▶ ANALYSIS

An analogous problem to that seen in the principal case above arises when an employer closes his plant and reopens elsewhere "because of the union." Such action will generally be found to violate § 8(a)(3) where the relocation is motivated by employer hostility to the union. Such a move is termed a "runaway shop" and cannot be allowed where the employer only seeks to deprive his employees of their § 7 rights. However, where the move is prompted by Adkins-style economic factors, the courts are more apt than the NLRB to okay the move when the union has substantially contributed to the economic difficulties.

■=■

## Quicknotes

**NLRA (NATIONAL LABOR RELATIONS ACT)** Guarantees employees the right to engage in collective bargaining, and regulates labor unions.

**NLRB (NATIONAL LABOR RELATIONS BOARD)** An agency established pursuant to the National Labor Relations Act for the purpose of prohibiting unfair labor practices by employers and unions.

■=■

# Textile Workers Union v. Darlington Mfg. Co.

## Union (P) v. Employer (D)

380 U.S. 263 (1965).

**NATURE OF CASE:** Appeal by NLRB from refusal by court of appeals to enforce its finding of an unfair labor practice by employer.

**FACT SUMMARY:** Darlington Mfg. Co. (D) was controlled by Deering Milliken (D) which controlled 16 other textile manufacturers; to avoid bargaining with a certified union, Darlington (D) went out of business.

🏛 **RULE OF LAW**
While an employer has the absolute right to terminate his entire business for any reason he pleases, it is an unfair labor practice if he closes part of his business to avoid unionization.

**FACTS:** The Milliken family controlled Deering Milliken (D) whose president was Roger Milliken. Deering Milliken (D), in turn, controlled 17 textile manufacturers, including Darlington Mfg. Co. (D), from which it received products for marketing. After the Textile Workers Union won a representation election at Darlington (D), Roger Milliken, who feared that the costs of unionization would be prohibitive, secured approval from the board of directors and the stockholders to sell all of Darlington's (D) plant machinery and equipment. The union filed charges with the NLRB (P) claiming that Darlington (D) had violated §§ 8(a)(1) and 8(a)(3) (which prohibit an employer from discouraging or encouraging membership in a union by discrimination with respect to hiring or tenure of employment, or any term or condition of employment) by closing its plant, and § 8(a)(5) by refusing to bargain with the union after the election. The Board (P) found that Darlington (D) had been closed because of the antiunion animus of Roger Milliken, and that it was part of a single integrated employer group controlled by the Milliken family; hence, Deering Milliken (D) could be held liable for the unfair labor practices of Darlington (D). The Board (P) ordered back pay for all Darlington (D) employees until they obtained substantially equivalent work or were put on preferential hiring lists at the other Deering Milliken (D) mills; Deering Milliken (D) was ordered to bargain with the union. The court of appeals refused to enforce the Board's (P) order, holding that a company has the absolute right to close out a part or all of its business regardless of antiunion motives. From this refusal, the Board (P) appealed.

**ISSUE:** Is an employer free to close part of his business to avoid bargaining with a union without committing an unfair labor practice?

**HOLDING AND DECISION:** (Harlan, J.) No. An employer is free to close his business without violating § 8(a)(1), since this involves a matter of management prerogative. However, a decision to close only part of the business, if motivated by discrimination against the union, is squarely encompassed within the literal language of § 8(a)(3). A complete liquidation of a business yields no future benefit for the employer, if the termination is bona fide. The personal satisfaction that the employer would receive, or the possibility that other employers would follow suit, is too remote to be guarded against by the NLRA. Certainly, a complete closing is no different than the right of employees to quit their employment en masse. On the other hand, a discriminatory partial closing may have the effect of discouraging employees from exercising their § 7 rights in other plants kept open by the same employer. An organizational integration of plants or corporations is not a necessary prerequisite to the establishment of a § 8(a)(3) violation. All that need be shown is that the employer: (1) has an interest in another business which may or may not be doing the same kind of activity as the closed plant, of sufficient substantiality to give promise of receiving a benefit from discouragement of unionization in that business; (2) has acted to close the plant with the purpose of producing such a result; and (3) may have reasonably foreseen that such closing will discourage employees in other plants from persisting in organizational activities. However, although the court of appeals' ruling must be reversed, the case is remanded to the Board (P) for further findings on the purpose and foreseeable effect of the Darlington (D) closing on other plants controlled by Deering Milliken (D), and not just its chilling effect on the Darlington (D) employees. Remanded.

▶ **ANALYSIS**

A "runaway shop" may be caused by the employer's anti-union animus, or out of a legitimate business reason. Often, both motivations may be present; in such cases, if the economic reason is sufficient, the employer will probably win. Where a "runaway shop" is found to constitute an unfair labor practice, the Board will not resort to the most extraordinary remedy of ordering the employer to return. Rather, it will usually order back pay, with reinstatement, plus reimbursement for the expense of relocating near to the new plant.

■=■

*Continued on next page.*

## *Quicknotes*

**NLRA (NATIONAL LABOR RELATIONS ACT)**  Guarantees employees the right to engage in collective bargaining, and regulates labor unions.

**NLRB (NATIONAL LABOR RELATIONS BOARD)**  An agency established pursuant to the National Labor Relations Act for the purpose of prohibiting unfair labor practices by employers and unions.

■▬■

# Phelps Dodge Corp. v. NLRB

Employer (D) v. Labor board (P)

313 U.S. 177 (1941).

**NATURE OF CASE:** Appeal from findings of § 8(a)(3) violations.

**FACT SUMMARY:** After the conclusion of a strike against Phelps Dodge Corp. (Phelps) (D), Phelps (D) refused to rehire 38 strikers or hire two men as new employees because they were union members.

## 🏛 RULE OF LAW
An employer subject to the NLRA cannot refuse to hire employees solely because of their affiliation with a union.

**FACTS:** Union workers struck the Phelps Dodge Corp. (Phelps) (D) mine. At the strike's conclusion, Phelps (D) denied reinstatement to 38 strikers because of their union affiliation. Two men, Curtis and Daugherty, who were not employees of Phelps (D) at the time of the strike, applied to work for Phelps (D), but were denied employment on the ground that they were union members. The question arose as to whether the NLRB (P) could order Phelps (D) to hire the two new men as well as reinstate the strikers.

**ISSUE:** Can an employer who is subject to the National Labor Relations Act refuse to hire employees solely because of their affiliation with a union?

**HOLDING AND DECISION:** (Frankfurter, J.) No. The Act does not require employers to favor union members when hiring. It is directed solely against the abuse by an employer of his right to hire whomever he pleases by interfering with the countervailing right of workers' self-organization. Reinstatement is the conventional remedy for discriminatory firing. Discrimination in hiring is the twin to discrimination in firing; it would be surprising if Congress provided a remedy for one, but not for the other. To differentiate between the two would be meaningless. The Act broadly defines "employee," unless where explicitly stated otherwise, and that, in consideration of the definition of "labor dispute," expressed Congress's view that disputes may arise regardless of whether the disputants stand in the proximate relation of employer and employee, and that self-organization of employees may extend beyond a single plant or employer. The NLRB (P) can neutralize discrimination even where workers have obtained compensatory employment elsewhere, for the Board does not exist for the adjudication of private acts alone, it must carry out public policy. To limit the significance of discrimination merely to questions of monetary loss to workers would thwart the Act's central purpose toward achievement and maintenance of workers' self-organization. As Congress could not be expected to figure every method for circumventing the Act or every remedy, the NLRB (P) was given the discretion to establish appropriate remedies. Therefore, it appropriately ordered the hiring of Curtis and Daugherty.

## ▶ ANALYSIS

The remedy of reinstatement is provided in § 10(c) of the Act. Even though Curtis and Daugherty were not currently working for Phelps (D), they were found to be "employees" within the meaning of the term in § 2(3) of the Act. Had this case gone the other way, the Court would have, in effect, legitimized the practice of blacklisting. As for lost wages, in so figuring, wages earned elsewhere before reinstatement, must be deducted. Additionally, if a worker failed to attempt to find work elsewhere without reasonable cause, the amount of wages he should have earned will be deducted. The Court admitted that this would be an administrative burden but was "socially desirable."

■■■

## Quicknotes

**DISCRIMINATION** Unequal treatment of a class of persons.

**NLRA (NATIONAL LABOR RELATIONS ACT)** Guarantees employees the right to engage in collective bargaining, and regulates labor unions.

**NLRB (NATIONAL LABOR RELATIONS BOARD)** An agency established pursuant to the National Labor Relations Act for the purpose of prohibiting unfair labor practices by employers and unions.

■■■

# Blue Man Vegas, LLC v. NLRB

Theatre production (D) v. Union (P)

529 F.3d 417 (D.C. Cir. 2008).

**NATURE OF CASE:** Petition for review of an NLRB decision.

**FACT SUMMARY:** Blue Man Vegas, LLC (BMV) (D), which produces a stage act, refused to bargain with the International Alliance of Theatrical Stage Employees, Moving Picture Technicians, Artists & Allied Crafts of the United States, AFL-CIO (Union) (P), which was elected to represent some of BMV's (D) employees.

> 🏛 **RULE OF LAW**
> If employees in a proposed unit share a community of interest, the unit is prima facie appropriate unless the employer can show the prima facie appropriate unit is truly inappropriate.

**FACTS:** Blue Man Vegas, LLC (BMV) (D) produces the Las Vegas production of the Blue Man Group, a show in which men wearing blue grease paint on their faces and heads and dressed entirely in black perform skits and dance routines using musical instruments, props, videos, and sets. Seven musicians are on stage during each show, and the stage crew includes audio, carpentry, electrics, props, video, wardrobe, and musical instrument technicians (MITs). There are also "swings," which are trained to do a variety of things in order to fill in for absent crewmembers. Blue Man Group performed at the Luxor Hotel between 2000 and 2005, and during that time, BMV (D) directly employed MITs, but the Luxor employed other stage crews. The MITs reported to BMV's (D) production manager, while other stage crews reported to the Luxor; MITs were paid salaries, while others were paid an hourly wage; and the MITs' pre-performance sign-in sheet was separate from the sign-in sheet for the others. BMV (D) left the Luxor and went to the Venetian Hotel in 2005. At that time, BMV (D) decided to employ the entire stage crew directly, but several differences between the MITs and the other crews carried over from the Luxor to the Venetian: MITs continued to report directly to the production manager, while the others reported to other supervisors; the two MITs who had been with BMV (D) at the Luxor were still paid a salary, whereas all others were paid a wage; and MITs' sign-in sheet remained separate from the sign-in sheet for the other crews. The International Alliance of Theatrical Stage Employees, Moving Picture Technicians, Artists & Allied Crafts of the United States, AFL-CIO (Union) (P) petitioned the Board for a representation election in a unit that consisted of all stage crew employees except MITs in March 2006. BMV (D) objected to the exclusion of the MITs. The Board determined that the unit proposed by the Union (P) was appropriate, as there were significant differences between the MITs and the other stage crews in supervision, form of payment, and sign-in sheets. The Board also found differences that didn't stem from BMV's (D) time at the Luxor: the MITs had separate substitutes during days off, separate skills, they do not swing, and they work in different areas and interact primarily with musicians, not stage crew members. The Board therefore ordered a representation election, and denied BMV's (D) petition for review. The Union (P) won the election and the Union (P) was certified as the exclusive bargaining representative. One month later, a complaint was filed against BMV (D) for failure to bargain with the Union (P), in violation of the NLRA. BMV (D) argued it was not required to bargain because the exclusion of MITs made the unit inappropriate. The Board found in favor of the Union (P). BMV (D) then petitioned for review in court, and the Board cross-applied for enforcement.

**ISSUE:** If employees in a proposed unit share a community of interest, is the unit prima facie appropriate unless the employer can show the prima facie appropriate unit is truly inappropriate?

**HOLDING AND DECISION:** (Ginsburg, J.) Yes. If employees in a proposed unit share a community of interest, the unit is prima facie appropriate unless the employer can show the prima facie appropriate unit is truly inappropriate. BMV's (D) argument that the standard conflicts with the NLRA, and was therefore rejected by the Fourth Circuit, is incorrect. First, the standard does not conflict with the NLRA. The main concern in evaluating a proposed bargaining unit is whether members of the proposed unit share a "community of interest" based on such factors as their different methods of compensation, hours of work, benefits, supervision, training, and skills. If the employees in a proposed unit share a community of interest, then the unit is prima facie appropriate unless the employer can show that it is truly inappropriate. To do that, the employer would have to show that there is no legitimate basis on which to exclude certain employees from it, such as where there are overwhelming similarities between the excluded and included employees—the so-called overwhelming-community-of-interest standard. But it does not follow that if the MITs have a community of interest to any degree with the other stage crews, they could not be excluded, as BMV (D) argued. Second, the case BMV (D) relies on to argue that the standard applied was wrong is the Fourth Circuit's decision to overrule the Board's decision in *Lundy Packing Co.*, 314 NLRB 1042

*Continued on next page.*

(1994), in which the court objected to the Board's application of a standard that presumed a unit proposed by the Union (P) was proper unless there was an overwhelming community of interest with excluded employees. As long as the Board applies the overwhelming-community-of-interest standard after the proposed unit has been shown to be prima facie appropriate—not presumed appropriate—the Board doesn't violate *Lundy*. In this case, the Board applied the overwhelming-community-of-interest standard correctly, after finding that the proposed unit was prima facie appropriate, and held that the unit was not truly inappropriate based on that standard. BMV's (D) argument that the unit determination was not supported by substantial evidence of differences between MITs and other crew is also rejected. The Board could reasonably conclude that the MITs had different employment interests from those of the rest of the crew. A unit consisting of all of the non-MIT stage crews is prima facie appropriate because even though there are differences among them, those employees share a community of interest. While a unit consisting of all stage crews including the MITs could also be prima facie appropriate because the MITS also share a community of interest with the other stage crew employees, that fact does not necessarily make the unit that excludes MITs truly inappropriate. Finally, BMV's (D) argument that the Board's decision is arbitrary and capricious because it creates an allegedly "disfavored residual unit" is also rejected. BMV (D) argued that because MITs share an obvious community of interest with other stage crews, the Board improperly created a residual unit of MITs by excluding them. But all employees who share a community of interest need not be included in the same unit.

## ▶ ANALYSIS

The criteria for valid unit determinations is whether the those employees included in the proposed unit share a community of interests, not whether all employees sharing a community of interest are included in the prosed unit. The MITs in this show work side-by-side with the rest of the crew, and therefore share a community of interests, but it wasn't necessary to include them in the unit. Arguably, if their votes for unionization were in doubt, they may have been excluded on that basis as well, but that fact doesn't change the fact that the unit as determined is valid based on current standards and precedent.

■═■

## Quicknotes

**NLRA (NATIONAL LABOR RELATIONS ACT)** Guarantees employees the right to engage in collective bargaining, and regulates labor unions.

**NLRB (NATIONAL LABOR RELATIONS BOARD)** An agency established pursuant to the National Labor Relations Act for the purpose of prohibiting unfair labor practices by employers and unions.

**PRIMA FACIE CASE** An action where the plaintiff introduces sufficient evidence to submit the issue to the judge or jury for determination.

■═■

# American Hospital Ass'n v. NLRB

Employer (P) v. Labor board (D)

499 U.S. 606 (1991).

**NATURE OF CASE:** Appeal from reversal of injunction against enforcement of an industry-specific, unit-defining rule.

**FACT SUMMARY:** After the NLRB (D) promulgated a substantive rule defining the employee units appropriate for collective bargaining for the entire industry, American Hospital Association (Hospital) (P) brought suit challenging the facial validity of the rule.

> 🏛 **RULE OF LAW**
> The NLRB has the authority under the NLRA to promulgate a general rule outlining the unit appropriate for the purposes of collective bargaining for an entire industry.

**FACTS:** For the first time since its inception in 1935, the NLRB (D) promulgated a substantive rule defining the employee units appropriate for collective bargaining in an entire industry. The rule was applicable to acute care hospitals and provided that eight and only eight units shall be appropriate in any such hospital. American Hospital Association (Hospital) (P) brought this action challenging the facial validity of the rule on three grounds: that § 9(b) of the NLRA prohibited the NLRB (D) from using general rules since it required the NLRB (D) to make separate bargaining unit determinations "in each case"; that the rule formulated by the NLRB (D) violated a congressional admonition to avoid the undue proliferation of bargaining units in the health care industry; and that the rule was arbitrary and capricious. The district court agreed with the second argument and enjoined enforcement of the rule. The court of appeals reversed, finding no merit in any of the three arguments.

**ISSUE:** Does the NLRB have the authority under the NLRA to promulgate a general rule outlining the unit appropriate for the purposes of collective bargaining for an entire industry?

**HOLDING AND DECISION:** (Stevens, J.) Yes. The NLRB has the authority under the NLRA to promulgate a general rule outlining the unit appropriate for the purposes of collective bargaining for an entire industry. The general mandate granted to the NLRB (D) by § 6 is unquestionably sufficient to authorize the rule at issue unless limited by some other provision in the Act. Contrary to Hospital's (P) first argument, § 9(b) does not provide such a limitation. Read in conjunction with § 6, § 9(a), and the context of the statute as a whole, the more natural reading of the three words "in each case" simply indicates that whenever there is a disagreement about the appropriateness of a unit, the NLRB (D) shall resolve the dispute. The NLRB (D) must still apply the rule "in each case." If Congress had intended to curtail the broad rulemaking authority granted in § 6, it would be expected to do so in language expressly describing an exception from that section or at least referring specifically to the section. Second, the admonition contained in both the House and Senate Committee Reports on NLRA Amendments of 1974, that due consideration should be given by the NLRB (D) to preventing proliferation of bargaining units in the health care industry, is best understood as a form of notice to the NLRB (D) that if it did not give appropriate consideration to the problem of proliferation in this industry, Congress might respond with a legislative remedy. Finally, as for the rule being arbitrary and capricious, the extensive notice and comment rulemaking conducted by the NLRB (D), its careful analysis of the comments that it received, and its well-reasoned justification for the new rule demonstrated that it was based on substantial evidence and supported by a "reasoned analysis." The NLRB's (D) conclusion that, absent extraordinary circumstances, "acute care hospitals do not differ in substantial, significant ways relating to the appropriateness of units" was thus based on a "reasoned analysis" of an extensive record. Affirmed.

▌ **ANALYSIS**

The Court declared that the language of § 6, "authority from time to time to make, amend, and rescind . . . such rules and regulations as may be necessary to carry out the provisions" of the Act, expressly contemplates the possibility that the NLRB (D) will reshape its policies on the basis of more information and experience in the administration of the Act. In addition, § 9(a)'s provision that the representative "designated or selected for the purposes of collective bargaining by the majority of the employees in a unit appropriate for such purposes" implies that the initiative in selecting an appropriate unit resides with the employees. The Court points out in this context, § 9(b)'s provision that the NLRB (D) shall decide "in each case" can be seen to apply to the obvious potential for disagreement concerning the appropriateness of the unit selected by the union seeking recognition by the employer under § 9(a) and not, as Hospital (P) contended, as a bar to the NLRB's (D) adoption of a general rule applicable to an entire industry.

■■■■

*Continued on next page.*

## *Quicknotes*

**COLLECTIVE BARGAINING** Negotiations between an employer and employee that are mediated by a specified third party.

**NLRA (NATIONAL LABOR RELATIONS ACT)** Guarantees employees the right to engage in collective bargaining, and regulates labor unions.

**NLRB (NATIONAL LABOR RELATIONS BOARD)** An agency established pursuant to the National Labor Relations Act for the purpose of prohibiting unfair labor practices by employers and unions.

# Charles D. Bonanno Linen Service, Inc. v. NLRB

Employer (D) v. Labor board (P)

454 U.S. 404 (1982).

**NATURE OF CASE:** Appeal of a finding of an unfair labor practice.

**FACT SUMMARY:** Charles D. Bonanno Linen Service, Inc. (Bonanno) (D) unilaterally withdrew from a multiemployer bargaining unit and refused to comply with the collective bargaining agreement subsequently reached.

## 🏛 RULE OF LAW
A bargaining impasse is not a sufficiently unusual circumstance to justify an employer's unilateral withdrawal from a multiemployer bargaining unit, and a failure to execute the resulting agreement is an unfair labor practice.

**FACTS:** The Union (P) charged Charles D. Bonanno Linen Service, Inc. (Bonanno) (D) with an unfair labor practice under §§ 8(a)(1) and (5) because of its refusal to execute a collective bargaining agreement reached between the Union (P) and a multiemployer bargaining unit from which Bonanno (D) unilaterally withdrew because of an impasse in negotiations. The administrative law judge found that no unusual circumstance excused the withdrawal and ordered Bonanno (D) to execute the agreement. The Board affirmed, and the court of appeals enforced the Board's order. Bonanno (D) appealed.

**ISSUE:** Is a bargaining impasse a sufficiently unusual circumstance to justify an employer's unilateral withdrawal from a multiemployer bargaining unit, thereby protecting him from an unfair labor practice charge?

**HOLDING AND DECISION:** (White, J.) No. A bargaining impasse is not a sufficiently unusual circumstance to justify an employer's unilateral withdrawal from a multiemployer bargaining unit, and a failure to execute the resulting agreement is an unfair labor practice. Because an impasse is a temporary deadlock, and because it is easily created by one party merely to justify withdrawal, it cannot be the basis for withdrawal without severely undercutting the efficacy of collective bargaining through multiemployer units. Further, although impasse is recognized as justifying withdrawal when an employer is the target of a selective strike, any agreement reached separately by the employer with the union expires upon execution of the agreement between the union and the multiemployer units. These interim agreements serve to deter fragmentation because the withdrawing employer maintains an equal interest in the overall agreement. Without this interest the use of multiemployer units is rendered meaningless. Therefore, the employer cannot be allowed to completely withdraw due to impasse. Affirmed.

## ▶ ANALYSIS

Once negotiations begin, withdrawal from a multiemployer bargaining unit upsets the relationships and assumptions upon which the parties have been relying. Usually the only unusual circumstances recognized to justify unilateral withdrawal have been impending bankruptcy or forced closing. Finally, this case ends the conflict over this issue of impasse which existed among several circuit courts.

∎══∎

## Quicknotes

**NLRB (NATIONAL LABOR RELATIONS BOARD)** An agency established pursuant to the National Labor Relations Act for the purpose of prohibiting unfair labor practices by employers and unions.

**UNFAIR LABOR PRACTICE** Conduct by labor unions and employers, which is proscribed by the National Labor Relations Act.

∎══∎

# General Electric Co. v. NLRB

## Employer (D) v. Labor board (P)

412 F.2d 512 (2d Cir. 1969).

**NATURE OF CASE:** Appeal from NLRB's finding of an unfair labor practice by employer.

**FACT SUMMARY:** General Electric Co. (GE) (D) refused to sit down at the collective bargaining table with a union committee which included nonvoting members of other unions.

### 🏛 RULE OF LAW
A mixed-union negotiating committee is not per se improper, and, absent a showing of substantial evidence of ulterior motive or bad faith, an employer commits an unfair labor practice unless it bargains with such a group.

**FACTS:** General Electric Co. (GE) (D) refused to meet with the International Union of Electrical, Radio and Machine Workers, AFL-CIO (IUE) because the IUE bargaining committee included, on an eight-man panel, seven nonvoting members of other unions. The avowed purposes of the members of this committee were to coordinate collective bargaining with GE (D) and its chief competitor, to formulate national goals, and otherwise to support one another. The NLRB (P) found that the committee was neither "locked in" (engaged in a conspiracy to obliterate bargaining unit lines) nor bent on joint bargaining. Finding no substantial evidence of the IUE committee's ulterior motive or bad faith, the NLRB (P) held that GE's (D) refusal to bargain with the committee was a violation of §§ 8(a)(1) and (5) of the NLRA. GE (D) appealed.

**ISSUE:** Does a union's inclusion of members of other unions on its bargaining committee, absent unusual or exceptional circumstances, justify an employer's refusal to bargain?

**HOLDING AND DECISION:** (Feinberg, J.) No. A union's inclusion of members of other unions on its bargaining committee, absent unusual or exceptional circumstances, does not justify an employers's refusal to bargain. Section 7 of the NLRA guarantees to employees and employers alike the right to choose whomever they wish to represent them in formal labor negotiations; neither side can control the other's selection. The exceptions to this rule have been rare and confined to situations so infected with ill will, usually personal, or conflict of interest as to make good faith bargaining impractical. Absent some showing of bad faith or ulterior motive, such as where an expanded bargaining committee seeks to force a single bargaining unit on different plants or crafts, a union has the right to select outsiders to sit in and assist a local bargaining committee. The specific policy reasons for such inclusion stem not only from the union's interest in using experts to bargain, but also from the union's desire to increase communications between all of them, and, thereby, to prevent the employer from playing one off against the other. In the present case, the IUE's purpose was to increase its bargaining strength. This is not objectionable since such a goal is a normal one for unions or employers. While the possibility exists that there will be improper attempts to ignore unit boundaries, it is not necessary at this time to consider the extent to which the law permits cooperation in bargaining among unions or employers; the risk is inherent in the bargaining process. Furthermore, the NLRB (P) is capable of making the determination when a case comes before it. Regardless, cooperation between unions is not illegal up to a point. GE (D) could have tested IUE's good faith by meeting with the committee; its failure to do so is its own fault. Affirmed.

## ▶ ANALYSIS

Prior to the commencement of negotiations, both management and labor may withdraw from collective bargaining involving multiemployer units by giving clear notice. However, once negotiations are under way, neither party can withdraw absent the other's consent or the presence of "unusual circumstances." A dropping off of a company's production or sales, or a real bargaining impasse is not considered "unusual" enough to justify a unilateral withdrawal by the employer.

■═■

### Quicknotes

**COLLECTIVE BARGAINING** Negotiations between an employer and employee that are mediated by a specified third party.

**NLRA (NATIONAL LABOR RELATIONS ACT)** Guarantees employees the right to engage in collective bargaining, and regulates labor unions.

**NLRB (NATIONAL LABOR RELATIONS BOARD)** An agency established pursuant to the National Labor Relations Act for the purpose of prohibiting unfair labor practices by employers and unions.

■═■

# Leedom v. Kyne

Parties not identified.

358 U.S. 184 (1958).

**NATURE OF CASE:** Appeal by employees from NLRB's determination of a collective bargaining unit.

**FACT SUMMARY:** Although the NLRA specifically required the NLRB (D) to secure the approval of professional employees before including them in the same bargaining unit as nonprofessional employees, the Board (D) issued a representation order without having done so.

## 🏛 RULE OF LAW
A federal district court has original jurisdiction of a suit to strike down a representation order of the NLRB made in excess of its delegated powers and contrary to a specific prohibition in the NLRA.

**FACTS:** Section 9(b)(1) of the NLRA provides that, in determining the unit appropriate for collective bargaining, "the Board shall not (1) decide that any unit is appropriate for such purposes if such unit includes both professional employees and employees who are not professional employees unless a majority of such professional employees vote for inclusion in such unit." The NLRB (D) had certified 233 professional employees and nine technical employees of a Westinghouse Electric plant as a bargaining unit without taking a vote of the professional employees to determine if they favored inclusion of the technical employees. An association (P) that represented the professional employees then filed an action against the Board (D) in federal district court charging them with violating § 9(b)(1), and praying that the Board's (D) action be set aside. The trial court, holding that it had jurisdiction, granted the association's (P) motion for summary judgment, and set aside the Board's (D) determination of the bargaining unit and also the resulting election and certification. The Board (D) appealed to the court of appeals which affirmed the district court's judgment.

**ISSUE:** Does a federal district court have jurisdiction over an original suit that seeks to strike down an NLRB representation order which is in direct violation of § 9(b)(1)?

**HOLDING AND DECISION:** (Whittaker, J.) Yes. The Court has previously held that a Board (D) order in certification proceedings under § 9 is not a "final order" and therefore, as a rule, is not subject to judicial review. However, the present suit is not one to "review" a decision of the Board (D) made within its jurisdiction. Rather, it is one to strike down a representation order of the Board (D) made in excess of its delegated powers and contrary to a specific prohibition in the Act. Section 9(b)(1) is clear and mandatory. Plainly, the Board's (D) refusal to take a vote among the professional employees and proceed with certification was an attempted exercise of power that Congress had specifically withheld. Surely, a federal district court has jurisdiction of an original suit to prevent deprivation of a right given by Congress to professional employees. Affirmed.

**DISSENT:** (Brennan, J.) There is nothing in the legislative history of the NLRA to suggest that Congress did not mean to drastically limit time-consuming court procedures which would seriously threaten to frustrate the basic national policy of preventing industrial strife and achieving industrial peace by promoting collective bargaining. After today's decision, ingenious counsel will find some ingenious way to use the tactic of litigation to delay the initiation of collective bargaining when it suits the purposes of either labor or management. Congress was fully aware of the hardship a union may suffer if review of a representation order is not open to it; nonetheless, Congress believed the disadvantages of broader review to be more serious than the difficulties which limited review posed for the parties. The Board (D), in the present case, did not blatantly ignore § 9(b)(1), but arguably construed it to be inapplicable where the professional employees outnumbered the nonprofessional employees. This construction should not be overturned by a federal district court.

## ▶ ANALYSIS

Where there is no charge before a court that the Board's representation was in excess, or contrary to its statutorily limited authority, § 9(d) and § 10 are given effect. Section 9(d) limits review of Board representation orders, i.e., certification and decertification, only when the rulings are incidental to prohibiting an unfair labor practice. Section 10 provides that a petition for review may be filed only by a "person aggrieved by an order." Courts have construed these two sections together to limit review only when a party challenges an election by charging an unfair labor practice, and the Board, in response to the charge, has issued a "final order." The upshot of all this is that if the Board, in its discretion, refuses to hear the charge, there can be no judicial review.

■▬■

### *Quicknotes*

**JUDICIAL REVIEW** The authority of the courts to review decisions, actions or omissions committed by another agency or branch of government.

*Continued on next page.*

**NLRA (NATIONAL LABOR RELATIONS ACT)** Guarantees employees the right to engage in collective bargaining, and regulates labor unions.

**NLRB (NATIONAL LABOR RELATIONS BOARD)** An agency established pursuant to the National Labor Relations Act for the purpose of prohibiting unfair labor practices by employers and unions.

**ORIGINAL JURISDICTION** The power of a court to hear an action upon its commencement.

# NLRB v. Gissel Packing Co.

Labor board (P) v. Employer (D)

395 U.S. 575 (1969).

**NATURE OF CASE:** Appeal from findings and orders under NLRA §§ 8(a)(1), 8(a)(3), and 8(a)(5).

**FACT SUMMARY:** In three consolidated cases, the extent of an employer's duty under the Act to recognize a union that bases its majority solely on authorization cards, and the steps an employer may take to resist such card-based recognition was considered.

## 🏛 RULE OF LAW
Where an employer commits independent and substantial unfair labor practices disruptive of election conditions, the NLRB may withhold the election or set it aside, and issue instead a bargaining order as a remedy for the various violations.

**FACTS:** In each of three consolidated cases from the Fourth Circuit, the union waged an organizational campaign, obtained authorization cards from a majority of employees in the appropriate bargaining unit, and then, on the basis of the cards, demanded recognition by the employer. All three employers refused to bargain on the ground that cards were inherently unreliable indicators; and they either began, or continued, strong antiunion campaigns that gave rise to numerous unfair labor practice charges. In each case, the NLRB (P) found: (1) that the union had a majority as shown by cards and was entitled to represent the appropriate bargaining unit; and (2) that the employers' refusal to bargain violated § 8(a)(5) as it was not motivated by a "good faith" doubt of the unions' majority status, but rather to dissipate that status. This was based on the employers' commission of substantial unfair labor practices during the antiunion campaign. Thus, there was restraint and coercion of employees in violation of § 8(a)(1), and a violation of § 8(a)(3) by wrongful discharge of employees engaged in union activities. The NLRB (P) ordered each employer to cease and desist, to reinstate with back pay the wrongfully discharged, and to bargain on request with the unions. On appeal, the Fourth Circuit upheld the findings of §§ 8(a)(1) and 8(a)(3) violations, but reversed the finding of § 8(a)(5) violations. The court said that only if the employer had independent knowledge that a majority existed was he required to bargain. The NLRB (P) appealed.

**ISSUE:** Where an employer commits independent and substantial unfair labor practices disruptive of elective conditions, may the NLRB withhold the election or set it aside, and issue instead a bargaining order as a remedy for the various violations?

**HOLDING AND DECISION:** (Warren, C.J.) Yes. Generally, when an employer is confronted by a recognition demand based upon authorization cards, an employer need not grant recognition immediately, but may, unless he has knowledge independently of the union's majority, decline the request to bargain and insist upon an election either by requesting the union to petition or petitioning himself, § 9(c)(1)(B). If, however, the employer commits independent and substantial unfair labor practices disruptive of election conditions, the NLRB (P) may withhold the election or set it aside, and issue instead a bargaining order as a remedy for the various violations. A bargaining order will not issue if the union obtained the cards through misrepresentation or coercion or if the employees unfair labor practices are unrelated generally to the representation campaign. A union can establish a bargaining obligation by means other than an NLRB (P) election. While the § 9(c) election and certification procedures are used most commonly, there was early recognition that an employer had a duty to bargain whenever the union representative presented "convincing evidence of union support." Such evidence includes union-called strikes, a strike vote, or authorization cards signed by a majority in the bargaining unit. Further, authorization cards are not such inherently unreliable indicators so as to be disallowed. While cards are admittedly inferior, both sides still have the opportunity to argue the pros and cons of unionizing. If the card itself is unambiguous, it will be counted unless the employee was told it would be used solely to obtain an election. As for § 8(a)(5) remedies, the court has long held that the NLRB (P) can issue a bargaining order without a showing that the union has maintained its majority and even when it is clear that the union has lost its majority. "The only effect of our holding here is to approve the NLRB's (P) use of the bargaining order in less extraordinary cases marked by less pervasive practices which nonetheless still have the tendency to undermine majority strength and impede the election processes." Reversed and remanded.

## ▶ ANALYSIS

On remand, the NLRB (P) upheld issuance of the bargaining order because the employers' unfair labor practices were so pervasive as to preclude the holding of a fair election. The NLRB's (P) position is that *Gissel* "contemplated that the propriety of a bargaining order would be judged as of the time of the commission of the unfair labor practices and not in the light of subsequent events."

*Continued on next page.*

Otherwise, an employer could gain from its wrongful conduct by keeping a union whose majority has been weakened from securing a bargaining order. *Gibson Products Co.,* 185 NLRB 352 (1970). In *Pacific Abrasive Supply Co.,* 182 NLRB 329 (1970), it was held that an employer could violate § 8(a)(5) by refusing to bargain if he has independent knowledge that the union has a majority, even though he commits no other unfair labor practices.

■══■

## Quicknotes

**COERCION** The overcoming of a person's free will as a result of threats, promises, or undue influence.

**NLRA (NATIONAL LABOR RELATIONS ACT)** Guarantees employees the right to engage in collective bargaining, and regulates labor unions.

**NLRB (NATIONAL LABOR RELATIONS BOARD)** An agency established pursuant to the National Labor Relations Act for the purpose of prohibiting unfair labor practices by employers and unions.

**WRONGFUL DISCHARGE** Unlawful termination of an individual's employment.

■══■

# Linden Lumber Div., Summer & Co. v. NLRB

## Employer (D) v. Union (P)

419 U.S. 301 (1974).

**NATURE OF CASE:** Appeal from a finding of an unfair labor practice.

**FACT SUMMARY:** The Union (P) argued that Linden Lumber Div., Summer & Co. (D) committed an unfair labor practice because it refused to accept authorization cards as evidence of the Union's (P) having gained majority status.

### 🏛 RULE OF LAW
An employer should not be found to have committed an unfair labor practice solely on the basis of its refusal to accept evidence of majority status other than the results of an NLRB election.

**FACTS:** The Union (P) obtained authorization cards from a majority of Linden Lumber Div., Summer & Co.'s (Linden) (D) employees and demanded recognition as the representative of those employees. Linden (D) doubted the Union's (P) majority status and suggested that it petition to the NLRB (P) for an election. The Union (P) did so but withdrew its petition when Linden (D), which claimed that the Union's (P) organizational campaign had been improperly assisted by company supervisors, declined to abide by an election. When Linden (D) continued to refuse to enter into collective bargaining, the Union (P) struck for recognition and filed an unfair labor practice action based upon Linden's (D) refusal to bargain. The NLRB (P) ruled that an unfair labor practice was not committed solely by Linden's (D) failure to accept evidence of majority status other than an election. The court of appeals reversed and Linden (D) appealed.

**ISSUE:** Should an employer be found to have committed an unfair labor practice solely on the basis of its refusal to accept evidence of majority status other than the results of an NLRB election?

**HOLDING AND DECISION:** (Douglas, J.) No. An employer should not be found to have committed an unfair labor practice solely on the basis of its refusal to accept evidence of majority status other than the results of an NLRB election. It has earlier been held that an employer who engages in "unfair" labor practices "likely to destroy the union's majority and seriously impede the election" may not insist that before it bargains, the union get a secret ballot election, *NLRB v. Gissel Packing Co.*, 395 U.S. at 600 (1969). No such unfair labor practices occurred here. The NLRB (P) in its decision did not believe whether the employer had good reasons or poor reasons was relevant to the inquiry. The question has become one of whether the union or the employer has the burden to request an election when the employer has committed no unfair labor practice. The NLRB's (P) belief that the Union (P) should petition should be the answer. An employer who wants to delay can do so through a petition, and an employer's petition would not obviate litigation over the sufficiency of the union's showing of interest. While a union petition requires a backing of 30%, the sufficiency of such showing is not litigable. Reversed.

**DISSENT:** (Stewart, J.) "The language and history of the Act clearly indicate that Congress intended to impose upon an employer the duty to bargain with a union that has presented convincing evidence of majority support, even though the union has not petitioned for and won a board-supervised election."

### ▌ *ANALYSIS*

An employer can refuse to accept authorization cards for various reasons. His objection can, of course, be a cover for his general dislike of unions. On the other hand, a good-faith objection may exist for not trusting authorization cards in a specific situation. Just because a majority of employees strikes and pickets does not mean that they support the particular union seeking recognition. Some employees will not cross picket lines out of sympathy or out of fear. These factors illustrate the difficulty in determining on what basis the employer was moved to decide. By placing the burden on the union to petition for an election where no unfair labor practice has been committed by the employer avoids consideration of this problem.

▪━▪

### *Quicknotes*

**COLLECTIVE BARGAINING** Negotiations between an employer and employee that are mediated by a specified third party.

**NLRB (NATIONAL LABOR RELATIONS BOARD)** An agency established pursuant to the National Labor Relations Act for the purpose of prohibiting unfair labor practices by employers and unions.

▪━▪

# Brooks v. NLRB

Employer (D) v. Labor board (P)

348 U.S. 96 (1954).

**NATURE OF CASE:** Appeal from court of appeals' enforcement of NLRB finding of unfair labor practice on part of employer.

**FACT SUMMARY:** Brooks' Chrysler-Plymouth agency (D) refused to bargain with newly certified union which, shortly after certification election, had been disavowed by a majority of the employees in the bargaining unit.

🏛 **RULE OF LAW**
An employer must bargain for a reasonable period with a union which has been selected by his employees in an NLRB-conducted election and certified by the NLRB, even if that union loses the support of the employees shortly after it has been certified.

**FACTS:** Brooks' Chrysler-Plymouth agency (Brooks) (D) employed 13 machinists. The union won an NLRB-conducted election there by a vote of 8-5 to be the exclusive bargaining representative of the agency's machinists. One week later, and just before the union was certified by the NLRB, Brooks (D) received a letter from 9 of the 13 employees in the bargaining unit which stated that they were no longer in favor of being represented by the union as a bargaining agent. Relying on this letter, Brooks (D) refused to bargain with the union. The NLRB (P) found that Brooks (D) was guilty of an unfair labor practice under §§ 8(a)(1) and 8(a)(5) of the NLRA. The court of appeals enforced the NLRB's (P) order to bargain, and Brooks (D) appealed.

**ISSUE:** Does an employer have a duty to bargain with a duly certified bargaining agent, if, shortly after the election which resulted in the certification, the union has lost, through no fault of the employer, a majority of the employees from its membership?

**HOLDING AND DECISION:** (Frankfurter, J.) Yes. There are five reasons in support of the rule that an employer must continue to bargain with a certified bargaining representative for a reasonable time after certification, even if the representative has lost the support of the employees: (a) as in the political and business spheres, a binding election promotes a sense of responsibility in the electorate and needed coherence in administration; (b) revocation of authority should occur by a procedure no less solemn than that of the initial designation. A petition or a public meeting is no substitute for the privacy and independence of the voting booth; (c) a union should be given ample time, free from pressures to produce hot-house results, to carry out its mandate; (d) an employer would be discouraged from serious bargaining it he knew that because of his own

dilly-dallies, or otherwise, the rank and file may, at the last moment, repudiate their agent; and (e) raiding and strife among competing unions will be minimized if elections are not subject to the hazard of informal and short-term recall. By refusing to bargain with the union, Brooks (D) is, in effect, seeking to vindicate the rights of his employees to select their bargaining representative. However, the employees' proper recourse is to submit their own grievance to the NLRB (P). An employer who has doubts must petition the NLRB (P) for relief, while continuing to bargain in good faith. It is up to the NLRB (P), and not the employer, to revoke a certification. To justify employer self-help would be to undermine industrial peace. The NLRB (P) has determined that certification must be recognized for, at the very least, a period of one year. Finally, it is not within the power of this court to require the NLRB (P) to make a distinction between an employer with many employees, and one who has only a few. Affirmed.

**► ANALYSIS**

The NLRB has defined "reasonable period," for the purpose of requiring an employer to extend good faith recognition to the certified union, as being at least one year following the time of certification. Once the year has expired, either the employer or the employees may petition the NLRB for a new election. However, the question has arisen whether an employer's deliberate attempt to delay good faith bargaining so as to gain a time advantage tells the running of the "reasonable period." The NLRB has concluded that it does in ruling that the one year applies only to actual, good faith bargaining.

■━━■

## Quicknotes

**COLLECTIVE BARGAINING** Negotiations between an employer and employee that are mediated by a specified third party.

**NLRA (NATIONAL LABOR RELATIONS ACT)** Guarantees employees the right to engage in collective bargaining, and regulates labor unions.

**NLRB (NATIONAL LABOR RELATIONS BOARD)** An agency established pursuant to the National Labor Relations Act for the purpose of prohibiting unfair labor practices by employers and unions.

■━━■

# Allentown Mack Sales and Service, Inc. v. NLRB

### Employer (D) v. Federal agency (P)

522 U.S. 359 (1998).

**NATURE OF CASE:** Appeal from order to bargain with a union.

**FACT SUMMARY:** Allentown Mack Sales (D) was accused of violating the National Labor Relations Act when it failed to recognize an incumbent union.

## RULE OF LAW
Conducting an internal poll of employee support for a union is an unfair labor practice if the employer cannot show that it had a good faith reasonable doubt about the union's majority support.

**FACTS:** Mack Trucks had a factory branch in Allentown, Pennsylvania, whose service and parts employees were represented by a union. When the branch was sold, Allentown Mack Sales (Allentown) (D) began operating it as an independent dealership. Some employees made statements to the new owners indicating that the incumbent union had lost support among the employees. The new employer (D) rejected the union's request that it be recognized as the employees' collective-bargaining representative, and arranged for an independent poll by secret ballot. The poll was conducted and the union lost. The union then filed an unfair-labor-practice charge with the NLRB (P). The administrative law judge (ALJ) concluded that Allentown (D) was a successor employer to Mack Trucks, and therefore inherited Mack's bargaining obligation and a presumption of continuing majority support for the union. The ALJ found that Allentown (D) did not have an objective reasonable doubt about the majority status of the union, and thus was not authorized to conduct a poll. The NLRB (P) adopted the ALJ's findings and ordered Allentown (D) to recognize and bargain with the union. The Court of Appeals for the District of Columbia enforced the NLRB's (P) bargaining order. The Supreme Court granted certiorari.

**ISSUE:** Is conducting an internal poll of employee support for a union an unfair labor practice if the employer cannot show that it had a good faith reasonable doubt about the union's majority support?

**HOLDING AND DECISION:** (Scalia, J.) Yes. Conducting an internal poll of employee support for a union is an unfair labor practice if the employer cannot show that it had a good faith reasonable doubt about the union's majority support. In this case, a reasonable jury could not have found that Allentown (D) possessed a genuine, reasonable uncertainty about the continuing support of a majority of unit employees, permitting it to conduct such a poll. The NLRB's (P) "reasonable doubt" test for employer polls is facially rational and consistent with the Act. However, the NLRB's (P) factual finding that Allentown Mack Sales (D) lacked such a doubt is not supported by substantial evidence on the record as a whole. Reversed and remanded.

**CONCURRENCE IN PART AND DISSENT IN PART:** (Rehnquist, C.J.) The NLRB's (P) standard is not rational and not consistent with the NLRA. The ability to poll employees provides the employer with a neutral and effective manner of obtaining information relevant to determining the employees' proper representative.

**CONCURRENCE IN PART AND DISSENT IN PART:** (Breyer, J.) The majority's interpretation departs from settled principles permitting agencies broad leeway to interpret their own rules.

## ANALYSIS

The court in this case found that the NLRB (P) had refused to credit probative circumstantial evidence. Statements made by two employees that the entire night shift did not want the union were excluded. Since only the existence of a reasonable doubt, and not the fact of disfavor itself, was at issue, this court found their testimony probative.

---

### Quicknotes

**COLLECTIVE BARGAINING** Negotiations between an employer and employee that are mediated by a specified third party.

**NLRA (NATIONAL LABOR RELATIONS ACT)** Guarantees employees the right to engage in collective bargaining, and regulates labor unions.

**NLRB (NATIONAL LABOR RELATIONS BOARD)** An agency established pursuant to the National Labor Relations Act for the purpose of prohibiting unfair labor practices by employers and unions.

**PRESUMPTION** A rule of law requiring the court to presume certain facts to be true based on the existence of other facts, thereby shifting the burden of proof to the party against whom the presumption is asserted to rebut.

**PROBATIVE** Tending to establish proof.

# Negotiation of the Collective Bargaining Agreement

## Quick Reference Rules of Law

# J.I. Case Co. v. National Labor Relations Board

Employer (D) v. Labor board (P)

321 U.S. 332 (1944).

**NATURE OF CASE:** Appeal from determination of an NLRA § 8(a)(5) violation.

**FACT SUMMARY:** J.I. Case Co. (D) refused to bargain collectively with about three quarters of its employees, with whom it had individual contracts, until those contracts expired.

## RULE OF LAW

Individual contracts, no matter what the circumstances that justify their execution or what their terms, may not be availed of to defeat or delay any procedures or rights under the NLRA.

**FACTS:** J.I. Case Co. (Case) (D) signed individual contracts of employment with about three quarters of its employees. Subsequently, a union was selected as the collective bargaining representative for Case (D) employees in a Board election. Case (D) refused to bargain on any matter covered in the individual contracts, claiming that those contracts had to be honored until they expired. However, Case (D) was willing to bargain on any matter not covered by those contracts. The NLRB (P) held that the refusal to bargain was a § 8(a)(5) violation. Case (D) appealed.

**ISSUE:** May individual contracts be availed of to defeat or delay any procedures or rights under the NLRA?

**HOLDING AND DECISION:** (Jackson, J.) No. Individual contracts, no matter what the circumstances that justify their execution or what their terms, may not be availed of to defeat or delay any procedures or rights under the NLRA. Neither can they be used to delay bargaining of limit or condition terms of the collective agreement. Private contracts must yield to the Act whenever they conflict. Advantages which may be given to some individuals over those given to the whole are fruitful in interfering with organization and choice of representation and are disruptive of the strength of the whole. Affirmed.

## ▶ ANALYSIS

This case has been called, perhaps, the most significant opinion interpreting the NLRA because it establishes the primacy of the collective bargaining representative over the individual employee's relation with his employer. Collective bargaining involves collective burdens as well as collective benefits. Thus, for the greater good of the whole, some employees may find that their pay, as established in an individual hiring agreement, may be reduced by a collective bargaining agreement even though the term of the individual contracts has not run.

◼▬◼

## Quicknotes

**COLLECTIVE BARGAINING** Negotiations between an employer and employee that are mediated by a specified third party.

**NLRA (NATIONAL LABOR RELATIONS ACT)** Guarantees employees the right to engage in collective bargaining, and regulates labor unions.

**NLRB (NATIONAL LABOR RELATIONS BOARD)** An agency established pursuant to the National Labor Relations Act for the purpose of prohibiting unfair labor practices by employers and unions.

◼▬◼

# Emporium Capwell Co. v.
# Western Addition Community Organization

Employer (D) v. Civil rights organization (P)

420 U.S. 50 (1975).

**NATURE OF CASE:** Complaint before NLRB initiated by civil rights organization, charging employer with committing an unfair labor practice.

**FACT SUMMARY:** Although a collective bargaining agreement provided for arbitration to resolve charges of racial discrimination by an employer (D), two black employees, attempting to bypass their union, sought to bargain with the employer (D) themselves.

## 🏛 RULE OF LAW
Despite the national policy against racial discrimination in employment, the NLRA does not protect concerted activity by a group of minority employees to bargain with their employer over issues of employment discrimination in circumvention of their elected bargaining representative.

**FACTS:** A collective bargaining agreement between the Emporium Capwell Co. (Emporium) (D), which operated a department store, and the union prohibited employment discrimination by reason of race, contained a no-strike or lockout clause, and established grievance and arbitration machinery for processing any violation of the antidiscrimination clause. A group of Emporium's black employees who were covered by the agreement met with Johnson, the Secretary-Treasurer of the union, to present a list of grievances charging Emporium (D) with discriminating on the basis of race in making assignments and promotions. The union agreed to press the charges, and in fact, notified Emporium (D) that it desired arbitration over the matter. Nonetheless, the black employees, objecting to reliance on correction of inequities on an individual basis, attempted to negotiate with Emporium (D) directly. When Emporium (D) refused to meet with them, two of the black employees picketed the store with signs urging a consumer boycott. Failing to heed Emporium's (D) warnings that they were subject to discharge unless they desisted, the two picketers were fired. The Western Addition Community Organization (P), a local civil rights association to which the two discharged employees belonged, filed a charge against Emporium (D) with the NLRB. The Board, however, concluded that the activity which was the basis of the firings was not protected by § 7, and that the discharges did not, therefore, violate § 8(a)(1). The court of appeals reversed and remanded, relying on the national labor policy against discrimination as expressed in both the NLRA, and Title VII of the Civil Rights Act of 1964. Emporium (D) appealed.

**ISSUE:** May a group of minority employees, who claim that they have been discriminated against on the basis of race by the employer, bypass their elected bargaining representative to deal directly with the employer?

**HOLDING AND DECISION:** (Marshall, J.) No. In securing a regime of majority rule, Congress sought to secure to all members of the unit the benefits of their collective strength and bargaining power, in full awareness that the superior strength of some individuals or groups might be subordinated to the interest of the majority. In vesting the representatives of the majority with this broad power, Congress did not, of course, authorize a tyranny of the majority over minority interests. First, it provided that bargaining units must be distinguished by a sufficient commonality of interests. Second, in the Landrum and Griffin amendments to the NLRA, it assured that minority voices are heard as they are in the functioning of a democratic institution. Third, it imposed on the chosen bargaining representative a duty to represent fairly and in good faith the interests of minorities in the unit. Against this background of long and consistent adherence to the principle of exclusive representation tempered by safeguards for the protection of minority interests, it is far from clear that separate bargaining is necessary to help eliminate discrimination. Indeed, as the facts of this case demonstrate, the proposed remedy might have just the opposite effect. The agreement here specifically provided for a grievance machinery and arbitration to resolve charges involving racial discrimination which was expressly prohibited. There is no reason to believe that the processing of grievances is inherently limited to the correction of individual cases of discrimination. One would hardly expect an employer to continue in effect an employment practice that routinely results in adverse arbitration decisions. Furthermore, an employer confronted with competing demands of each of several groups would be unable to agree to remedial steps to all at once, particularly where the claims are for assignment or promotion to a limited number of positions. The result will only be rancor and division among the employees thereby undermining the potential effectiveness of the bargaining representative. Thus, the likelihood of making headway against discriminatory practices would be minimal. Finally, if it can be determined that the discharges were discriminatorily motivated, the two fired picketers have a recourse under Title VII for judicial relief by filing a charge with the EEOC. Reversed.

*Continued on next page.*

**DISSENT:** (Douglas, J.) The black employees' picketing against racial discrimination was a "concerted activity" under NLRA § 7. It was a traditional form of labor protest directed at matters unquestionably a proper subject of employee concern. While the NLRB held that they were unprotected because the employee grievance procedure was under union control, in the area of racial discrimination the union is hardly in the position to demand exclusive control, for the employee's right to nondiscriminatory treatment does not depend upon union demand but is based on the law.

## ▶ *ANALYSIS*

Section 9(a) of the NLRA provides that a labor organization which is designated as the bargaining representative by a majority of the employees in the appropriate bargaining unit shall serve as the exclusive representative for all of the unit's employees. Courts have interpreted this right to include a duty on the union's part to fairly represent all the employees, whether or not they were members of the union. Section 9(a) also authorizes employees to deal directly with the employer in presenting and adjusting their grievances so long as any adjustment is not inconsistent with the provisions of the collective bargaining contract.

■══■

## *Quicknotes*

**ARBITRATION**  An agreement to have a dispute heard and decided by a neutral third party, rather than through legal proceedings.

**BOYCOTT**  A concerted effort to refrain from doing business with a particular person or entity.

**NLRA (NATIONAL LABOR RELATIONS ACT)**  Guarantees employees the right to engage in collective bargaining, and regulates labor unions.

**NLRB (NATIONAL LABOR RELATIONS BOARD)**  An agency established pursuant to the National Labor Relations Act for the purpose of prohibiting unfair labor practices by employers and unions.

■══■

# Steele v. Louisville & Nashville R. Co.

## Black firemen (P) v. Employer (D)

### 323 U.S. 192 (1944).

**NATURE OF CASE:** Action under Railway Labor Act by black employees for declaratory and injunctive relief, and for damages, against the union and employers.

**FACT SUMMARY:** The Union (D), which was the exclusive bargaining representative, as provided by statute, for all craft employees, sought to have black employees (P), who were not members of the Union (D), removed from service by the employers (D).

---

### 🏛 RULE OF LAW
The Railway Labor Act imposes on the union, in collective bargaining and in making contracts with the carrier, the duty to represent nonunion or minority union members of the craft without hostile discrimination, fairly, impartially, and in good faith.

---

**FACTS:** The Railway Labor Act, in requiring carriers to bargain with the representative chosen by a majority of the employees in a craft, operates to exclude any other union from representing that craft. The Act is silent as to the manner in which the bargaining representative shall discharge its duties. The Brotherhood (D) was chosen by a majority of railroad firemen as the exclusive bargaining representative of the craft. Black firemen (P), who were thereby bound, under the terms of the Act, to accept the Brotherhood (D) as their representative also, were excluded from membership in the Brotherhood (D). The railroads (D) and the Brotherhood (D) entered into a collective bargaining agreement which provided for the gradual phasing out of all black firemen from the service. The black firemen (P) thereupon brought suit in an Alabama state court for an injunction against enforcement of the agreements, for an injunction against the Brotherhood (D) from purporting to act as their representative so long as the discrimination continues, for a declaratory judgment and for damages. From the trial court's judgment sustaining a demurrer to their complaint, the black firemen (P) appealed.

**ISSUE:** Does the Railway Labor Act impose on the bargaining representative of a craft or class of employees the duty to exercise fairly the power conferred upon it on behalf of all those for whom it acts, without hostile discrimination against them?

**HOLDING AND DECISION:** (Stone, C.J.) Yes. The labor union representing a craft owes some duty to represent nonunion members of the craft, at least to the extent of not discriminating against them as such in the contracts which it makes as their representative. The Act clearly provides that a union chosen by the majority repre-

sents the whole craft or class and not just the majority. The exercise of a granted power to act on behalf of others involves the assumption toward them of a duty to exercise the power in their interest and behalf. The Act imposes on the statutory representative of a craft at least as exacting a duty, with respect to minority craft members, as the Constitution imposes on a legislature to give equal protection to all those for whom it legislates. While the Act does not bar a union from making contracts that may have unfavorable effects on some members, these distinctions may be made on the basis of seniority, the type of work performed, and the competence and skill required, and not, as here, on the basis of race. The representative which unlawfully discriminates may be enjoined from doing so. Furthermore, the union is required to consider the requests of nonunion members of the craft, and to give them notice of and opportunity for hearing upon its proposed action. Accordingly, the black firemen (P) are entitled to the injunctive relief they have prayed for. Reversed.

---

### ▶ ANALYSIS

In *Railroad Trainmen v. Howard*, 343 U.S. 768 (1952), the issue was whether the *Steele* doctrine applies where the discriminatory union is not the bargaining representative of those discriminated against. There, the union, representing white brakemen, sought to have the railroads discharge all black train porters who were operating as brakemen. The Supreme Court concluded that, "The federal act ... prohibits bargaining agents it authorizes from using their position and power to destroy colored workers' jobs in order to bestow them on white workers."

---

### Quicknotes

**COLLECTIVE BARGAINING** Negotiations between an employer and employee that are mediated by a specified third party.

**DUTY** An obligation owed by one individual to another.

**FIFTH AMENDMENT** Provides that no person shall be compelled to serve as a witness against himself, or be subject to trial for the same offense twice, or be deprived of life, liberty, or property without due process of law.

# NLRB v. A-1 King Size Sandwiches, Inc.

## Labor board (P) v. Employer (D)

732 F.2d 872 (11th Cir.), *cert. den.*, 469 U.S. 1035 (1984).

**NATURE OF CASE:** Appeal from enforcement of an NLRB order.

**FACT SUMMARY:** The NLRB (P) held A-1 King Size Sandwiches, Inc. (A-1) (D) failed to bargain in good faith by engaging in surface bargaining and not attempting to reach an agreement.

---

### 🏛 RULE OF LAW

An employer engages in surface bargaining where its proposals are so unusually harsh, vindictive, or unreasonable that they are predictably unacceptable.

---

**FACTS:** A-1 King Size Sandwiches, Inc. (A-1) (D) entered into collective bargaining with the Union (D) regarding workers in its sandwich preparation plant. A-1 (D) insisted on a management rights clause that gave to the employer the sole right to set salaries, grant increases, and hire and fire. It also demanded full control over work schedules and working conditions. The Union (P) charged such demands constituted surface bargaining with no good faith attempt to reach an agreement. The administrative law judge found A-1 (D) guilty of an unfair labor practice, and the NLRB (P) adopted his findings. The Board (P) now seeks enforcement of its order.

**ISSUE:** Does an employer engage in surface bargaining where its proposals are so unusually harsh, vindictive, or unreasonable that they are predictably unacceptable?

**HOLDING AND DECISION:** (Dyer, J.) Yes. An employer engages in surface bargaining where its proposals are so unusually harsh, vindictive, or unreasonable that they are predictably unacceptable. Maintaining such fundamental control over these main subjects of collective bargaining leaves no room for good faith negotiations. Thus, in this case, any bargaining is merely a facial attempt to fulfill statutory requirements without actually giving up control over the issues. As a result, the order must be enforced.

---

### ▌ *ANALYSIS*

Surface bargaining occurs where the fundamental areas of bargaining are closed off due to entrenched positions on one side. Entrenchment forecloses areas of negotiation and the bargaining energies are wasted. Only where such basic areas of employment are subject to discussion can true collective bargaining occur.

---

### *Quicknotes*

**COLLECTIVE BARGAINING** Negotiations between an employer and employee that are mediated by a specified third party.

**NLRB (NATIONAL LABOR RELATIONS BOARD)** An agency established pursuant to the National Labor Relations Act for the purpose of prohibiting unfair labor practices by employers and unions.

---

# Detroit Edison Co. v. NLRB

## Employer (D) v. Labor board (P)

440 U.S. 301 (1979).

**NATURE OF CASE:** Action on a complaint charging failure to bargain in good faith.

**FACT SUMMARY:** Detroit Edison Co. (D) refused to give the union representing its employees copies of employee test questions and answers it used and the scores of individual employees.

## 🏛 RULE OF LAW
An employer does not violate his duty to bargain in good faith by refusing to divulge to the union representing its employees tests and test scores achieved by individual employees, in a statistically validated psychological aptitude testing program, unless the union obtains individual employee consent.

**FACTS:** In order to ascertain aptitude to fill certain job vacancies, Detroit Edison Co. (P) gave its employees a statistically validated psychological aptitude test. As none of the ten employees in the job unit who bid for the vacancies received a passing score, the jobs were filled with applicants from outside the bargaining unit. The union representing these ten employees asked for copies of the test and the answers and a list of the scores each employee received. Detroit Edison (P) refused, saying it would divulge individual test scores only if the union obtained consent from an individual employee to such revelation. The union then brought a complaint charging that failure to divulge this information constituted a violation of Detroit Edison's (P) duty to bargain in good faith because it denied the union the information it needed to adequately represent its members. From a decision enforcing a Board order requiring the information be divulged, Detroit Edison (P) appealed.

**ISSUE:** Is an employer's duty to bargain in good faith violated by his refusal to give the union representing its employees tests and test scores achieved by individual employees on a statistically validated psychological aptitude test, unless the union obtains individual employee consent?

**HOLDING AND DECISION:** (Stewart, J.) No. The employer's duty to bargain in good faith does not require him to divulge to the union representing its employees the tests and test results achieved by individual employees in a statistically validated psychological aptitude testing program in the absence of individual employee consent to such revelation. Secrecy of test questions and answers is necessary to continued validity of the test, which Detroit Edison (P) spent large sums in perfecting, and federal policy favors use of such validated, standardized and nondiscriminatory employee selection procedures.

There simply are not sufficient sanctions available to ensure that secrecy would be maintained after divulgence to the union. As to employee scores, each individual should have the option of deciding if his score, which may hold him up to scorn or harassment, is to be divulged. Vacated and remanded.

**DISSENT:** (White, J.) The Board cannot be said to have abused its discretion in ordering revelation of these various items to the union. Its judgment that the sanctions available are sufficient to insure continued secrecy as to the test should be given great deference. That same deference should be given the decision regarding divulgence of individual scores instead of presuming that such will result in harm to individual employees.

**DISSENT IN PART:** (Stevens, J.) The Court should respect the Board's discretion insofar as ordering revelation of the test and test answers to the union, but conditioning revelation of individual scores on individual consent is also appropriate.

## ▶ ANALYSIS

In general, the courts have not considered individual rights of confidentiality as a sufficient basis for an employer's withholding relevant information, e.g., job evaluations. They believe in giving due deference to the Board's decision on what weight should be given that interest and enforce disclosure orders issued by the Board on that basis.

∎▬∎

## Quicknotes

**DUTY** An obligation owed by one individual to another.

**GOOD FAITH** An honest intention to abstain from any unconscientious advantage of another.

**NLRB (NATIONAL LABOR RELATIONS BOARD)** An agency established pursuant to the National Labor Relations Act for the purpose of prohibiting unfair labor practices by employers and unions.

∎▬∎

# NLRB v. Insurance Agents' International Union

## Labor board (P) v. Union (D)

### 361 U.S. 477 (1960).

**NATURE OF CASE:** Appeal from denial of enforcement of an NLRB order finding a § 8(b)(3) violation.

**FACT SUMMARY:** The NLRB (P) argued that the Insurance Agents' International Union (Union) (D) failed to bargain collectively in good faith because it sponsored employee work slowdowns at the same time as it was involved in contract negotiations.

🏛 **RULE OF LAW**
A union does not fail to bargain in good faith in violation of § 8(b)(3) by sponsoring on-the-job conduct designed to interfere with the employer's business and place economic pressure upon him at the same time that it is negotiating a contract.

**FACTS:** The Insurance Agents' International Union (Union) (D) was negotiating a contract between its members and their employer, Prudential Insurance. During contract negotiations, the Union (D) announced that if agreement was not reached by a certain date, it would begin using tactics designed to place economic pressure on Prudential. When an agreement was not achieved by the deadline and while negotiations continued, Union (D) members stopped soliciting insurance policies, failed to follow company procedures and engaged in "sit-in mornings," amongst other things, amounting to "doing what comes naturally." Prudential charged that such conduct was a refusal by the Union (D) to bargain in good faith, and the NLRB (P) found that the Union (D) violated § 8(b)(3). The court of appeals denied enforcement of the order, and the NLRB (P) appealed.

**ISSUE:** Does a union fail to bargain in good faith in violation of § 8(b)(3) by sponsoring on-the-job conduct designed to interfere with the employer's business and place economic pressure upon him at the same time that it is negotiating a contract?

**HOLDING AND DECISION:** (Brennan, J.) No. A union does not fail to bargain in good faith in violation of § 8(b)(3) by sponsoring on-the-job conduct designed to interfere with the employer's business and place economic pressure upon him at the same time that it is negotiating a contract. Collective bargaining presupposes a desire to reach an ultimate agreement; both sides have the duty to bargain collectively. Congress intended parties to have wide latitude in their negotiations, unrestricted by any governmental power to regulate substantive solutions of their differences. Collective bargaining is not an idealistic forum; each side proceeds from contrary viewpoints and concepts of self-interest. The necessity for good faith bar-

gaining and the use of economic pressure exist side-by-side. The scope of § 8(b)(3) does not include the NLRB's (P) determining good faith upon use of economic pressure tactics, otherwise the NLRB (P) could go as far as to determine which economic weapons are permissible. An ordinary economic strike is not evidence of a failure to bargain in good faith, not because it constitutes a protected activity, but because there is no inconsistency between the application of economic pressure and good faith collective bargaining. Similarly, economic pressure applied through tactics not amounting to a strike do not evidence a failure to bargain in good faith. Congress has been specific in those economic weapons that it has outlawed, but a general work slowdown has never been specifically prohibited. Affirmed.

▶ **ANALYSIS**

Note that the tactics of economic pressure used by the Union (D) were not protected concerted activities under § 7 of the Act. However, unprotected activities which can be lawful grounds for discharge are not also deemed to be unfair labor practices. Employees, by engaging in unprotected activities, risk suffering the consequences of participating in such activities. But as long as the negotiations are conducted in good faith, unprotected activities outside of the negotiations will not taint the bargaining sessions.

■═■

### Quicknotes

**BAD FAITH** Conduct that is intentionally misleading or deceptive.

**COLLECTIVE BARGAINING** Negotiations between an employer and employee that are mediated by a specified third party.

**NLRB (NATIONAL LABOR RELATIONS BOARD)** An agency established pursuant to the National Labor Relations Act for the purpose of prohibiting unfair labor practices by employers and unions.

■═■

# NLRB v. Katz

### Labor board (P) v. Employer (D)

369 U.S. 736 (1962).

**NATURE OF CASE:** Appeal by NLRB from court of appeals' refusal to enforce its finding of an unfair labor practice by employer.

**FACT SUMMARY:** The NLRB (P) found that Katz (D), an employer who had instituted unilateral changes on mandatory subjects of bargaining during the course of negotiations with union, had violated his statutory duty to bargain.

## 🏛 RULE OF LAW
An employer's refusal to negotiate in fact as to any mandatory subject about which the union seeks to negotiate violates his statutory duty to bargain, even though the employer has every good faith desire to reach agreement with the union upon a collective bargaining agreement.

**FACTS:** The duty "to bargain collectively" enjoined by NLRA § 8(a)(5) is defined by § 8(d) as the duty to "meet . . . and confer in good faith with respect to wages, hours, and other terms and conditions of employment." In the course of bona fide contract negotiations with the union, Katz (D), the employer, unilaterally instituted three new changes: (1) without first notifying or consulting the union, Katz (D) reduced the number of sick leave days per year, but raised the number which could be carried over to the next year; (2) Katz (D) created an automatic wage increase system which was considerably more generous than that which had shortly theretofore been offered to and rejected by the union; and (3) without notice to the union, Katz (D) granted merit increases to 20 employees out of the 50 in the unit. The NLRB (P), expressly disclaiming any finding that the totality of Katz's (D) conduct manifested bad faith in the pending negotiations, held that Katz (D) had violated § 8(a)(5) by his unilateral changes. The court of appeals refused to enforce the Board's (P) order, ruling that the statutory duty to bargain cannot be held to be violated, when bargaining is in fact being carried on, without a finding of the employer's subjective bad faith in negotiating. The NLRB (P) appealed.

**ISSUE:** Is an employer's unilateral changes in conditions of employment under negotiation, though made in good faith, a violation of his duty under § 8(a)(5) to bargain collectively?

**HOLDING AND DECISION:** (Brennan, J.) Yes. The Board (P) may hold unilateral action by the employer on mandatory subjects during bona fide negotiations to be an unfair labor practice in violation of § 8(a)(5), without also finding the employer guilty of overall subjective bad

faith. Unilateral action by an employer without prior discussion with the union amounts to a refusal to negotiate about the affected conditions of employment under negotiation, and must of necessity obstruct bargaining, contrary to the congressional policy. As the present case indicates, such unilateral action not only discloses an unwillingness to negotiate, but also is rarely justified by any reason of substance. With respect to the sick-leave days change, since employees will be split over whether this is an improvement or a diminution of benefits, Katz (D) will have either aggravated the issue, or forced the union to take a vague, equivocal stand on the issue. As for the automatic wage increase system, while an employer is not required to lead with his best offer, such action is necessarily inconsistent with a sincere desire to conclude an agreement with the union. In fact, this change conclusively manifested bad faith in the negotiations and so would have violated § 8(a)(5) even in the court of appeals' interpretation. Similarly, there is no way for the union to know whether the merit increases had been a substantial departure from past practice, and, therefore, the union may properly insist that the company negotiate as to the procedures and criteria for determining such increases. Thus, in light of the dangers unilateral changes pose for true collective bargaining, subjective bad faith is immaterial. Reversed and remanded.

## ▶ ANALYSIS

Once labor and management negotiators have reached an "impasse," the employer may make unilateral changes which do not confer more benefits than those offered at the collective bargaining table. This is not allowed, however, where the employer's failure to engage in good faith bargaining was the direct cause of the impasse. Furthermore, the more fact that a collective bargaining agreement has expired does not sanction unilateral action by the employer.

■=■

### Quicknotes

**BAD FAITH** Conduct that is intentionally misleading or deceptive.

**COLLECTIVE BARGAINING** Negotiations between an employer and employee that are mediated by a specified third party.

**NLRB (NATIONAL LABOR RELATIONS BOARD)** An agency established pursuant to the National Labor Relations

*Continued on next page.*

Act for the purpose of prohibiting unfair labor practices by employers and unions.

**UNFAIR LABOR PRACTICE** Conduct by labor unions and employers, which is proscribed by the National Labor Relations Act.

■=■

# McClatchy Newspapers, Inc. v. NLRB

## Employer (D) v. Government agency (P)

131 F.3d. 1026 (D.C. Cir. 1997).

**NATURE OF CASE:** Appeal from orders to enforce government agency finding of unfair labor practices.

**FACT SUMMARY:** The NLRB (P) found that McClatchy Newspapers, Inc. (D) had committed unfair labor practices when it unilaterally implemented a discretionary merit pay proposal after it had bargained to impasse with the union.

> 🏛 **RULE OF LAW**
> Implementation of an offer after impasse is legitimate only as a method for breaking the impasse.

**FACTS:** After McClatchy Newspapers, Inc. (D), the publisher of two California newspapers, had reached an impasse in its negotiations with the labor union representing editorial, advertising, and telephone switchboard employees, it began implementing its own discretionary merit pay proposal. The union filed an unfair labor practice charge against McClatchy (D), alleging that implementing "merit" increases without the union's consent violated McClatchy's (D) duty to bargain with the union over wages. The NLRB (P) found for the union, and McClatchy (D) petitioned the court for review of the orders. The NLRB (P) cross-petitioned for enforcement.

**ISSUE:** Is implementation of an offer after impasse legitimate only as a method for breaking the impasse?

**HOLDING AND DECISION:** (Silberman, J.) Yes. Implementation of an offer after impasse is legitimate only as a method for breaking the impasse. In this case, where McClatchey (D) has refused to state any definable objective procedures and criteria for defining merit, McClatchey's (D) ongoing ability to exercise its economic force in setting wage increases would simultaneously disparage the union's ability to act as the employee's representative and deprive the union of its ability to bargain knowledgeably. Here, the NLRB (P) has denied the employer a particular economic tactic for the sake of preserving the stability of the collective bargaining process. Assessing the significance of impasse and the dynamics of collective bargaining is precisely the kind of judgment that should be left to the NLRB (P). Affirmed.

## ▶ ANALYSIS

The court in this case discussed and rejected the employer's arguments. It found that it was within the NLRB's (P) authority to prevent the employer from undermining the bargaining process. The employer's implementation of its proposal could be seen as seeking de-collectivization of bargaining.

■■■

## Quicknotes

**COLLECTIVE BARGAINING** Negotiations between an employer and employee that are mediated by a specified third party.

**IMPASSE** Deadlock; inability to come to an agreement or compromise.

**NLRB (NATIONAL LABOR RELATIONS BOARD)** An agency established pursuant to the National Labor Relations Act for the purpose of prohibiting unfair labor practices by employers and unions.

■■■

# NLRB v. American National Insurance Co.

## Labor board (P) v. Employer (D)

### 343 U.S. 395 (1952).

**NATURE OF CASE:** Appeal from reversal of an NLRB determination of §§ 8(a)(1) and (5) violations.

**FACT SUMMARY:** American National Insurance Co. (American) (D) refused to bargain with the union on certain issues which American (D) included in a management functions clause proposed by it.

## 🏛 RULE OF LAW
An employer may bargain for a management functions clause covering any condition of employment guaranteed by NLRA § 7 without violating per se the requirement to bargain in good faith.

**FACTS:** In bargaining begun January 10, 1945, American National Insurance Co. (American) (D) rejected a union proposal for unlimited bargaining and countered with a proposed management functions clause dealing with promotions, discipline, and work scheduling as management's responsibility to be excluded from arbitration. The union claimed that the excluded matters were subject to the duty to bargain collectively under the Act and would not accept American's (D) proposal. The NLRB (P) filed a complaint against American (D) on this question. Meanwhile, negotiations continued with an agreement reached on January 13, 1950, after a trial examiner reached a decision on the complaint, but before the NLRB (P) announced its opinion. The 1950 agreement contained a management functions clause removing discipline and work schedules from arbitration and left promotions and demotions to a union-management joint committee. The trial examiner concluded that American (D) had the right to bargain for a management functions clause, but the NLRB (P) held that any such clause was a per se violation of NLRA §§ 8(a)(1) and (5). The court of appeals reversed the NLRB's (P) decision, and the NLRB (P) appealed.

**ISSUE:** May an employer bargain for a management functions clause covering any condition of employment guaranteed by NLRA § 7 without violating per se the requirement to bargain in good faith?

**HOLDING AND DECISION:** (Vinson, C.J.) Yes. An employer may bargain for a management functions clause covering any condition of employment guaranteed by NLRA § 7 without violating per se the requirement to bargain in good faith. Section 8(d) requires a good faith test for bargaining. Any fears the NLRB (P) may have that use of management function clauses will lead to evasion of an employer's duty to bargain collectively as to rates of pay, wages, hours, and employment conditions do not justify prohibiting all bargaining in such areas where an employer proposes conditions or removal of such areas from bargaining. It is equally clear that the NLRB (P) may not, either directly or indirectly, compel concessions or otherwise sit in judgment upon the substantive terms of collective bargaining agreements. Applying this standard, it was proper to find that American (D) did not bargain in bad faith by proposing a management functions clause. Affirmed.

**DISSENT:** (Minton, J.) Not all proposed management function clauses are automatically valid. Where, as here, an employer tells a union that the only way to obtain a contract as to wages is to agree not to bargain about certain other working conditions, the employer has refused to bargain about those other working conditions, which is a plain refusal to bargain in violation of § 8(a)(5).

## ▶ ANALYSIS

One of the most troublesome areas in industrial relations is determining the respective responsibilities of management and unions which are of practical concern to both employer and employees. The decisions are classified in three general groups: (1) matters as to which management makes the final decision, e.g., types of products, pricing, plant locations, work assignments; (2) matters for joint management-union determination, e.g., wages, hours, seniority, vacations, union status, provisions; and (3) matters within the union's exclusive control, e.g., admission or exclusion of members, whether or not to operate as an unincorporated association or to obtain a corporate charter. In the past, the topics have been allocated to one category or another by mutual acquiescence, but the NLRB has in its decisions begun to define the scope of collective bargaining. Cox and Dunlop, Regulation of Collective Bargaining, 63 Harv. L. Rev., 389 (1950).

■━■

## Quicknotes

**ARBITRATION** An agreement to have a dispute heard and decided by a neutral third party, rather than through legal proceedings.

**COLLECTIVE BARGAINING** Negotiations between an employer and employee that are mediated by a specified third party.

**NLRA (NATIONAL LABOR RELATIONS ACT)** Guarantees employees the right to engage in collective bargaining, and regulates labor unions.

*Continued on next page.*

**NLRB (NATIONAL LABOR RELATIONS BOARD)** An agency established pursuant to the National Labor Relations Act for the purpose of prohibiting unfair labor practices by employers and unions.

■═■

# NLRB v. Wooster Division of Borg-Warner Corp.

Labor board (P) v. Employer (D)

356 U.S. 342 (1958).

**NATURE OF CASE:** Appeal from a finding of an NLRA § 8(a)(5) violation.

**FACT SUMMARY:** Wooster (D) insisted that the collective bargaining agreement contain a ballot clause calling for a prestrike secret vote of employees, and it refused to bargain with the certified international union although it was willing to bargain with the uncertified local.

## RULE OF LAW

Insistence on inclusion in a collective bargaining agreement of proposals that are not mandatory subjects of collective bargaining is, in effect, a refusal to bargain about subjects that are within the scope of mandatory bargaining and, hence, a § 8(a)(5) violation.

**FACTS:** Wooster (D), an employer, insisted on including in a collective bargaining agreement two clauses. One was a "ballot" clause calling for a prestrike secret vote of all employees, union and nonunion, as to the employer's last offer. In the event the employees rejected the last offer, Wooster (D) would have 72 hours to present a new proposal and a new vote would be taken. The second, a "recognition" clause, would have required Wooster (D) to negotiate with the uncertified local union rather than with the board-certified international union. Wooster (D) refused to agree to any contract not containing these clauses, while the union refused to agree to any contract containing them. The NLRB (P), upon the international union's complaint, found Wooster (D) in violation of the § 8(a)(5) requirement to bargain in good faith. The court of appeals enforced as to the recognition clause, but it reversed as to the ballot clause. The NLRB (P) appealed.

**ISSUE:** Is insistence on inclusion in a collective bargaining agreement of proposals that are not mandatory subjects of collective bargaining, in effect, a refusal to bargain about subjects that are within the scope of mandatory bargaining, and, hence, a § 8(a)(5) violation?

**HOLDING AND DECISION:** (Burton, J.) Yes. Insistence on inclusion in a collective bargaining agreement of proposals that are not mandatory subjects of collective bargaining is, in effect, a refusal to bargain about subjects that are within the scope of mandatory bargaining and, hence, a § 8(a)(5) violation. Together, §§ 8(a)(5) and (d) establish the obligation to bargain in good faith with respect to wages, hours, and other terms of employment. The duty is limited to those subjects and neither side is legally obligated to yield. Good faith does not permit an employer to refuse to enter into agreements on the ground that they

do not include some proposal which is not a mandatory subject of collective bargaining. It does not follow that because an employer may propose clauses outside the scope of mandatory subjects, that it can lawfully insist upon them as a condition to any agreement. As it is lawful to insist upon matters within the scope of mandatory subjects, the issue here was whether either the "ballot" or "recognition" clauses were subject to mandatory bargaining. The ballot clause was not a mandatory subject as it related only to a procedure to be followed by the employees alone. The recognition clause also was not a mandatory subject because an employer cannot refuse to recognize the certified negotiating representative. Affirmed in part; reversed in part.

**CONCURRENCE:** (Frankfurter, J.) Insistence by the company on the recognition clause was an unfair labor practice, but as Justice Harlan states in his dissent, the clause is not so clearly outside the reasonable range of bargaining as to establish a refusal to bargain.

**CONCURRENCE AND DISSENT:** (Harlan, J.) The right to bargain becomes illusory if one is not free to press a proposal in good faith to the point of insistence. The ballot clause appeared to be a mandatory subject because it would affect the employer-employee relationship by determining the timing of strikes. As for the recognition clause, Wooster's (D) insistence upon it was an unfair labor practice because by its terms it directly contravened the specific requirements of the Act.

## ANALYSIS

In *Utility Workers Local 111*, 203 NLRB 230 (1973), several union locals were the certified bargaining agents at several plants operated by three subsidiaries of an electric company. Some locals refused to sign agreements until all units with which collective bargaining was then taking place reached agreement also. This was held to be outside the scope of negotiation. It was an unlawful insistence that the employer agree to consolidate the various units into one for purposes of collective bargaining. The smaller units had been certified by the NLRB, and it was irrelevant that a larger unit may have been more appropriate.

## Quicknotes

**COLLECTIVE BARGAINING** Negotiations between an employer and employee that are mediated by a specified third party.

*Continued on next page.*

**GOOD FAITH** An honest intention to abstain from taking advantage of another.

**NLRB (NATIONAL LABOR RELATIONS BOARD)** An agency established pursuant to the National Labor Relations Act for the purpose of prohibiting unfair labor practices by employers and unions.

■═■

# Fibreboard Paper Products Corp. v. NLRB

Employer (D) v. Labor board (P)

379 U.S. 203 (1964).

**NATURE OF CASE:** Appeal by employer from NLRB finding that it had committed an unfair labor practice.

**FACT SUMMARY:** Upon expiration of collective bargaining agreements, an employer (D) decided, for legitimate business reasons, to contract out work previously performed by union members to independent contractors, and refused to negotiate this matter with the union.

> # RULE OF LAW
> (1) "Contracting out"—the replacement of employees in the existing bargaining unit with those of an independent contractor to do the same work under similar conditions of employment—even if planned for legitimate business reasons, is a mandatory subject of collective bargaining.
> (2) Where the employer has failed to bargain in good faith, the NLRB may order resumption of discontinued operations and reinstatement of employees with back pay.

**FACTS:** Section 8(a)(5) of the NLRA provides that it is an unfair labor practice for an employer "to refuse to bargain collectively with the representatives of his employees." Section 8(d) defines collective bargaining as "the mutual obligation . . . to confer in good faith with respect to wages, hours, and other terms and conditions of employment." Upon the expiration of a collective bargaining agreement with the union which was the exclusive bargaining representative for a unit of Fibreboard Paper Products Corporation's (D) maintenance employees, Fibreboard (D) looked into the possibility of "contracting out" its maintenance work. Receiving assurances from independent contractors that economies could be derived by reducing the work force, decreasing fringe benefits, and eliminating overtime payments, Fibreboard (D) informed the union that in view of its decision to contract out the maintenance work, further negotiations of a new collective bargaining agreement would be "pointless." When the independent contractors took over, and the existing employees were released, the union established a picket line at Fibreboard's (D) plant. The NLRB (P) found that even though Fibreboard's (D) motive in contracting out the maintenance work was economic rather than anti-union, its failure to negotiate with the union over its decision to do so constituted a violation of § 8(a)(5). The Board (P) ordered Fibreboard (D) to reinstate the previous operation performed by the employees represented by the Union, to

reinstate these employees, and to give them back pay. The court of appeals granted the Board's (P) petition for enforcement, and Fibreboard (D) appealed.

**ISSUE:**
(1) Is "contracting out" a mandatory subject of collective bargaining within the meaning of §§ 8(a)(5) and 8(d)?
(2) In a case involving only a refusal to bargain, is the Board empowered to order the resumption of operations discontinued for legitimate reasons and reinstatement with back pay for affected employees?

**HOLDING AND DECISION:** (Warren, C.J.)
(1) Yes. "Contracting out," albeit for economic reasons, is well within the literal meaning of the phrase "terms and conditions of employment" of § 8(d), particularly where such "contracting out" necessitates termination of employment. Holding that contracting out is a mandatory subject of collective bargaining would serve to promote the Act's purpose in furthering the peaceful settlement of industrial disputes. Looking to prevailing industrial practices, it is apparent that provisions relating to contracting out exist in numerous agreements. While the Act does not encourage an employer to engage in fruitless marathon discussions at the expense of frank statement and support of his position, the union must be afforded an opportunity to meet management's legitimate complaints that its performance was unduly costly. Accordingly, Fibreboard (D) was guilty of violating § 8(a)(5).
(2) Yes. Section 10(c) of the NLRA empowers the Board (P), upon a finding that an unfair labor practice has been committed, to take any "affirmative action including reinstatement of employees with or without back pay, as will effectuate the policies of" the Act. A Board (P) order will be disturbed only when it is shown that the order is a patent attempt to achieve ends other than those which can fairly be said to effectuate the Act. Here, there is no showing that the Board's (P) order restoring the status quo ante to insure meaningful bargaining is not well designed to promote the policies of the Act, or would place an undue burden on Fibreboard (D). Nor does the order exceed the Board's (D) powers under § 10(c), which provides that reinstatement is an inappropriate remedy where an individual has been suspended or discharged for cause. That provision relates only to employee misconduct. Affirmed.

*Continued on next page.*

**CONCURRENCE:** (Stewart, J.) The Court holds no more than that Fibreboard's (D) decision to subcontract this work, "involving the replacement of employees in the existing bargaining unit with those of an independent contractor to do the same work under similar conditions of employment" is the subject of the duty to bargain collectively. "The Court most assuredly does not decide that every managerial decision which necessarily terminates an individual's employment is subject to the duty to bargain. Nor does the Court decide that subcontracting decisions are as a general matter subject to that duty." Nothing in the decision should be understood as imposing a duty to bargain collectively regarding managerial decisions which are at the core of entrepreneurial control. An employer's subcontracting practices are not, as a general matter, in themselves conditions of employment. But on the facts of the case here, all that was involved was the substitution of one group of workers for another to perform the same task in the same plant under the ultimate control of the same employer. This situation is closely analogous with other traditional collective bargaining situations including compulsory retirement, layoffs according to seniority, and work assignments.

## ▶ ANALYSIS

After *Fibreboard*, a confusing and inconsistent set of opinions, particularly among the courts of appeals, emerged over the issue of when an employer must negotiate with the union before "contracting out" work. Thus, it has been held that the assumption of production work by supervisory personnel which deprives employees of overtime pay is a mandatory subject of bargaining. However, a court of appeals has held that a publisher is not guilty of a failure to bargain where he contracts out work while the union is conducting an economic strike.

■══■

## Quicknotes

**COLLECTIVE BARGAINING** Negotiations between an employer and employee that are mediated by a specified third party.

**INDEPENDENT CONTRACTOR** A party undertaking a particular assignment for another who retains control over the manner in which it is executed.

**NLRB (NATIONAL LABOR RELATIONS BOARD)** An agency established pursuant to the National Labor Relations Act for the purpose of prohibiting unfair labor practices by employers and unions.

**UNFAIR LABOR PRACTICE** Conduct by labor unions and employers, which is proscribed by the National Labor Relations Act.

■══■

# First National Maintenance Corp. v. NLRB

## Employer (D) v. Labor board (P)

452 U.S. 666 (1981).

**NATURE OF CASE:** Appeal from finding of violations of NLRA §§ 8(a)(1) and (5).

**FACT SUMMARY:** The union, which was was selected as the bargaining unit for First National Maintenance Corp.'s (FNM's) (D) Greenpark employees just when FNM (D) was in the process of shutting down its Greenpark operation, argued that FNM's (D) failure to bargain with the union was an unfair labor practice in violation of NLRA §§ 8(a)(1) and (5).

## 🏛 RULE OF LAW
An employer's decision to shut down part of its business purely for economic reasons is not a term and condition for mandatory bargaining under the NLRA.

**FACTS:** First National Maintenance Corp. (FNM) (D) was a provider of maintenance and custodial services for various enterprises in the New York City area. It would hire employees and provide equipment and supplies for each location for which its services were contracted. FNM (D) paid the employees and taxes, and did not transfer employees between its work sites. One of FNM's (D) customers was Greenpark Care Center, a nursing home. FNM (D) originally charged Greenpark $500 per week, but that was later reduced to $250. FNM (D) began losing money on Greenpark and gave a 30-day cancellation notice unless Greenpark agreed to pay $500 per week again. During this time, the union conducted an organizing campaign among FNM's (D) Greenpark employees and was certified as their bargaining agent at an NLRB (P) conducted election. The union asked FNM (D) to bargain with it, but FNM (D) never responded. Meanwhile, Greenpark did not accede to FNM's (D) request for a $500 fee; FNM (D) fired its Greenpark employees and refused the offer to bargain, saying its action was taken purely on the basis of prohibitive financial losses. The union filed a complaint alleging violations of NLRA §§ 8(a)(1) and (5). The NLRB (P) adopted an administrative law judge's finding that FNM (D) failed to satisfy its duty to bargain concerning both its decision to terminate the Greenpark contract and the effect of the change on unit employees. The court of appeals affirmed, and FNM (D) appealed.

**ISSUE:** Is an employer's decision to shut down part of its business, purely for economic reasons, a term and condition for mandatory bargaining under the NLRA?

**HOLDING AND DECISION:** (Blackmun, J.) No. An employer's decision to shut down part of its business purely for economic reasons is not a term and condition for mandatory bargaining under the NLRA. In this case, FNM's (D) business decision involved a change in the scope and direction of the enterprise and was akin to the decision whether to be in business at all. This was "not in (itself) primarily about conditions of employment, though the effect of the decision may be necessarily to terminate employment." Bargaining over management decisions that have a substantial impact on continued availability of employment should be required only if the benefit, for labor-management relations and the collective bargaining process, outweighs the burden placed on the conduct of the business. Here, there was no anti-union animus behind FNM's (D) decision to shut down the Greenpark operation. The dispute with Greenpark was over the size of the fee, something over which the union had no control. Further, the union was not elected or certified until well after FNM's (D) difficulties with Greenpark had begun. FNM's (D) decision to halt work at Greenpark represented a significant change in its operation not unlike opening a new line of business or going out of business entirely. Reversed and remanded.

**DISSENT:** (Brennan, J.) The Court's test in this case takes into consideration only the interests of management without considering the legitimate interests of the employees or their union. "The primary responsibility to determine the scope of the statutory duty to bargain has been entrusted to the NLRB (P), which should not now be reversed by the courts merely because they might prefer another view of the statute."

## ▶ ANALYSIS

The Court distinguished the above case from that of *Fibreboard Paper Products Corp. v. NLRB*, 379 U.S. 203 (1964). That case involved an employer's decision to subcontract out for maintenance work, rather than the business of a maintenance company which accepts the subcontract. However, in *Fibreboard*, it was held that a decision to subcontract was a subject of mandatory bargaining; it involved replacing existing employees with those of an independent contractor and stemmed from a desire to reduce labor costs. Note, that in the above case, FNM (D) recognized its duty to bargain about the effects or results to stop its Greenpark operation and consented to an NLRB order concerning the same. FNM (D) had already reached an agreement with the union on severance pay while this appeal was pending before the Supreme Court.

*Continued on next page.*

## *Quicknotes*

**COLLECTIVE BARGAINING** Negotiations between an employer and employee that are mediated by a specified third party.

**INDEPENDENT CONTRACTOR** A party undertaking a particular assignment for another who retains control over the manner in which it is executed.

**NLRA (NATIONAL LABOR RELATIONS ACT)** Guarantees employees the right to engage in collective bargaining, and regulates labor unions.

**NLRB (NATIONAL LABOR RELATIONS BOARD)** An agency established pursuant to the National Labor Relations Act for the purpose of prohibiting unfair labor practices by employers and unions.

∎▬∎

# United Food & Commercial Workers, Local 150-A v. NLRB (Dubuque Packing Co.)

Union (P) v. Labor board (D)

1 F.3d 24 (D.C. Cir. 1993).

**NATURE OF CASE:** Petition for review of a ruling by the NLRB on an unfair labor practices complaint.

**FACT SUMMARY:** After the Dubuque Packing Company (Dubuque) (D) had extracted major concessions from its workers, the company relocated part of its operations to another state, eliminating many jobs, whereupon the Union of Food & Commercial Workers (UFCW) (P) filed a complaint with the Board (D), claiming that Dubuque (D) had refused to bargain in good faith.

## 🏛 RULE OF LAW
Plant relocations are exempt from a duty to bargain where they are entrepreneurial in nature, are motivated by something other than labor costs, or where bargaining would be futile or impossible.

**FACTS:** After the Dubuque Packing Company (Dubuque) (D) extracted major concessions from workers at its home plant because it was losing money, it gave notice of its intention to relocate part of its operations to another state. The United Food & Commercial Workers (UFCW) (P) then requested detailed financial information, which the company refused to provide. Dubuque (D) relocated. The UFCW (P) filed unfair labor practice complaints with the Board (D), claiming that Dubuque (D) had refused to bargain in good faith. An administrative law judge (ALJ) ruled in Dubuque's (D) favor. Much later, the Board (D) affirmed the ALJ. This court remanded because the Board's (D) opinion was inadequately explained. On remand, the Board (D) adopted a new test and, applying it retroactively, ordered Dubuque (D) to pay back wages to all employees terminated due to the relocation. Dubuque (D) petitioned for review.

**ISSUE:** Are plant relocations exempt from a duty to bargain where they are entrepreneurial in nature, are motivated by something other than labor costs, or where bargaining would be futile or impossible?

**HOLDING AND DECISION:** (Buckley, J.) Yes. Plant relocations are exempt from a duty to bargain where they are entrepreneurial in nature, are motivated by something other than labor costs, or where bargaining would be futile or impossible. There is no evidence that the relocation decision here was accompanied by a basic change in the nature of Dubuque's (D) operation. The ALJ stated that Dubuque (D) used the new facility to substantially replace the old facility. Since the UFCW (P) could, would, and did make concessions, the Board's (D) finding that good-faith bargaining might not have been futile was substantially

supported by the record. Moreover, where an agency ruling seeks only to clarify established doctrine, its retroactive application will be allowed. Thus, Dubuque's (D) petition for review is denied, and the Board's (D) remedial order is enforced.

## ▶ ANALYSIS

Given the deference owed the Board's (D) policy choices, its test does not impermissibly fail to protect management's prerogatives over capital investment. The test establishes rules on which management may plan with a large degree of confidence. While it leaves some areas of uncertainty as to which relocation decisions are clearly subject to negotiation, these will be narrowed in time through future adjudications.

◼◼◼

## Quicknotes

**COLLECTIVE BARGAINING** Negotiations between an employer and employee that are mediated by a specified third party.

**NLRB (NATIONAL LABOR RELATIONS BOARD)** An agency established pursuant to the National Labor Relations Act for the purpose of prohibiting unfair labor practices by employers and unions.

◼◼◼

# Allied Chemical and Alkali Workers v. Pittsburgh Plate Glass Co.

Union (P) v. Employer (D)

404 U.S. 157 (1971).

**NATURE OF CASE:** Appeal from denial of enforcement of an NLRB order.

**FACT SUMMARY:** Allied Chemical and Alkali Workers (P) unilaterally modified the union-negotiated pension and insurance plan as to retirees and appealed an order to engage in collective bargaining on that matter and the court of appeals refused enforcement.

## 🏛 RULE OF LAW
A company's unilateral modification of pension and insurance benefits negotiated by a union for all employees is merely a permissive subject of collective bargaining and such a modification is not an unfair labor practice which must be resolved through collective bargaining as to retirees.

**FACTS:** Allied Chemical and Alkali Workers (Allied) (P) negotiated a pension and insurance plan for employees in its ranks with Pittsburgh Plate Glass Co. (Pittsburgh) (D). After the agreement was reached, Pittsburgh (D) announced its intentions to cancel the agreement with respect to retirees and offered an alternative plan of paying a supplemental Medicare premium for those retirees. Pittsburgh (D) was ordered to bargain collectively on the issue of these benefits and the cancellation and appealed.

**ISSUE:** Is a company's unilateral modification of pension and insurance benefits negotiated by a union for all employees merely a permissive subject of collective bargaining not making such a modification an unfair labor practice as to retirees?

**HOLDING AND DECISION:** (Brennan, J.) Yes. The question in this case centers in large part around who is an "employee" within the meaning of the agreement and the collective bargaining requirements. The NLRB has the task of determining contours of the term "employee," within the constraints of the law. In this case, the NLRB found that the retirees in question were employees for the purposes of this agreement and dispute. The Labor Relations Act, however, defines employees and workers in such a way as to exclude retirees. Thus, an order to cease and desist from refusing to collectively bargain was improper. A company's unilateral modification of pension and insurance benefits negotiated by a union for all employees is merely a permissive subject of collective bargaining and such a modification as to retirees is not an unfair labor practice. Affirmed.

## ▶ ANALYSIS

The retirees would not of course be entirely without remedy. If certain of them did not wish to participate in the alternative plan, the cancellation of the agreement would be actionable in a private action as a breach of contract. It is here held that the cancellation did not work an unfair labor practice requiring collective bargaining under federal law.

■■■

## Quicknotes

**BREACH OF CONTRACT** Unlawful failure by a party to perform its obligations pursuant to contract.

**CEASE AND DESIST ORDER** An order from a court or administrative agency prohibiting a person or business from continuing a particular course of conduct

**COLLECTIVE BARGAINING** Negotiations between an employer and employee that are mediated by a specified third party.

**NLRB (NATIONAL LABOR RELATIONS BOARD)** An agency established pursuant to the National Labor Relations Act for the purpose of prohibiting unfair labor practices by employers and unions.

■■■

# Land Air Delivery, Inc. v. NLRB

Employer (D) v. Labor board (P)

862 F.2d 354 (D.C. Cir. 1988).

**NATURE OF CASE:** Appeal of administrative finding of unfair labor practice.

**FACT SUMMARY:** Land Air Delivery, Inc. (D), faced with a strike, replaced the striking employees permanently with subcontractors.

## 🏛 RULE OF LAW
An employer may not permanently replace striking workers with subcontractors.

**FACTS:** Land Air Delivery, Inc. (Land Air) (D) operated an air freight motor carrier business. It used the services of both employees and independent contractors. For various reasons, the employees, members of a certified Union, went on strike. Land Air (D) used a mix of employees from other locations, its regular contractors, and new employees to continue in operation. Land Air (D) then terminated the new employees and engaged the services of new subcontractors. When Union (P) members agreed to return to work, they were told no positions were available. The new subcontractors' services were being used on a permanent basis. The Union (P) filed an unfair labor practice complaint with the NLRB. The Board found an unfair practice to have been committed, and Land Air (D) appealed.

**ISSUE:** May an employer permanently replace striking workers with subcontractors?

**HOLDING AND DECISION:** (Silberman, J.) No. An employer may not permanently replace striking workers with subcontractors. It is true that an employer faced with an economic strike is entitled to replace strikers permanently with new employees. It is also true, however, that an employer is obliged to bargain in good faith with the union before deciding to subcontract. A material difference exists between replacing strikers with employees and subcontractors. In the event of the former, the union, in theory at least, may be able to win the allegiance of the new employees. This cannot occur with subcontractors. An employer may not unilaterally decertify a union; to hire subcontractors on a permanent basis would be doing precisely that. In light of these considerations, it would appear that the proper rule is that an employer may not permanently replace strikers with subcontractors. Review denied.

## ▶ ANALYSIS

The court allowed the possibility of exceptions to this rule. Economic necessity might dictate the use of subcontractors, said the court. Here, however, the company had used employee replacements but terminated them in favor of subcontractors.

■=■

## *Quicknotes*

**INDEPENDENT CONTRACTOR** A party undertaking a particular assignment for another who retains control over the manner in which it is executed.

**NLRB (NATIONAL LABOR RELATIONS BOARD)** An agency established pursuant to the National Labor Relations Act for the purpose of prohibiting unfair labor practices by employers and unions.

**SUBCONTRACTOR** A contractor who enters into an agreement with a principal contractor, or other subcontractor, to perform all or a part of a contract.

■=■

# H. K. Porter Co. v. NLRB

Employer (D) v. Labor board (P)

397 U.S. 99 (1970).

**NATURE OF CASE:** Appeal from an NLRB order compelling an employer to accept a union contract proposal.

**FACT SUMMARY:** The NLRB (P) ordered an employer, H. K. Porter Co. (the Company) (D), to bargain in good faith over a union checkoff proposal; later, the NLRB (P) expanded its order and required the Company (D) to accept that proposal.

> 🏛 **RULE OF LAW**
> While the NLRB does have the authority to require employers and employees to negotiate, it is without power to compel a company or a union to agree to any substantive contractual provision of a collective bargaining agreement.

**FACTS:** Section 8(d) of the NLRA provides that "(the) obligation (to bargain collectively) does not compel either party to agree to a proposal or require the making of a concession." Section 10(c) provides that when a party is found to have failed to bargain in good faith, the NLRB may take "such action as will effectuate the policies of the Act." At the collective bargaining table, the union proposed that the employer, H. K. Porter Co. (the Company) (D), deduct ("check off") the dues owed to the union periodically from the Company's (D) wage payments to the employees. The Company (D) objected, not on the ground of inconvenience, but solely because it was "not going to aid and comfort the union." Efforts by the union to obtain some kind of compromise on the checkoff request evoked little response from the Company (D). The NLRB (P) found that the Company (D) had refused to bargain in good faith, and issued a cease and desist order with respect to the union's checkoff provision. Later, the NLRB (P) issued a new opinion in which it required the Company (D) to "grant to the union a contract clause providing for the check off of union dues." The court of appeals granted enforcement of this order, holding that § 8(d) did not forbid the Board (P) from compelling an agreement since that section relates only to "a determination of whether a ... violation has occurred and not the scope of the remedy which may be necessary to cure violations which have occurred." The Company (D) appealed.

**ISSUE:** Does the NLRB have the statutory authority to order a negotiating party to accept a substantive contractual provision of a collective bargaining agreement?

**HOLDING AND DECISION:** (Black, J.) No. The framers of the NLRA never intended that the government would, in cases where agreement has become impossible,

step in, become a party to the negotiations and impose its own views of a desirable settlement. Section 8(d) clearly indicates that the Board (P) may not either directly or indirectly compel concessions or otherwise sit in judgment upon the substantive terms of a collective bargaining agreement. It would be anomalous indeed to hold that while § 8(d) prohibits the Board (P) from relying on a refusal to agree as the sole evidence of bad faith bargaining, the NLRA permits the Board (P) to compel agreement in that same dispute. The Board (P) may order good faith bargaining. However, it must also, as required by the Act, respect the parties' freedom of contract. To allow the Board (P) to compel agreement when the parties themselves are unable to do so would violate the fundamental premise on which the Act is based—private bargaining under governmental supervision of the procedure alone, without any official compulsion over the actual terms of the contract. If the present remedial powers of the Board (P) are insufficiently broad to cope with important labor problems, it is up to Congress, and not the Board (P) or the courts, to effect a change. Accordingly, the Board (P) exceeded its statutory authority when it required the Company (D) to accept the union's checkoff proposal. Reversed and remanded.

**DISSENT:** (Douglas, J.) Here, H.K. Porter (D) refused to provide a checkoff only to avoid reaching any agreement with the union. "In those narrow and specialized circumstances, I see no answer to the power of the Board (P) in its discretion to impose the checkoff as 'affirmative action' necessary to remedy the flagrant refusal of the employer to bargain in good faith. The case is rare, if not unique, and will seldom arise."

---

▶ **ANALYSIS**

When the Board finds a violation of § 8(a)(5), it usually issues a cease and desist order accompanied by an affirmative order requiring the employer to engage in collective bargaining with the certified representative. Some commentators worry that such orders lack any real meat because the parties against whom they are directed are virtually free to ignore them. However, at least one empirical study has concluded that after the issuance of these orders employers and employees have gone on to establish real and effective collective bargaining sessions. Despite this conclusion, there still exists a legitimate concern that the conventional Board remedy provides a new,

*Continued on next page.*

uncertified union, struggling for recognition, with considerably less than adequate protection.

■■■■

## *Quicknotes*

**CEASE AND DESIST ORDER**  An order from a court or administrative agency prohibiting a person or business from continuing a particular course of conduct.

**COLLECTIVE BARGAINING**  Negotiations between an employer and employee that are mediated by a specified third party.

**GOOD FAITH**  An honest intention to abstain from taking advantage of another.

**NLRA (NATIONAL LABOR RELATIONS ACT)**  Guarantees employees the right to engage in collective bargaining, and regulates labor unions.

**NLRB (NATIONAL LABOR RELATIONS BOARD)**  An agency established pursuant to the National Labor Relations Act for the purpose of prohibiting unfair labor practices by employers and unions.

■■■■

# Ex-Cell-O Corporation

## Employer (D) v. Union (P)

185 NLRB 107 (1970).

**NATURE OF CASE:** NLRB review of trial examiner's recommended order against employer.

**FACT SUMMARY:** Employer refused to bargain after union won election. Trial examiners awarded compensatory damages to employees, and employer sought review of that order.

## 🏛 RULE OF LAW
A trial examiner's recommended remedy calling for the company to compensate its employees for any monetary losses suffered because of the company's unlawful refusal to bargain exceed the trial examiner's authority.

**FACTS:** The United Auto Workers (P) requested recognition in 1964, but Ex-Cell-O Corporation (the Company) (D) refused. The Union (P) petitioned for an election, which was held and won two months after Ex-Cell-O's (D) refusal. The NLRB held a hearing at the Company's (D's) request, and the Union (P) was certified by the NLRB in 1965. The Company (D) then refused to bargain as a way to secure court review of the NLRB's action, and the Union (P) brought unfair labor practice charges in 1966. The Company (D) tried unsuccessfully to enjoin the regional director and trial examiner, but the trial examiner closed the hearing and issued his decision in 1967. The trial examiner found a refusal to bargain and recommended an order to bargain as well as compensatory damages for the employees, who suffered monetary loss because of the employer's refusal to bargain.

**ISSUE:** Does a trial examiner's recommended remedy calling for the company to compensate its employees for any monetary losses suffered because of the company's unlawful refusal to bargain exceed the trial examiner's authority?

**HOLDING AND DECISION:** [Member name not stated in casebook excerpt.] Yes. A trial examiner's recommended remedy calling for the company to compensate its employees for any monetary losses suffered because of the company's unlawful refusal to bargain exceeds the trial examiner's authority. The NLRB's authority to order an employer to take affirmative action to rectify damage caused by its unfair labor practice is broad, but not so broad as to permit the punishment of a particular employer or class of employers. Here, the employer did not flagrantly violate the NLRA, but refused to bargain until it obtained judicial affirmation of the NLRB's decision that the election should not be set aside.

**DISSENT IN PART:** (McCulloch, Member) The compensatory remedy recommended by the trial examiner should be granted, because the NLRB has the statutory authority to direct such relief, and such relief would effectuate the policies of the NLRA. The order to bargain is not adequate to remedy the effects of an unlawful refusal to bargain. The employees were deprived of their legal right to collective bargaining through the union it elected for five years and should be compensated for the employer's illegal deprivation of their rights.

## ▶ ANALYSIS

Note that the majority found that the employer in this case did not intend to violate the NLRA by stalling on the bargaining progress, but merely sought to postpone bargaining until judicial affirmation of the NLRB's decision.

■━■

## Quicknotes

**COMPENSATORY DAMAGES** Measure of damages necessary to compensate victim for actual injuries suffered.

**ENJOIN** The ordering of a party to cease the conduct of a specific activity.

**NLRA (NATIONAL LABOR RELATIONS ACT)** Guarantees employees the right to engage in collective bargaining, and regulates labor unions.

**NLRB (NATIONAL LABOR RELATIONS BOARD)** An agency established pursuant to the National Labor Relations Act for the purpose of prohibiting unfair labor practices by employers and unions.

■━■

# Strikes, Picketing, and Boycotts

## *Quick Reference Rules of Law*

# NLRB v. City Disposal Systems, Inc.

Labor board (P) v. Employer (D)

465 U.S. 822 (1984).

**NATURE OF CASE:** Appeal from decision upholding discharge.

**FACT SUMMARY:** Brown (P) appealed from a decision of the court of appeals that his action in refusing to drive a truck for safety reasons was not a concerted activity within the meaning of § 7 of the NLRA, thereby upholding his discharge.

---

🏛 **RULE OF LAW**
An individual employee's reasonable and honest invocation of a right grounded in a collective bargaining agreement is "concerted activity" within the meaning of § 7 of the NLRA.

---

**FACTS:** Brown (P), a refuse truck driver for City Disposal Systems, Inc. (City) (D), experienced difficulties with the wheels of his truck and brought it in for repairs. Since it could not be repaired that day, he was initially told to go home, but was then asked to drive a truck which Brown (P) had reason to believe was unsafe due to faulty brakes, and which had been brought in for repairs. Brown (P) stated his belief that the brake system on that particular truck was unsafe and refused to drive it. He did not refer to the collective bargaining agreement, which provided that a justified refusal to operate unsafe equipment would not be a violation of the agreement. After continually refusing to drive the truck, Brown (P) was sent home and was later informed that he was discharged. Brown (P) filed a written grievance which the Union declined to process, so he filed suit with the NLRB. The administrative law judge found that Brown (P) had been discharged for his refusal to operate the truck, that the refusal was covered by § 7 of the NLRA, and that City's (D) discharge of Brown (P) violated § 8(a)(1) of the NLRA. He held that even though an employee acts alone in asserting a contractual right, he is, nevertheless, engaged in "concerted activity" within the meaning of § 7. The NLRB affirmed this decision, but the court of appeals characterized the refusal as an action taken solely on his own behalf, and held that the refusal was not concerted activity within the meaning of § 7 of the NLRA. Brown (P) appealed from this decision.

**ISSUE:** Is an individual employee's reasonable and honest invocation of a right grounded in a collective bargaining agreement "concerted activity" within the meaning of § 7 of the NLRA?

**HOLDING AND DECISION:** (Brennan, J.) Yes. An individual employee's reasonable and honest invocation of a right grounded in a collective bargaining agreement is "concerted activity" within the meaning of § 7 of the

NLRA. This is the essence of the NLRB's longstanding "Interboro doctrine." The assertion of such a right is recognized as an extension of the concerted action that produced the collective bargaining agreement and affects the rights of all employees covered. A reading of the NLRA does not preclude individual action from the scope of § 7. The process that gave rise to the collective bargaining agreement, from union organization to enforcement, can be seen as a single concerted activity. The NLRB's policy is also consistent with the purposes of the NLRA, which is to protect certain activities so as to give employers the opportunity to deal with equality with their employers. The refusal by Brown (P) in the present case may be seen as a reasonable first step in enforcing the collective bargaining agreement, prior to filing a grievance, and no one seriously contends that if the grievance were filed alone, that this would be concerted activity. Since judicial review of the NLRB's construction of the NLRA is limited to whether the construction is reasonable, there is no justification for overturning the NLRB's reasonable judgment that in the present case Brown (P) had engaged in "concerted activity" by refusing to drive. The question of whether this method of enforcing this particular right was protected is not considered; it is clear that enforcing the right was "concerted activity." Reversed and remanded.

**DISSENT:** (O'Connor, J.) The proper focus for "concerted activity" issues revolves around the precise nature of the relationship that must exist between the action of an individual employee and the actions of the group. The fact that the right enforced is grounded in the collective bargaining agreement is not sufficient to make the activity a "concerted activity," but is only relevant to whether that type of activity is protected. "Concerted activity" refers to group activity or activity for the group's benefit, and in no sense of the term "concerted" can Brown's (P) refusal be characterized as "concerted activity" within the meaning of § 7 of the NLRA.

---

▶ **ANALYSIS**

The NLRB has recently repudiated its theory of "constructive concerted" activity in connection with the vindication of statutory rights enforced by individual employees in unorganized plants. A finding of "concerted activity" now requires that the employee's activity be engaged in with or on the authority of other employees. See *Meyers Industries, Inc.*, 268 NLRB No. 73, 115 L.R.R.M. 1025 (1984).

---

■■■

*Continued on next page.*

## *Quicknotes*

**COLLECTIVE BARGAINING** Negotiations between an employer and employee that are mediated by a specified third party.

**NLRA (NATIONAL LABOR RELATIONS ACT)** Guarantees employees the right to engage in collective bargaining, and regulates labor unions.

**NLRB (NATIONAL LABOR RELATIONS BOARD)** An agency established pursuant to the National Labor Relations Act for the purpose of prohibiting unfair labor practices by employers and unions.

■=■

# IBM Corp.

## Employees (P) v. Employer (D)

341 NLRB 1288 (2004).

**NATURE OF CASE:** NLRB review of its own previous decision on employee rights.

**FACT SUMMARY:** Employees (P) brought unfair labor practice charges against IBM Corp. (D) for failing to allow them to have co-workers present at their interviews in an investigation of harassment by another employee.

> ## RULE OF LAW
> Nonunionized employees do not have the right to have a co-worker present at an investigatory interview that might lead to discipline.

**FACTS:** IBM Corp. (D) received a letter from a former contract employee alleging harassment by regular employees and began interviewing employees about the allegations. The three employees (P) who eventually filed unfair labor practice charges were initially interviewed on Oct. 15, 2001. None of the three employees (P) asked to have a co-worker present during their first interview, but they each made the request prior to their second interview on Oct. 23, 2001. An IBM manager denied the requests. The company fired the three employees (P) about a month later. They then filed unfair labor practice charges in connection with IBM's (D) denial of their request to have a co-worker present during their second interviews. An administrative law judge applied the Board's decision in *Epilepsy Foundation* and found that IBM (D) violated § 8(a)(1). IBM (D) urged the Board to overrule *Epilepsy Foundation*, arguing that the considerations supporting *Weingarten* rights in unionized workplaces are not present in nonunion workplaces. IBM (D) asserted that co-workers, unlike union representatives, do not represent the interests of the entire unit, cannot redress the perceived imbalance of power between the employer and employees, and cannot facilitate the interview process like a union representative. IBM (D) also argued that extending *Weingarten* rights to nonunion settings may compromise the investigation process.

**ISSUE:** Do nonunionized employees have the right to have a co-worker present at an investigatory interview that might lead to discipline?

**HOLDING AND DECISION:** (Battista, Chairman) No. Nonunionized employees do not have the right to have a co-worker present at an investigatory interview that might lead to discipline. The NLRB acknowledged that extending *Weingarten* rights to nonunion workplaces or limiting them to union workplaces are both permissible interpretations of the NLRA. However, the NLRB found that policy considerations support overruling *Epilepsy Foundation*. The employer must be allowed to conduct its required investigations in a thorough, sensitive, and confidential manner. This can best be accomplished by permitting an employer in a nonunion setting to investigate an employee without the presence of a co-worker. Complaint dismissed.

**DISSENT:** (Liebman, Member) The U.S. Court of Appeals for the District of Columbia Circuit upheld the board's decision in *Epilepsy Foundation* as "both clear and reasonable" [268 F.3d 1095 (D.C. Cir. 2001)]. NLRA § 7 gives "all workers, union-represented or not," the right to engage in concerted activities for the purpose of mutual aid or protection.

## ▶ ANALYSIS

The decision marks the fourth time in the past 23 years that the NLRB has changed positions on the issue of whether *Weingarten* rights are limited to workplaces where the employees are represented by a union. The Supreme Court held in *NLRB v. J. Weingarten Inc.*, 420 U.S. 251, 88 LRRM 2689 (1975), that employees in unionized workplaces are entitled to representation during investigatory interviews. The NLRB first extended *Weingarten* rights to nonunion settings in *Materials Research Corp.*, 262 NLRB 1010, 110 LRRM 1401 (1982). However, the NLRB reversed that position a few years later in *Sears, Roebuck & Co.*, 274 NLRB 230, 118 LRRM 1329 (1985), and modified its rationale in *E.I. DuPont & Co.*, 289 NLRB 627, 128 LRRM 1233 (1988). In *Epilepsy Foundation of Northeast Ohio*, 331 NLRB 676, 164 LRRM 1233 (2000), the NLRB 3-2 overruled *Sears* and *DuPont* and returned to its position in *Materials Research*.

■━■

## Quicknotes

**HARASSMENT** Conduct directed at a particular person with the intent to inflict emotional distress and with no justification therefor; a criminal prosecution commenced without a reasonable expectation of its resulting in a conviction.

**NLRA (NATIONAL LABOR RELATIONS ACT)** Guarantees employees the right to engage in collective bargaining, and regulates labor unions.

**NLRB (NATIONAL LABOR RELATIONS BOARD)** An agency established pursuant to the National Labor Relations Act for the purpose of prohibiting unfair labor practices by employers and unions.

■━■

# Eastex, Inc. v. NLRB

## Employer (D) v. Employees (P)

437 U.S. 556 (1978).

**NATURE OF CASE:** Action on an unfair labor practice charge.

**FACT SUMMARY:** Employees of Eastex, Inc. (P) sought to distribute a union newsletter in nonworking areas during nonworking time.

> ## 🏛 RULE OF LAW
> The NLRB is not required to distinguish among distributions of protected matter by employees on an employer's property on the basis of the content of each distribution.

**FACTS:** The union newsletter that employees of Eastex, Inc. (P) sought to distribute in nonworking areas of the company property during nonworking time urged support of the union and discussed a proposal to incorporate the state "right-to-work" statute into the state constitution and a presidential veto of an increase in the federal minimum wage. It also called on employees to take action to protect their interests as employees with respect to these two issues. Eastex (P) argued that its refusal to permit such dissemination on its property was not a violation of employee rights under the NLRA because the material in question was not directed at conditions in the workplace over which the employer had control and that distributions were not, for that reason, for the "mutual aid and protection" of the employees. The NLRB and court of appeals found the argument wanting and ordered Eastex (P) to permit distribution.

**ISSUE:** Must the NLRB distinguish among distributions of protected matter by employees on an employer's property on the basis of content?

**HOLDING AND DECISION:** (Powell, J.) No. There simply is no requirement that the NLRB distinguish on the basis of content among distributions of protected matter by employees on an employer's property. The NLRA envisions activity in furtherance of the mutual interests of all employees and does not restrict protected activity to that specifically involving particular employees and a particular employer. The type of generalized political activity urged by the newsletter here at issue is, therefore, protected. Furthermore, even if the employer had rights with regard to distribution, they would not be to ban distribution on the basis of content, but to ban distribution of all types. Distribution was properly ordered. Affirmed.

**DISSENT:** (Rehnquist, C.J.) It has never been held that employees have a protected right to engage in anything other than organizational activity on the employer's property. While Congress might be able to require submission of all owner property rights to such political advocacy, it never has.

> ## ▶ ANALYSIS
>
> One of the purposes in protecting employees' rights under the NLRA was to permit precisely this type of concerted activity in furtherance of the general goals of all workers. It was believed that this type of protection would enable employers and employees to meet and bargain effectively as equals.
>
> ■=■

## Quicknotes

**NLRA (NATIONAL LABOR RELATIONS ACT)** Guarantees employees the right to engage in collective bargaining, and regulates labor unions.

**NLRB (NATIONAL LABOR RELATIONS BOARD)** An agency established pursuant to the National Labor Relations Act for the purpose of prohibiting unfair labor practices by employers and unions.

■=■

# NLRB v. Local 1229, IBEW (Jefferson Standard Broadcasting Co.)

## Labor board (P) v. Union (D)

346 U.S. 464 (1953).

**NATURE OF CASE:** Writ of certiorari.

**FACT SUMMARY:** The members of Local 1229 (D), which represented 22 television technicians, manned picket lines on their off-duty hours while continuing to hold their regular jobs and to perform their regular duties after an impasse in negotiations occurred. Later, the technicians published 5,000 handbills denouncing the television station as giving second-rate service. The employees were fired.

## 🏛 RULE OF LAW
An employer may discharge for cause employees who have deliberately attacked in a public way the quality of a product or service provided by their employer, even though such an attack comes in the midst of a labor controversy but without reference to that controversy.

**FACTS:** After an impasse in negotiations occurred, the members of Local 1229 (D), which represented 22 television technicians, began to picket peacefully on their off-duty hours while continuing to hold their regular jobs and to perform their regular duties. The picket signs identified the union and charged the company with unfairness to its technicians and emphasized the company's refusal to renew the provision for arbitration of discharges. Later, the technicians under the heading, WBT Technicians, published 5,000 handbills denouncing the television station as giving second-rate service. Some of these handbills were mailed to local businessmen and others were handed out in restaurants, barber shops, on the public square and in buses. WBT, the employer, felt this attack jeopardized its advertising income. Ten days later, with no sign of abatement of the union's tactics, WBT fired ten employees by letter, explaining that they had pursued a tactic of turning customers against WBT, even though they were receiving full pay and benefits while they continued to work. The company also explained that they had been retained even though other untruths had been published before the handbills. It also pointed out that it was not required by law to retain employees who disparaged their employer. After a hearing, the trial examiner held that all employees should be reinstated with back pay, but the NLRB (P) found that only one of the ten was innocent of any involvement with the handbill and ordered his reinstatement. The NLRB (P) found no unfair labor practice in the discharge of the other nine.

**ISSUE:** May an employer discharge for cause employees who have deliberately attacked in a public way the quality of the product or service provided by their employer, even

though such attack comes in the midst of a labor controversy but without reference to that controversy?

**HOLDING AND DECISION:** (Burton, J.) Yes. An employer may discharge for cause employees who have deliberately attacked in a public way the quality of the product or service provided by their employer even though such attack comes in the midst of a labor controversy but without reference to that controversy. Section 10(c) of the Taft-Hartley Act (Act) provides that the employer has the right to discharge employees for cause. Case law and congressional history uphold this interpretation. The question becomes whether the discharge was for cause or because the employees engaged in other concerted activities protected by § 7. Here, the employees' attack did not relate to a labor practice of the company. It did not refer to wages, working conditions or hours. It did not ask for public support. It attacked policies of finance and public relations for which management, not technicians, is responsible. It was an off-duty, continuous attack upon the interests the employees were being paid to conserve and develop. Nothing could be further from the purposes of the Act. The fortuity of a labor dispute affords the employees no defense because the handbill omitted all reference to it. It was merely the undisclosed motive, disclosure of which might have cost them the support of the public. The NLRB (P) effectively separated in its findings the handbill and labor controversy. The NLRB's (P) decision is upheld. Order set aside and cause remanded with instructions.

**DISSENT:** (Frankfurter, J.) The Court bar pointed to the employees' "disloyalty" and found sufficient "cause" to justify the discharges, but did not approach the issue of whether the handbill was a "concerted activity" within § 7. Just because certain activity in connection with a protected "concerted activity" under § 7 can be so improper as to be denied § 7 protection does not obviate the need to first analyze whether the distribution of the handbill was a legitimate activity. It is for the NLRB (P) to make these judgments, and the courts do not go beyond their proper bounds in asking for greater clarity in light of the correct legal standards for judgment. This case will not lend guidance for future cases beyond the specific facts of this case.

## ▶ ANALYSIS

Whether strikers fall into the two basic categories of "economic strikers" or "unfair labor practice strikers" is irrelevant when they have been discharged or suspended

*Continued on next page.*

"for cause." Section 10(c) provides that the NLRB (P) may not order reinstatement or back pay for striking employees discharged or suspended for cause. As illustrated by this case, "disloyalty" is sufficient "cause" although the case does not define that term.

■■■■

## Quicknotes

**NLRB (NATIONAL LABOR RELATIONS BOARD)** An agency established pursuant to the National Labor Relations Act for the purpose of prohibiting unfair labor practices by employers and unions.

■■■■

# NLRB v. Mackay Radio & Telegraph Co.

Labor board (P) v. Employer (D)

304 U.S. 333 (1938).

**NATURE OF CASE:** Appeal from reversal of findings of NLRA §§ 8(a)(1) and (3) violations.

**FACT SUMMARY:** Mackay Radio & Telegraph Co. (D), after filling six of 11 vacancies created by striking employees, only rehired strikers who were not otherwise active in union activities.

## RULE OF LAW
Discrimination in rehiring striking employees on account of their union activity violates §§ 8(a)(1) and (3) in regard to tenure of employment.

**FACTS:** After a strike against Mackay Radio & Telegraph Co.'s (Mackay's) (D) San Francisco office, Mackay (D) transferred employees from its other offices to keep the struck office operating. The transferred employees were told that they could remain permanently in San Francisco if they chose, and that striking employees would not be rehired except as vacancies arose. Out of the 11 vacancies filled by transfers, 6 opened at the close of the strike. Mackay (D), in rehiring striking employees, did not rehire the five who were most active in union activities. The NLRB (P) held that such discrimination violated §§ 8(a)(1) and (3) in regard to tenure of employment. The court of appeals reversed, and the NLRB (P) appealed.

**ISSUE:** Does discrimination in rehiring striking employees on account of their union activity violate §§ 8(a)(1) and (3) in regard to tenure of employment?

**HOLDING AND DECISION:** (Roberts, J.) Yes. Discrimination in rehiring striking employees on account of their union activity violates §§ 8(a)(1) and (3) in regard to tenure of employment. Here, it was unnecessary to determine whether the strike was advisable or justified in order to determine whether the strike was a consequence of a current labor dispute because the alleged discrimination occurred afterwards. Within the act, strikers remain employees and are protected against unfair labor practices even while on strike. It was not an unfair labor practice for Mackay (D) to replace strikers, nor to retain transferred employees at strike's end. However, any discrimination solely for participating in union activity, which is protected under the Act, violates the Act. The five who were not rehired solely for their union activity should have been reinstated. Reversed.

## ▶ ANALYSIS

It is important to note that striking employees, whether involved in an unfair labor practice strike or an economic strike, are fully protected during the strike by the Act.

However, those protections may operate differently depending on whether the strike was economic in nature or based upon an unfair labor practice. For example, as seen in *Mackay*, economic strikers have the right to nondiscriminatory reinstatement, while unfair labor practice strikers will generally be awarded back pay if their strike was justified, but not if an employer is not found to have committed an unfair practice.

■━■

## Quicknotes

**DISCRIMINATION** Unequal treatment of a class of persons.

**NLRA (NATIONAL LABOR RELATIONS ACT)** Guarantees employees the right to engage in collective bargaining, and regulates labor unions.

**NATIONAL LABOR RELATIONS BOARD (NLRB)** An agency established pursuant to the National Labor Relations Act for the purpose of prohibiting unfair labor practices by employers and unions.

■━■

# NLRB v. Erie Resistor Corp.

Labor board (P) v. Employer (D)

373 U.S. 221 (1963).

**NATURE OF CASE:** Appeal from reversal of findings of NLRA §§ 8(a)(1) and (3) violations.

**FACT SUMMARY:** Erie Resistor Corp. (D), in order to encourage strikers to return to work and to hire replacements, offered 20 years "super-seniority" to those who would stay on the job.

## 🏛 RULE OF LAW

A legitimate business purpose is not always a defense to an unfair labor practice charge because some conduct by its very nature may contain the implications of illegal intent or motive to discriminate or interfere with union rights.

**FACTS:** During a strike, Erie Resister Corp. (Erie) (D), under intense competitive pressure, continued production with nonstrikers and later hired replacements promising extra seniority at the strike's end. During the strike, Erie (D) added 20 years of "super-seniority" to each non-striker's and replacement's actual service record for the purpose of determining lay-off priorities according to seniority. The offer of super-seniority was extended to any striker who would return to work. After this offer, the strike collapsed. The NLRB (P) found violations of §§ 8(a)(1) and (3), i.e., discrimination in regard to tenure, without the need of specific evidence of Erie's (D) discriminatory motive. The court of appeals reversed on the ground that employer action solely to protect and continue its business did not violate the Act without a showing of illegal motivation. The NLRB (P) appealed.

**ISSUE:** Is a legitimate purpose always a defense to an unfair labor practice charge without a specific showing of illegal motivation?

**HOLDING AND DECISION:** (White, J.) No. A legitimate business purpose is not always a defense to an unfair labor practice charge because some conduct by its very nature may contain the implications of illegal intent or motive to discriminate or interfere with union rights. Existence of discrimination may be inferred. While proof is obviously helpful, intent may be found in the inherently discriminatory or destructive nature of the conduct itself. The employer in such cases must be found to intend the very consequences which foreseeably flow from his action, and which, if unexplained, is an unfair labor practice on its face. While an employer can counter that his actions were in pursuit of legitimate business ends, and that his dominant purpose was not to discriminate or invade union rights, his conduct can speak otherwise for itself. Here, super-seniority discriminated between strikers and nonstrikers during and after the strike and had a destructive impact. Reversed.

## ▶ ANALYSIS

Two things are required to find a § 8(a)(3) violation: (1) encouraging or discouraging union membership, and (2) discrimination. Note the destructive effects of Erie's (D) offer of super-seniority. The offer necessarily operated to the detriment of strikers. It, in effect, was an offer of extra benefits to induce abandonment of the strike. It undermined the strikers' mutual interest and clearly caused the strike's collapse. Finally, it made future collective bargaining difficult because employees were divided into two opposing groups—those who wanted to retain their super-seniority and those who did not obtain it and wanted those who had it to give it up.

■■■■

## Quicknotes

**COLLECTIVE BARGAINING** Negotiations between an employer and employee that are mediated by a specified third party.

**NLRA (NATIONAL LABOR RELATIONS ACT)** Guarantees employees the right to engage in collective bargaining, and regulates labor unions.

**NLRB (NATIONAL LABOR RELATIONS BOARD)** An agency established pursuant to the National Labor Relations Act for the purpose of prohibiting unfair labor practices by employers and unions.

**UNFAIR LABOR PRACTICE** Conduct by labor unions and employers, which is proscribed by the National Labor Relations Act.

■■■■

# American Ship Building Co. v. NLRB

### Employer (D) v. Labor board (P)

380 U.S. 300 (1965).

**NATURE OF CASE:** Appeal by employer from NLRB finding of an unfair labor practice.

**FACT SUMMARY:** American Ship Building (D), reasonably fearful that a strike, despite unions' protestations to the contrary, was imminent, and that an impasse could not be resolved, laid off its employees.

> ## 🏛 RULE OF LAW
> An employer violates neither § 8(a)(1) nor § 8(a)(3) when, after a bargaining impasse has been reached, he temporarily shuts down his plant and lays off his employees for the sole purpose of bringing economic pressure to bear in support of his legitimate bargaining position.

**FACTS:** American Ship Building (American) (D), which operated some shipyards on the Great Lakes, reached an impasse in August of 1961 with eight unions at the collective bargaining. Previous contracts with these unions had all been preceded by strikes. What little work was obtained during the summer months had to be performed quickly to prevent immobilizations of the ships. Fearing that a strike would endanger its ability to finish ship repairs before the lake would become frozen, American (D) gradually laid off almost all employees. Shortly thereafter, negotiations resumed, and a new agreement was reached. Employees were recalled. The unions filed a complaint with the NLRB (P) charging American (D) with continuing unfair labor practices in violation of §§ 8(a)(1) and (3). Although the trial examiner found that American (D) could reasonably anticipate a strike in spite of the unions' assurances to the contrary, and concluded that American (D) was justified in laying off its employees when it did, the Board (P) rejected these conclusions. The Board (P) found that the layoff was motivated solely by a desire to bring economic pressure and secure settlement of the dispute on favorable grounds, and accordingly, held that American (D) had violated §§ 8(a)(1) and (3). American (D) appealed.

**ISSUE:** Is an employer free to temporarily lay off employees solely as a means to bring economic pressure to bear in support of its bargaining position after an impasse has been reached?

**HOLDING AND DECISION:** (Stewart, J.) Yes. The employer's use of a lockout solely in support of a legitimate bargaining position is in no way inconsistent with the right to bargain collectively or with the right to strike. A lockout is not inherently discriminatory against concerted union activity. Nothing in the NLRA guarantees a union the "right" to insist on its position free from economic disadvantage. As for the contention that a lockout preempts the possibility of a strike, thus leaving the union with nothing to strike against, this is specious reasoning since the work stoppage that would have been the subject of the strike has in fact occurred. Nor is the kind of lockout prohibited by § 8(a)(3) pursuant to which the Board (P) is entitled to look at an employer's motivation. There is no claim here that American (D) locked out only union members, or locked out any employee simply because he was a union member, or that American (D) conditioned rehiring upon resignation from the union. The mere possibility that some member felt himself discouraged or discriminated against is too remote to justify a finding that § 8(a)(3) has been violated. While an employer has other economic weapons at his disposal, e.g., stockpiling and subcontracting, or permanently replacing strikers, the NLRA does not give the Board (P) a general authority to assess the relative economic power of the adversaries in the bargaining process and to deny weapons to one party or the other because of its assessment of that party's bargaining power. Reversed.

**CONCURRENCE:** (White, J.) An employer, whether or not a strike is imminent, has the right to inform his customers that he in fact anticipates one so as to protect their property.

**CONCURRENCE:** (Goldberg, J.) The tests as to whether an employer's conduct violates § 8(a)(1) or § 8(a)(3) without a showing of antiunion motive is whether the legitimate economic interests of the employer justify his interference with the rights of his employees—a test involving the balancing of the conflicting legitimate interests. Thus, it is unnecessary to reach the broad question of whether an employer may lock out his employees solely to bring economic pressure to bear in support of his bargaining position. Certainly, an employer may lock out his employees in the face of a threatened strike under circumstances where, had the choice of timing been left solely to the unions, the employer and his customers would have been subject to economic injury over and above the loss of business normally incident to an impasse.

## ▶ ANALYSIS

Conversely, an employer who engages in a lockout does commit an unfair labor practice if in doing so he was attempting to harm the ability of his employees to participate in protected concerted activities, or to get out of his

*Continued on next page.*

statutory duty to bargain. A clearcut example of a violation is where the employer announces his antiunion animus for the lockout. Such sentiments may also be shown by extrinsic evidence.

■━■

## *Quicknotes*

**COLLECTIVE BARGAINING** Negotiations between an employer and employee that are mediated by a specified third party.

**EXTRINSIC EVIDENCE** Evidence that is not contained within the text of a document or contract but which is derived from the parties' statements or the circumstances under which the agreement was made.

**NLRA (NATIONAL LABOR RELATIONS ACT)** Guarantees employees the right to engage in collective bargaining, and regulates labor unions.

**NLRB (NATIONAL LABOR RELATIONS BOARD)** An agency established pursuant to the National Labor Relations Act for the purpose of prohibiting unfair labor practices by employers and unions.

■━■

# NLRB v. Great Dane Trailers, Inc.

Labor board (P) v. Employer (D)

388 U.S. 26 (1967).

**NATURE OF CASE:** Appeal from reversal of an NLRB finding of §§ 8(a)(1) and (3) violations.

**FACT SUMMARY:** After employees of Great Dane Trailers, Inc. (Great Dane) (D) went on strike, Great Dane (D) decided to pay nonstriking employees their contractually agreed-upon vacation benefits while denying those benefits to otherwise qualified strikers.

## RULE OF LAW
Once it has been proved that an employer engaged in discriminatory conduct which could have adversely affected employee rights to some extent, the burden is upon the employer to establish that it was motivated by legitimate objectives since such proof is most accessible to him.

**FACTS:** The collective bargaining agreement between Great Dane Trailers, Inc. (Great Dane) (D) and the union, which expired on March 31, 1963, provided that vacation benefits would be paid to employees who met certain qualifications. These benefits were to be paid on the Friday closest to July 1 of every year. The agreement was temporarily extended to April 30, 1963, but the union went on strike on May 16, 1963. Great Dane (D) continued operating with nonstrikers and replacements. On July 12, 1963, a number of striking employees demanded their vacation benefits, but Great Dane (D) refused on the grounds that all contractual obligations were terminated by the strike. Subsequently, Great Dane (D) unilaterally decided to pay vacation benefits to all those who had reported for work on July 1, 1963. The NLRB (P) found such action to violate §§ 8(a)(1) and (3); i.e., discrimination in terms and conditions of employment which would discourage union membership and which unlawfully interferes with a protected activity. The court of appeals reversed, and the NLRB (P) appealed.

**ISSUE:** Once it has been proved that an employer engaged in discriminatory conduct which could have adversely affected employee rights to some extent, is the burden upon the employer to establish that it was motivated by legitimate objectives?

**HOLDING AND DECISION:** (Warren, C.J.) Yes. A finding of a § 8(a)(3) violation requires both a finding of discrimination and a resulting discouragement of union membership. Paying benefits to nonstrikers and not to strikers was such a discrimination. Discouraging membership in a labor organization includes discouraging participation in concerted activities such as a legitimate strike. Not paying benefits to strikers may have such a discouraging effect.

Such discrimination means that the finding of a violation would ordinarily depend on whether the discrimination was motivated by an antiunion purpose. Principles aiding in determining motivation include: (1) if it is reasonable to conclude that the conduct is inherently destructive then no proof of motivation is needed and an unfair labor practice can be found even if the employer shows evidence of motivation by business considerations; and (2) if the adverse effect of discriminatory conduct is "comparatively slight," an antiunion motivation must be proved to sustain the charge if the employer has given evidence of legitimate and substantial business justification. In either situation, once it has been proved that an employer engaged in discriminatory conduct which could have adversely affected employee rights to some extent, the burden is upon the employer to establish that it was motivated by legitimate objectives since such proof is most accessible to him. Here, Great Dane (D) did not meet that burden of proof. As discriminatory conduct was shown without Great Dane (D) providing evidence of justifiable business motivation, the court of appeals was reversed, and the NLRB (P) decision was reinstated.

**DISSENT:** (Harlan, J.) Employers have always been free to take reasonable measures which discourage a strike by pressuring the economic interests of employees, including the extreme measure of hiring permanent replacements, without having the NLRB (P) inquire into the substantiality of their business justifications. "If the Court means to change this rule, though I assume it does not, it surely should not do so without argument of the point by the parties and without careful discussion."

## ANALYSIS

The Court believed that it was not necessary for it to decide the degree to which the challenged conduct might have affected employee rights. This was because Great Dane (D) came forward with no evidence of legitimate motives for its discriminatory conduct. Because the company did not meet its burden of proof, the court concluded that the court of appeals misconstrued the function of judicial review because it speculated in its reversal of the NLRB (P) as to what might have motivated the employer.

◼▆◼

## Quicknotes

**BURDEN OF PROOF** The duty of a party to introduce evidence to support a fact that is in dispute in an action.

*Continued on next page.*

**COLLECTIVE BARGAINING** Negotiations between an employer and employee that are mediated by a specified third party.

**DISCRIMINATION** Unequal treatment of a class of persons.

**NLRA (NATIONAL LABOR RELATIONS ACT)** Guarantees employees the right to engage in collective bargaining, and regulates labor unions.

**NLRB (NATIONAL LABOR RELATIONS BOARD)** An agency established pursuant to the National Labor Relations Act for the purpose of prohibiting unfair labor practices by employers and unions.

# Local 15 IBEW v. NLRB

## Union (P) v. NLRB (D)

429 F.3d 651 (7th Cir. 2005).

**NATURE OF CASE:** Appeal from NLRB decision in favor of the employer.

**FACT SUMMARY:** [Facts not stated in casebook excerpt.]

---

🏛 **RULE OF LAW**
An employer violates §§ 8(a)(1) and (3) of the NLRA by locking out and/or refusing to reinstate those employees who were on strike at the time of a union's unconditional offer to return to work, while not locking out and/or reinstating those employees who, prior to the union's unconditional offer to return to work, had ceased participating in the strike by making an offer to return to work, and had either returned to work or scheduled a return to work.

---

**FACTS:** [Facts not stated in casebook excerpt.]

**ISSUE:** Does an employer violate §§ 8(a)(1) and (3) of the NLRA by locking out and/or refusing to reinstate those employees who were on strike at the time of a union's unconditional offer to return to work, while not locking out and/or reinstating those employees who, prior to the union's unconditional offer to return to work, had ceased participating in the strike by making an offer to return to work, and had either returned to work or scheduled a return to work?

**HOLDING AND DECISION:** (Flaum, C.J.) Yes. An employer violates §§ 8(a)(1) and (3) of the NLRA by locking out and/or refusing to reinstate those employees who were on strike at the time of a union's unconditional offer to return to work, while not locking out and/or reinstating those employees who, prior to the union's unconditional offer to return to work, had ceased participating in the strike by making an offer to return to work, and had either returned to work or scheduled a return to work. In reaching its decision, the court applied the test from *NLRB v. Great Dane Trailers Inc.*, 388 U.S. 26 (1967). Under the *Great Dane* test, a harmful action by an employer is either inherently destructive or comparatively slight. Inherently destructive conduct is conduct that harms the collective bargaining process, interferes with employees' right to strike, or is taken against employees based on union status, and its effect on the collective bargaining process is more than temporary, instead establishing a barrier to future collective bargaining. Where inherently destructive conduct exists, no proof of an anti-union motivation is required. Such actions are permissible only if business justification is superior when weighed against employee rights. Action that is comparatively slight encompasses all other harmful action and will be justified on a showing by the employer that the action satisfies a legitimate and substantial business need. If an action cannot be justified under the comparatively slight harm standard, it clearly cannot be justified under the inherently destructive standard. The court held that Midwest's operational needs did not justify the partial lockout. The company successfully maintained operations throughout the strike without the use of crossover employees or non-strikers. The court also held that the partial lockout was not justified as a lawful means of economically pressuring holdouts. Once the employer, Midwest, announced the selective lockout, all of the employees in the bargaining unit removed themselves from the economic strike by offering to return to work, and the only distinction between employees was whether an individual employee made his offer to return as part of the union's activity or individually. Thus, there was no need to pressure holdouts, because there were no holdouts. The court also held that if the employer were free to exercise economic penalties selectively against those employees against whom they believe economic coercion would be most effective, an employer could take discriminatory actions that have traditionally been barred, which is not a legitimate and substantial business justification for a partial lockout. In instituting the partial lockout, Midwest displayed anti-union animus; either employees were locked out in a completely blind fashion, thereby offering no legitimate and substantial business justification for selective lockout, or they were chosen on the basis of their union activities and therefore the action was based on invalid anti-union motivations. Such an action has a natural tendency to discourage participation in concerted union activities in violation of § 8(a)(3) of the NLRA. Reversed and remanded.

▌**ANALYSIS**

The court remanded the case to the NLRB to determine whether the employer's unfair labor practices rendered the collective bargaining agreement void. As of the date of publication, the case has not yet reached the NLRB for rehearing. The employer petitioned for rehearing, which was denied, rehearing en banc, which was denied, and on April 4, 2006, filed a petition for certiorari with the Supreme Court.

◼▬◼

*Continued on next page.*

## Quicknotes

**ANIMUS** Intention, will.

**CERTIORARI** A discretionary writ issued by a superior court to an inferior court in order to review the lower court's decisions; the Supreme Court's writ ordering such review.

**COLLECTIVE BARGAINING** Negotiations between an employer and employee that are mediated by a specified third party.

**EN BANC** The hearing of a matter by all the judges of the court, rather than only the necessary quorum.

**NLRA (NATIONAL LABOR RELATIONS ACT)** Guarantees employees the right to engage in collective bargaining, and regulates labor unions.

**NLRB (NATIONAL LABOR RELATIONS BOARD)** An agency established pursuant to the National Labor Relations Act for the purpose of prohibiting unfair labor practices by employers and unions.

# Laidlaw Corp.

## Employer (D) v. Striking workers (P)

### 171 NLRB 1366 (1968).

**NATURE OF CASE:** Appeal by employer who fired striking workers.

**FACT SUMMARY:** Striking workers who made unconditional offers to return to work were denied positions by the employer.

## 🏛 RULE OF LAW
(1) **An individual whose work ceases due to a labor dispute remains an employee if he has not obtained other regular or substantially equivalent employment. The right to reinstatement does not depend on job availability as of the time when applications are filed.**
(2) **An employer refusing to reinstate strikers must show that the action was due to a legitimate and substantial business justification.**

**FACTS:** [The names of most of the parties are not stated in casebook excerpt.] A union (P) voted to reject Laidlaw Corp.'s (D) wage offer and notified the company (D) of its plan to strike. One striker, Massey (P), applied for reinstatement two days after the strike began, but was told that his job had been filled. Four days later, he was informed of an opening in his job classification and was asked by Laidlaw (D) to return, but with the pay rate of a new hire. He refused the offer and continued to strike. The union (P) met a month after the strike began and many strikers voted to return to work, and applied for jobs with the employer. Some of the strikers were rehired, but others were sent termination notices. Laidlaw (D) instituted a policy of rehiring a striking worker if a job were available as of the date of the application, but terminating the striking worker permanently if no job was available at the time of his application. The worker's application would not be kept on file to fill a future job post. Laidlaw (D) continued to advertise for help, however, and the strikers renewed their strike effort to protest against the employer's alleged unfair labor practice. The trial examiner found that Massey (P) was not entitled to reinstatement two days after the strike began when his job was filled by a replacement, but that he remained an employee within § 2(3) of the NLRA, and was therefore entitled to full reinstatement when he reapplied at a time when the position was vacant. The trial examiner also found that the termination of the other strikers (P) also violated the NLRA, because they remained employees under the NLRA, and that the failure to reinstate strikers as of February 11 (the day after they voted to end the original strike)

converted the strike as of that date from an economic strike to an unfair labor practice strike.

**ISSUE:**
(1) Does an individual whose work ceases due to a labor dispute remain an employee if he has not obtained other regular or substantially equivalent employment?
(2) Must an employer refusing to reinstate strikers show that the action was due to a legitimate and substantial business justification?

**HOLDING AND DECISION:** [Member name not stated in casebook excerpt.]
(1) Yes. An individual whose work ceases due to a labor dispute remains an employee if he has not obtained other regular or substantially equivalent employment. The right to reinstatement does not depend on job availability as of the time when applications are filed. Therefore, Massey (P) remained an employee when he rejoined the strike after his first effort to be reinstated was rejected even though at that particular moment he had been replaced. His right to reinstatement did not expire when the original application was made.
(2) Yes. An employer refusing to reinstate strikers must show that the action was due to a legitimate and substantial business justification. No such justifications existed here, and the employer's decision to pay Massey (P) at the rate of a new hire could only be interpreted as punishment for engaging in protected activity of striking. In addition, refusing to reinstate the other strikers while continuing to advertise for and hire new unskilled employees was not justified by the employer, and it thereby violated §§ 8(a)(3) and (1) of the NLRA.

## ▶ ANALYSIS

Clearly, the threat of permanent termination would have a chilling effect on an employee's motivation to strike in order to improve his or her working conditions. But the court's requirement that the employer provide a legitimate and substantial business justification for refusing to rehire strikers does not seem to be a very tall order; the employer could conceivably come up with any number of reasons why the operation of the business required the replacement of striking workers in a short period of time. This case seems to allow the employer to easily curb union activity.

■=■

*Continued on next page.*

# *Quicknotes*

**CHILLING EFFECT**  Any practice which results in discouraging the exercise of a right.

**NLRA (NATIONAL LABOR RELATIONS ACT)**  Guarantees employees the right to engage in collective bargaining, and regulates labor unions.

■■━■

# Metropolitan Edison Co. v. NLRB

## Employer (D) v. Labor board (P)

460 U.S. 693 (1983).

**NATURE OF CASE:** Appeal of an order finding commission of an unfair labor practice.

**FACT SUMMARY:** Metropolitan Edison Co. (D) disciplined union officials more severely than other employees, for failing to comply with a no-strike clause in the collective bargaining agreement.

---

### 🏛 RULE OF LAW
NLRA §§ 8(a)(1) and (3) prohibit employers from disciplining union officials more severely than other employees unless the employers' legitimate reasons for such discipline outweigh the invasion of the officials' rights to equal treatment.

---

**FACTS:** Lang (P), an official of the IBEW, filed an unfair labor practice charge against his employer, Metropolitan Edison Co. (D), who imposed a more severe punishment on him than on other employees for his role in a labor action. Lang (P) refused to obey the company's instructions to cross a picket line and thus induce his membership to end their work stoppage, which violated the no-strike clause of their collective bargaining agreement. Metropolitan Edison (D) justified the increased punishment claiming Lang (P) breached his duty as a union official to enforce the no-strike clause by refusing to follow the company's instruction, and that the union waived any right to equal punishment by impliedly agreeing to undertake action to enforce the no-strike clause. The Board adopted the holding of the administrative law judge and held the punishment violated §§ 8(a)(1) and (3), and the court of appeals enforced the order. Metropolitan Edison (D) appealed.

**ISSUE:** Do §§ 8(a)(1) and (3) prohibit employers from disciplining union officials more severely than other employees unless the legitimate reasons for the discipline outweigh the invasion of the officials' right to equal treatment?

**HOLDING AND DECISION:** (Powell, J.) Yes. Sections 8(a)(1) and (3) prohibit employers from disciplining union officials more severely than other employees unless the employer's legitimate reasons for such discipline outweigh the invasion of the officials' rights to equal treatment. Punishing union officials more severely than others discriminates solely on the basis of union activity and is inherently destructive of individual rights, as it dissuades individuals from taking an active part in their union's government. In this case, Metropolitan Edison's (D) justification for increased punishment does not outweigh the invasion of Lang's (P) right to equal treatment because although officials have an implied duty to uphold the collective bargaining agreement, they have no duty to follow the employer's instructions as to how best to fulfill their duty and then suffer increased punishment for their failure to abide by them. To rule otherwise gives employers unreasonable leverage over the manner in which officials discharge their union duties, in derogation of the basic policies of labor law. Finally, the union did not clearly waive its right to equal punishment by failing to change the collective bargaining agreement after two unsuccessful arbitrations over the issue of disparate punishment because such arbitrations do not establish a sufficient pattern of decision to render the union's acquiescence a clear waiver of a statutory right. Affirmed.

## ▌ ANALYSIS

The validity of a refusal to cross a picket line depends upon the legality of the strike. If the strike is itself an unfair labor practice, a worker who honors the picket is considered to join in the prohibited action. If the strike is valid, the refusal to cross the picket line is protected on the theory that the support shown the strikers may be reciprocated later.

■■■

## *Quicknotes*

**ARBITRATION** An agreement to have a dispute heard and decided by a neutral third party, rather than through legal proceedings.

**COLLECTIVE BARGAINING** Negotiations between an employer and employee that are mediated by a specified third party.

**NLRA (NATIONAL LABOR RELATIONS ACT)** Guarantees employees the right to engage in collective bargaining, and regulates labor unions.

**NLRB (NATIONAL LABOR RELATIONS BOARD)** An agency established pursuant to the National Labor Relations Act for the purpose of prohibiting unfair labor practices by employers and unions.

**UNFAIR LABOR PRACTICE** Conduct by labor unions and employers, which is proscribed by the National Labor Relations Act.

■■■

# International Bhd. of Teamsters, Local 695 v. Vogt, Inc.

## Union (D) v. Employer (P)

354 U.S. 284 (1957).

**NATURE OF CASE:** Action for a state court injunction to enjoin peaceful picketing.

**FACT SUMMARY:** When the Teamsters (D) were unsuccessful in their organization drive, they peacefully picketed the employer's (P) business; the employer obtained an injunction in state court on the basis of a state statute which prohibited employees from forcing an employer to violate the legal rights of his employees.

## 🏛 RULE OF LAW
A state, in enforcing some public policy, may constitutionally enjoin peaceful picketing aimed at preventing effectuation of that policy.

**FACTS:** Wisconsin statute § 111.06(2) made it an unfair labor practice for an employee individually or in concert with others to "coerce, intimidate or induce any employer to interfere with any of his employees in the employment of their legal rights ... or to engage in any practice with regard to his employees which would constitute an unfair labor practice if undertaken by him on his own initiative." When the Teamsters (D) sought unsuccessfully to induce some of Vogt, Inc.'s (P) employees to join a union, it commenced to picket the entrance to Vogt's (P) business with signs reading, "the men on this job are not 100% affiliated with the AFL." As a result of this picketing, truck drivers refused to deliver and haul goods to and from Vogt's (P) plant, thereby injuring its business. Vogt (P), claiming that the purpose of the picketing was to force it to induce its employees to become members of the Teamsters (D), and to injure it for refusing to do so, sought an injunction in state court. The trial court did not consider Vogt's (P) claim, but nonetheless issued the injunction on the basis of a state statute which prohibited picketing in the absence of a "labor dispute." On appeal, the Wisconsin Supreme Court reversed, holding the statute in question unconstitutional. However, upon reargument, the court withdrew its original opinion, and this time basing its decision on § 111.06(2), affirmed the issuance of the injunction. The Teamsters (D) appealed, challenging the authority of Wisconsin to enjoin peaceful picketing.

**ISSUE:** May a state enjoin peaceful picketing where the purpose of such picketing is in violation of some state public policy?

**HOLDING AND DECISION:** (Frankfurter, J.) Yes. In *Thornhill v. Alabama*, 310 U.S. 88 (1940), the Court made sweeping pronouncements about the right to picket in holding unconstitutional a statute that had been applied to ban all picketing, peaceful or otherwise. The Court in that case based its decision on the Due Process Clause of the Fourteenth Amendment. In *AFL v. Swing*, 312 U.S. 321 (1941), the Court held that a state may not enjoin picketing in the absence of an immediate dispute between employer and employee. However, since these two decisions, the Court has retreated from its broad pronouncements against state regulation. Picketing, even though peaceful, involves more than just communication of ideas and could not be immune from all state regulation. Thus, subsequent cases involved not so much questions of free speech as review of the balance struck by a state between picketing that involved more than "publicity" and competing interests of state policy. State public policies, either criminal or civil, legislative or judicially announced, which have been sanctioned by this Court as the basis for a state's exercise of injunctive power against peaceful picketing include the following: statutory policy against employer coercion of employees' choice of bargaining representative; policy against involuntary employment on racial lines; state antitrust laws prohibiting a conspiracy in restraint of trade; and "right to work" law. Thus, this Court will sustain state injunctions against peaceful picketing, even when arising in the course of a labor controversy, when such picketing is counter to valid state policy in a domain open to state regulation. In the present case, the policy of Wisconsin enforced by the prohibition of the picketing here is a valid one. Affirmed.

**DISSENT:** (Douglas, J.) Where, as here, there is no rioting, no mass picketing, no violence, no disorder, no fisticuffs, no coercion, indeed nothing but speech, the principles announced in *Thornhill* and *Swing* should give the advocacy of one side of a dispute first amendment protection. This form of expression can be regulated or prohibited only to the extent that it forms an essential part of a course of conduct that the state can regulate or prohibit.

## ▶ ANALYSIS

A picket line has often been characterized as involving "speech plus." The various attempts to regulate peaceful picketing have evoked considerable controversy among labor law commentators. On the one hand, supporters of the "speech plus" theory argue that since a picket line has the effect of inducing many persons who would otherwise enter the business premises to turn back, the fact that the picketing may be peacefully conducted is immaterial. On the other hand, the "free speech" proponents, who

*Continued on next page.*

oppose extensive regulation, respond that the decision of persons who approach a picket line to refuse to cross it is entirely volitional, and should not, for this reason, make otherwise protected First Amendment activity unlawful.

■━━■

## Quicknotes

**DUE PROCESS CLAUSE** Clauses found in the Fifth and Fourteenth Amendments to the United States Constitution providing that no person shall be deprived of "life, liberty, or property, without due process of law."

**ENJOIN** The ordering of a party to cease the conduct of a specific activity.

**FIRST AMENDMENT** Prohibits Congress from enacting any law respecting an establishment of religion, prohibiting the free exercise of religion, abridging freedom of speech or the press, the right of peaceful assembly and the right to petition for a redress of grievances.

**FOURTEENTH AMENDMENT** Declares that no state shall make or enforce any law which shall abridge the privileges and immunities of citizens of the United States.

■━━■

# Edward J. DeBartolo Corp. v. Florida Gulf Coast Bldg. & Constr. Trades Council

Employer (P) v. Union (D)

485 U.S. 568 (1988).

**NATURE OF CASE:** Appeal from order denying enforcement of NLRB order.

**FACT SUMMARY:** The NLRB held that the distribution of handbills by the Florida Gulf Coast Bldg. & Constr. Trades Council (Council) (D) constituted coercive conduct and was therefore an unfair labor practice.

🏛 **RULE OF LAW**
Distributing handbills that puts secondary pressure on nonstruck employers is protected speech and not an unfair labor practice.

**FACTS:** The Florida Gulf Coast Bldg. & Constr. Trades Council (Council) (D) distributed handbills requesting customers of a shopping mall not to patronize any store there because one store used nonunion labor on a construction job. The handbills described the dispute but did not indicate that the other stores and the owner, Edward J. DeBartolo Corp. (DeBartolo) (P), had nothing to do with the nonunion work. DeBartolo (P) filed a petition charging the Council (D) with an unfair labor practice. The NLRB held that the distribution of the handbills constituted coercive conduct against secondary employers. The court of appeals refused enforcement of the Board's order, holding the speech was protected under the First Amendment.

**ISSUE:** Is the distribution of handbills that puts secondary pressure on nonstruck employers protected speech?

**HOLDING AND DECISION:** (White, J.) Yes. The distribution of handbills that puts secondary pressure on nonstruck employers is protected speech and does not constitute an unfair labor practice. The information contained in the handbills was truthful and peaceful. It was closely targeted to the struck employer. Thus, it was protected speech and not an unfair labor practice. Affirmed.

▶ *ANALYSIS*

This opinion was written after the case had been remanded once. The NLRB had originally held that the speech was protected by the publicity proviso. The Supreme Court held that DeBartolo (P) did not constitute a distributor of any product produced by the struck employer, and thus the proviso did not apply.

■■■

## Quicknotes

**FIRST AMENDMENT** Prohibits Congress from enacting any law respecting an establishment of religion, prohibiting the free exercise of religion, abridging freedom of speech or the press, the right of peaceful assembly and the right to petition for a redress of grievances.

**NLRB (NATIONAL LABOR RELATIONS BOARD)** An agency established pursuant to the National Labor Relations Act for the purpose of prohibiting unfair labor practices by employers and unions.

**UNFAIR LABOR PRACTICE** Conduct by labor unions and employers, which is proscribed by the National Labor Relations Act.

■■■

# Carpenters Local No. 1506 (Eliason & Knuth of Arizona, Inc.)

## NLRB (P) v. Union (D)

355 N.L.R.B. 159 (2010).

**NATURE OF CASE:** Unfair labor practice action against a union.

**FACT SUMMARY:** [A union (D) displayed a banner to protest substandard wages. There was no chanting or yelling. The NLRB (P) brought an unfair labor practice action against the union (D).]

## 🏛 RULE OF LAW
A union practice of displaying large stationary banners in front of a secondary employer's business is not coercive, and thus does not violate the secondary boycott provisions of federal labor law.

**FACTS:** [Members of the Carpenters and Joiners of America (D) held 16-foot-long banners near two medical centers and a restaurant to protest work being performed by construction contractors that the union claimed paid substandard wages and benefits. The banners said, "SHAME ON [the name of the employer]!" in large letters, flanked on either side with the words "Labor Dispute" in smaller letters. As they were displaying the banners, union (D) representatives offered fliers that explained the nature of the labor dispute to interested members of the public. The fliers explained that the union's complaint was with the construction companies, but asserted that the employer was contributing to the undermining of area labor standards by using the services of those construction companies.]

**ISSUE:** Is a union practice of displaying large stationary banners in front of a secondary employer's business coercive, and thus in violation of the secondary boycott provisions of federal labor law?

**HOLDING AND DECISION:** (Liebman, Chairman) No. A union practice of displaying large stationary banners in front of a secondary employer's business is not coercive, and thus does not violate the secondary boycott provisions of federal labor law. The language of the NLRA and its legislative history do not suggest that Congress intended Section 8(b)(4)(ii)(B) to prohibit the peaceful stationary display of a banner. That section of the NLRA prohibits a union from threatening, coercing, or restraining a secondary employer not directly involved in a primary labor dispute. The Supreme Court in *Edward DeBartolo Corp. v. Florida Gulf Coast Building & Construction Trades Council*, 485 U.S. 568, 128 LRRM 2001 (1988), instructed the Board to avoid, if possible, construing the "threaten, coerce, or restrain" language in a way that would "raise serious questions under the First Amendment." In *DeBartolo*, the Supreme Court held that Congress did not

intend to bar all forms of union protest activity aimed at a secondary employer even when its objective is to persuade the secondary to stop doing business with the primary employer. The Court held that more than mere persuasion is necessary to find a violation, and ruled that distribution of handbills urging consumers not to patronize a secondary employer is not unlawful. Based on the Supreme Court decision, the issue is whether the display of the stationary banners on public sidewalks was "intimidation or persuasion." Conduct that makes picketing coercive is the combination of carrying picket signs and persistent walking of the picketers back and forth in front of an entrance to a worksite so that a physical or symbolic confrontation with workers entering the worksite exists. The banner displays did not constitute picketing because they did not create a confrontation.

**DISSENT:** (Schaumber, Member) The majority ruling creates a new standard that exempts other types of secondary activity from the NLRA's reach unless it causes or can be expected to cause some unknown quantum of disruption of the secondary's operation. The new standard will result in a dramatic increase in secondary boycott activity. The board has long held that the use of picket signs and patrolling are not prerequisites for finding a union's conduct is the equivalent of traditional picketing. The coercion element exists when a union posts its agents outside a business to advance the cause of the union. "Bannering" has the same coercive impact as traditional picketing. The size and placement of the banners, the stationing of union agents to hold them, and other direct similarities to picketing are all factors contributing to the confrontational impact of "bannering," sharply distinguishing that conduct from hand-billing's mere persuasion. In addition, the majority's decision is inconsistent with the text of the statute, its legislative history, decades of precedent, and sound and well-established policy.

## ▶ ANALYSIS

This is a significant decision. Under this ruling, unions that are careful not to picket may display large stationary banners—including inflatable rats, which have been used in some cases—in front of a neutral employer's business to alert the public that the neutral employer is doing business with a nonunion employer with whom the union has a dispute, all without violating the NLRA. It could easily encourage unions to engage in more secondary boycott

*Continued on next page.*

actions to pressure neutral employers to cease doing business with certain primary employers.

■═■

## Quicknotes

**BOYCOTT** A concerted effort to refrain from doing business with a particular person or entity, usually to achieve a particular result.

**NLRA (NATIONAL LABOR RELATIONS ACT)** Guarantees employees the right to engage in collective bargaining, and regulates labor unions.

**NLRB (NATIONAL LABOR RELATIONS BOARD)** An agency established pursuant to the National Labor Relations Act for the purpose of prohibiting unfair labor practices by employers and unions.

**UNFAIR LABOR PRACTICE** Conduct by labor unions and employers, which is proscribed by the National Labor Relations Act.

■═■

# Hudgens v. NLRB

Employer (D) v. Labor board (P)

424 U.S. 507 (1976).

**NATURE OF CASE:** Appeal from a finding of an unfair labor practice under NLRA § 7.

**FACT SUMMARY:** Hudgens (D) appealed from a decision holding that it was an unfair labor practice to threaten labor union members, who were engaged in peaceful primary picketing within the confines of a privately owned shopping center, with arrest for criminal trespass if they did not depart.

## 🏛 RULE OF LAW
The First Amendment poses no bar to a shopping center owner's prohibiting speech within his shopping center.

**FACTS:** Hudgens (D) owned a large enclosed shopping center and mall housing 60 retail stores and provided parking for 2,640 automobiles. Butler Shoe Company, which had a store in the shopping center, was being struck by its warehouse employees. The warehouse was not located in the center. The strikers picketed the warehouse and all of Butler's retail stores, including the one in Hudgens's (D) center. Hudgens's (D) shopping center manager told the picketers to leave or they would be arrested for trespassing. They departed. The union filed unfair labor practice charges under NLRA § 7 against Hudgens (D). The NLRB (P) entered a cease and desist order against Hudgens (D) on grounds of a First Amendment right to picket and violation of NLRA § 8(a)(1). The court of appeals remanded the case to the NLRB (P) in light of subsequent Supreme Court decisions. An administrative law judge then found the question to be governed by *NLRB v. Babcock & Wilcox Co.*, 351 U.S. 105 (1956), that union organizers who seek to solicit for union membership may intrude on an employer's private property if no alternative means exist for communicating with employees. The NLRB (P) accepted this but with the reasoning that the picketers were within the scope of Hudgens's (D) invitation to the public. The court of appeals upheld the NLRB (P) on the basis of *Republic Aviation Corp. v. NLRB*, 324 U.S. 793 (1945), where no-solicitation rules were acceptable only in case of special circumstances, which had not here been shown, and upon *Lloyd Corp. v. Tanner*, 407 U.S. 551 (1972), saying that the NLRB (P) had met the burden of showing that alternative picketing sites were earlier unavailable or ineffective. Hudgens (D) appealed using *Babcock & Wilcox* as his standard. The NLRB (P) argued that the balance between private property rights and employee marketing rights must be determined under the First Amendment using *Lloyd Corp. v. Tanner*.

**ISSUE:** Does the First Amendment pose any bar to a shopping center owner's prohibiting speech within his shopping center?

**HOLDING AND DECISION:** (Stewart, J.) No. The First Amendment poses no bar to a shopping center owner's prohibiting free speech within his shopping center. The free speech guarantee is put upon the government only, not private corporations or persons. In *Marsh v. Alabama*, 326 U.S. 501 (1946), a privately owned company town, indistinguishable from any public municipality by its facilities and services except for its private ownership, was held to the First Amendment guarantee of free speech. In *Amalgamated v. Logan Valley Plaza, Inc.*, 391 U.S. 308 (1968), it was held that Marsh required picketing to be allowed against a nonunion store in a privately owned shopping center as an expression of free speech, and that the shopping center was the functional equivalent of a business district. Later, in *Lloyd Corp.*, it was decided that protesters had no right to handbill in a shopping center. *Lloyd Corp.* thus overruled *Logan Valley*. In *Marsh*, the company town provided a full range of municipal services and functions, but here there was no such assumption of duties. Accordingly, the First Amendment played no part in this case, and the rights of the parties had to be determined exclusively under the Act. The resolution of conflicts between § 7 rights and private property rights may largely depend upon the content and context of the § 7 right being asserted. "Accommodation . . . must be obtained with as little destruction of one as is consistent with the maintenance of the other.'" Applying *Babcock & Wilcox*, the NLRB (P) should consider various factors such as the lawfulness of the economic strike activity, the fact that the activity was carried on by Butler employees, and that the property interests impinged upon were Hudgens's (D) and not the employer's, in reaching an accommodation. Vacated and remanded.

**DISSENT:** (Marshall, J.) The court of appeals should have been affirmed on statutory grounds. *Logan Valley* should not have been overruled. The traditional public channels of communication should remain free, regardless of the incidence of ownership. "The roadways, parking lots and walkways of the modern shopping center may be as essential for effective speech as the streets and sidewalks in the municipal or company-owned town." When a property owner opens his property to public use, the force of the

*Continued on next page.*

values of privacy and individual autonomy traditionally associated with private property ownership diminish.

## ▌ ANALYSIS

The confusing aspect of the way in which *Lloyd Corp.* was found to have overruled *Logan Valley* was that the court never said in the former case that the latter case was unsound. In fact, it appeared that *Logan Valley* was limited by *Lloyd Corp.* to the situation where union picketers "would have been deprived of all reasonable opportunity to convey their message to the patrons of the Weiss store had they been denied access to the shopping center." This case was heard by an eight-man court.

■═■

## Quicknotes

**FIRST AMENDMENT** Prohibits Congress from enacting any law respecting an establishment of religion, prohibiting the free exercise of religion, abridging freedom of speech or the press, the right of peaceful assembly and the right to petition for a redress of grievances.

**NLRA (NATIONAL LABOR RELATIONS ACT)** Guarantees employees the right to engage in collective bargaining, and regulates labor unions.

**NLRB (NATIONAL LABOR RELATIONS BOARD)** An agency established pursuant to the National Labor Relations Act for the purpose of prohibiting unfair labor practices by employers and unions.

**TRESPASS** Unlawful interference with, or damage to, the real or personal property of another.

**UNFAIR LABOR PRACTICE** Conduct by labor unions and employers, which is proscribed by the National Labor Relations Act.

■═■

# Hod Carriers Local 840 (Blinne Construction Co.)

## NLRB (P) v. Union (D)

135 NLRB 1153 (1962).

**NATURE OF CASE:** NLRB complaint against union for unlawful picketing.

**FACT SUMMARY:** An uncertified union (D) picketed to demand recognition by Blinne Construction Co. as the company's employees' bargaining agent for more than the statutory limit of 30 days without filing a petition for representation.

> 🏛 **RULE OF LAW**
> An uncertified union violates § 8(b)(7)(C) of the NLRA if it pickets as a means of demanding recognition for more than 30 days, and fails to file a representation petition before the expiration of the 30 days.

**FACTS:** All three laborers employed by Blinne Construction Co. signed cards designating the union (D) as their representative. The union (D) demanded that Blinne recognize the union (D) as their bargaining agent. Blinne refused, and told the union (D) it would transfer one of the laborers in order to destroy the union's majority. (Blinne's belief that transferring one employee would destroy the union's majority was erroneous, but the error is irrelevant.) Blinne transferred one employee five days later. The union (D) then began picketing, for three stated reasons: (1) recognition of the union; (2) payment of the Davis–Bacon pay scale; and (3) protest against Blinne for unfair labor practices in refusing to recognize the union and in threatening to transfer and transferring one employee. Peaceful picketing continued for more than a month. The three employees on the job—including the transferred employee's replacement—struck when the picketing started. The NLRB (P) charged that the union violated § 8(b)(7)(C) because (1) the union's picketing was for obtaining recognition, (2) the union was not currently certified as the representative of the employees involved, and (3) no petition for representation was filed within 30 days of the beginning of the picketing.

**ISSUE:** Does an uncertified union violate § 8(b)(7)(C) of the NLRA if it pickets as a means of demanding recognition for more than 30 days, and fails to file a representation petition before the expiration of the 30 days?

**HOLDING AND DECISION:** [Member not stated in casebook excerpt.] Yes. An uncertified union violates § 8(b)(7)(C) of the NLRA if it pickets as a means of demanding recognition for more than 30 days, and fails to file a representation petition before the expiration of the 30 days. Under the NLRA, not all picketing for recognition or organization is proscribed. A "currently certified" union may picket for recognition or organization of employees for whom it is certified.

But in this case the union was not certified. Unions not certified may picket for recognition or organization unless (1) another union has been lawfully recognized and a question concerning representation cannot appropriately be raised; (2) within the previous 12 months a "valid election" has been held; or (3) a representation petition was not filed prior to the expiration of a reasonable period of picketing not to exceed 30 days. In this case, the union was not certified, and picketed for more than 30 days without filing a representation petition. Had the union confined its picketing to the Davis–Bacon pay scale issue and the discriminatory transfer of an employee, § 8(b)(7)(C) would not have applied. Violation occurred and original Order is therefore reaffirmed.

## ▶ ANALYSIS

There are situations in which an uncertified union may picket for more than 30 days without filing a petition for representation. In *Smith v. NLRB (Crown Cafeteria Case)*, 327 F.2d 351 (9th Cir. 1964), the court held that an uncertified union may picket for more than 30 days without filing a representation petition if the picketing is for informational purposes, even if the picketing has an additional organizational or recognition objective, provided that the picketing is addressed mainly to the public, is truthful, and does not significantly interfere with deliveries or with services performed by other employers.

■■■

## Quicknotes

**AGENT** An individual who has the authority to act on behalf of another.

**NLRA (NATIONAL LABOR RELATIONS ACT)** Guarantees employees the right to engage in collective bargaining, and regulates labor unions.

**NLRB (NATIONAL LABOR RELATIONS BOARD)** An agency established pursuant to the National Labor Relations Act for the purpose of prohibiting unfair labor practices by employers and unions.

■■■

# NLRB v. Local 3, International Bhd. of Electrical Workers

## Labor board (P) v. Union (D)

317 F.2d 193 (2d Cir. 1963).

**NATURE OF CASE:** Action to enforce a NLRB order.

**FACT SUMMARY:** The NLRB (P) sought enforcement of its order holding that picketing engaged in by Local 3 (D) violated the National Labor Relations Act.

🏛 **RULE OF LAW**
Union picketing that is "for the purpose of truthfully advising the public" is not unlawful, but union picketing whose tactical purpose is to signal economic action backed by organized group discipline is.

**FACTS:** Picoult had been awarded a contract to renovate the Federal Post Office Building in Brooklyn. Local 3 (D) protested the award since Picoult chose to deal with another union, and it instituted picketing of the building, including side and rear delivery areas not frequented by the general public. There were two instances when the picket line turned away deliveries by employees of other companies. Local 3 (D) argued that the object of said picketing was to push for award of the subcontract to a company that recognized it as bargaining representative or, if that failed, to oust Picoult. The NLRB (P) issued an order finding the picketing violative of the NLRA and sought court enforcement.

**ISSUE:** Does a union violate the NLRA by engaging in picketing whose tactical purpose is to signal economic action backed by organized group discipline?

**HOLDING AND DECISION:** (Anderson, J.) Yes. The NLRA permits picketing that is "for the purpose of truthfully advising the public," but prohibits picketing whose object is forcing or requiring an employer to recognize or bargain. So-called "signal picketing" is generally prohibited except when an object thereof is not forcing or requiring an employer to recognize or bargain. "Publicity picketing" is generally permitted when it is "for the purpose of truthfully advising the public" and does not have the purpose of advising organized labor groups or their members as shown by signaling effects. The case is remanded for a determination as to whether or not the picketing was "for the purpose of truthfully advising the public" or for the impermissible tactical purpose of signaling economic action, backed by organized group discipline. Remanded.

▶ **ANALYSIS**

Picketing was not always recognized as legitimate. At the turn of the century, many states treated such organizational pressure as tortious and enjoinable. However, by the time the Wagner Act was passed, the tide had turned and the concern was with encouraging union organization and collective bargaining. It was not until 1947 that anti-picketing amendments were added.

■=∎

## Quicknotes

**COLLECTIVE BARGAINING** Negotiations between an employer and employee that are mediated by a specified third party.

**NLRA (NATIONAL LABOR RELATIONS ACT)** Guarantees employees the right to engage in collective bargaining, and regulates labor unions.

**NLRB (NATIONAL LABOR RELATIONS BOARD)** An agency established pursuant to the National Labor Relations Act for the purpose of prohibiting unfair labor practices by employers and unions.

■=∎

# NLRB v. Denver Bldg. & Const. Trades Council

Labor board (P) v. Union (D)

341 U.S. 675 (1951).

**NATURE OF CASE:** Action alleging an unfair labor practice under § 8(b)(4)(A) of the National Labor Relations Act.

**FACT SUMMARY:** The Denver Building & Construction Trades Council (Council) (D), which had a dispute with nonunionized subcontractor, picketed a construction site of the unionized general contractor in order to force the latter to release the subcontractor.

## RULE OF LAW
A union commits an unfair labor practice within the meaning of § 8(b)(4)(A) of the NLRA by engaging in a secondary strike, an object of which is to force the unionized general contractor on a construction project to terminate its contract with a nonunion subcontractor on that project.

**FACTS:** Section 8(b)(4)(A) of the NLRA provides that it is "an unfair labor practice for a labor organization . . . to engage in . . . a strike . . . where an object thereof is forcing or requiring . . . any employer or other person . . . to cease doing business with any other person." Doose & Lintner, the general contractor for the construction of a commercial building, awarded a subcontract for electrical work to Gould & Preisner. Doose & Lintner, and all the other subcontractors it engaged, were unionized; only Gould & Preisner was nonunion, and for a long period had been involved with a dispute with the Denver Building & Construction Trades Council (Council) (D). The Council (D) advised Doose & Lintner that if Gould & Preisner's men did work on the job, the Council (D) and its affiliates would picket the construction site. When Doose & Lintner refused to release Gould & Preisner, the Council (D) posted a picket at the project carrying a placard stating, "This Job Unfair to (the Council)." During the time this picketing was in effect, only Gould & Preisner's men reported to work. As a result, Doose & Lintner ordered Gould & Preisner off the job so it could continue with the project. Gould & Preisner thereupon filed charges with the NLRB (P). The Board (P) found that an object, if not the only object, of what transpired with respect to Doose & Lintner was to force or require them to cease doing business with Gould & Preisner. It rejected the Council's (D) argument that since Doose & Lintner supervised the work of Gould & Preisner, the employees of one were the employees of the latter. The Board (P) also rejected the Council's (D) contention that its picketing was protected by the free speech provisions of § 8(c) of the NLRA. On appeal from the Board's (P) finding that the Council (D) had violated § 8(b)(4)(A),

the court of appeals refused to enforce the Board's (P) order, holding that the picketing involved was primary and not secondary. The Board (P) appealed.

**ISSUE:** Does a union violate § 8(b)(4)(A) when it pickets a construction site, the object of which is to force a unionized general contractor to terminate its working relationship with a nonunion subcontractor?

**HOLDING AND DECISION:** (Burton, J.) Yes. A review of the legislative history of § 8(b)(4)(A) indicates that its sponsors intended to make it an unfair labor practice for a union to engage in a strike against employer A for the purpose of forcing that employer to cease doing business with employer B. The union here maintains that it engaged in a primary dispute with Doose & Lintner alone to force it to make the project an all-union job. This argument ignores, however, the contractual relationship between Doose & Lintner, and Gould & Preisner. The Council's (D) strike, in order to obtain its ultimate purpose, must have included among its objects that of forcing Doose & Lintner to terminate the subcontract with Gould & Preisner. The business relationship between independent contractors is too well established in the law to be overridden without clear language doing so. Here, Doose & Lintner and Gould & Preisner were "doing business" together; they did not share the status of employer and employee. Finally, § 8(c) is inapplicable here. That section does not apply to a mere signal by a labor organization to its members to engage in an unfair labor practice such as a strike proscribed by § 8(b)(4)(A). Reversed and remanded.

**DISSENT:** (Douglas, J.) The protest here was against the employment of union and nonunion men on the same job. The Council (D) was neither out to destroy Doose & Lintner, nor pursuing it to other jobs. The situation here is the same as if Doose & Lintner itself had put nonunion men on the job. The right to strike, guaranteed by § 13, should not be dependent on fortuitous business arrangements that have no significance so far as the evils of the secondary boycott are concerned.

## ANALYSIS

Contractor-subcontractor relationships, because of the presence of both types of employers at the same job site, pose special problems in § 8(b)(4) cases. However, courts have largely resorted to the same accommodating test as is employed in other common situs instances, namely, the right of the union to picket the primary employer at the

*Continued on next page.*

place of most effect balanced against the right of the neutral, secondary employer not to be drawn into the dispute.

■══■

## Quicknotes

**BOYCOTT**  A concerted effort to refrain from doing business with a particular person or entity.

**NLRA (NATIONAL LABOR RELATIONS ACT)**  Guarantees employees the right to engage in collective bargaining, and regulates labor unions.

**NLRB (NATIONAL LABOR RELATIONS BOARD)**  An agency established pursuant to the National Labor Relations Act for the purpose of prohibiting unfair labor practices by employers and unions.

**SUBCONTRACTOR**  A contractor who enters into an agreement with a principal contractor, or other subcontractor, to perform all or a part of a contract.

**UNFAIR LABOR PRACTICE**  Conduct by labor unions and employers, which is proscribed by the National Labor Relations Act.

■══■

# Sailors Union of the Pacific (Moore Dry Dock Co.)

## Third party (P) v. Union (D)

92 NLRB 547 (1950).

**NATURE OF CASE:** Ruling on NLRA § 8(b)(4) charges against a union.

**FACT SUMMARY:** A sailors' union picketed against the use of nonunionized sailors on a ship tied to a third-party's dock. Picketing took place in front of the third-party business. The third-party business sought to ban the picketing on its property.

**RULE OF LAW**

🏛 Where the situs of a labor dispute is not fixed, but ambulatory, and it comes to rest temporarily at the premises of another employer, the right to picket follows the situs while it is stationed at the premises of a secondary employer, when the only way to picket that situs is in front of the secondary employer's premises.

**FACTS:** A contract to transport gypsum was taken from an American ship with crew who were members of the Sailors Union of the Pacific (D), and given to a Panamanian ship called the S.S. Phopho, owned by the corporation Samsoc. The Phopho was tied at the Moore Dry Dock (P) for preparation to transport the gypsum. None of the crew hired for the voyage were members of the Sailors Union (D), and the wages paid were less than half union scale. The union demanded that Samsoc recognize it as the bargaining agent for the crew, but Samsoc refused. Picketers then arrived at the entrance to Moore Dry Dock (P), carrying signs against Phopho. The union asked permission to picket on Moore (P) property near the ship, but was denied. The union also sent letters to the unions representing Moore (P) employees requesting that no work be done on the Phopho. The picket signs and the letters emphasized that the dispute was with Samsoc and limited to the Phopho. Eventually, all work on the Phopho stopped. Moore (P) then filed § 8(b)(4) charges against the Sailors Union (D).

**ISSUE:** Where the situs of a labor dispute is not fixed, but ambulatory, and it comes to rest temporarily at the premises of another employer, does the right to picket follow the situs while it is stationed at the premises of a secondary employer, when the only way to picket that situs is in front of the secondary employer's premises?

**HOLDING AND DECISION:** [Member not stated in casebook excerpt.] Yes. Where the situs of a labor dispute is not fixed, but ambulatory, and it comes to rest temporarily at the premises of another employer, the right to picket follows the situs while it is stationed at the premises of a secondary employer, when the only way to picket that situs is in front of the secondary employer's premises. Picketing is primary if it is limited to times when the primary employer is engaged in normal business, is limited to places close by the primary employer's activity, and clearly discloses the union's dispute is with the primary employer. Failure to comply with one or more of the standards "creates a strong but rebuttable presumption that the picketing had an unlawful secondary object." Because the picketing here was primary and not secondary, there was not violation of Section 8(b)(4)(A) of the Act.

**ANALYSIS**

More recently, the NLRB ruled that a union violated the NLRA by picketing a gate reserved for neutral employers at a construction site. See *Local 7, Sheet Metal Workers' Int'l Ass'n*, 345 N.L.R.B. 119 (2005). The NLRB decided that the union's picketing the reserved neutral gate, even though the union had no reason to believe that the non-union employer or its employees had used the gate, violated *Moore Dry Dock* and gave rise to a presumption that the picketing had an unlawful secondary motive.

**Quicknotes**

**NLRA (NATIONAL LABOR RELATIONS ACT)** Guarantees employees the right to engage in collective bargaining, and regulates labor unions.

**NLRB (NATIONAL LABOR RELATIONS BOARD)** An agency established pursuant to the National Labor Relations Act for the purpose of prohibiting unfair labor practices by employers and unions.

**SITUS** Location.

# Douds v. Metropolitan Federation of Architects

## Labor board (P) v. Union members (D)

75 F. Supp. 672 (S.D.N.Y. 1948).

**NATURE OF CASE:** Petition to enjoin an alleged violation of NLRA § 8(b)(4)(A).

**FACT SUMMARY:** When Ebasco's architects (D) went on strike, Ebasco subcontracted its work to Project, a design firm. The architects (D) then protested the action.

🏛 **RULE OF LAW**
The term "doing business" does not include the situation where a struck employer subcontracts its work to another employer in order to keep the struck business going during the work stoppage.

**FACTS:** Employees of Ebasco, a design firm, went on strike when Ebasco and the Metropolitan Federation of Architects (MFA) (D), the union, could not agree on a contract. Ebasco then began subcontracting its work to Project, another design firm, whose work during the strike was 75% from Ebasco. The agreement between Ebasco and Project provided that Project be paid according to the salaries due its employees for hours spent on Ebasco work multiplied by a factor for overhead, and that all work be done on Ebasco forms so that Ebasco clients would appear to be receiving work from Ebasco employees. It also stated that Ebasco was not an employer as to Project's employees. The MFA (D) began picketing Project as a strikebreaking firm. Douds (P), the regional director of the NLRB, sought to enjoin the picketing of Project as a secondary boycott in violation of NLRA § 8(b)(4)(A) which provides: "It shall be an unfair labor practice for a labor organization . . . to . . . encourage the employees of any employer to engage in a strike . . . where the object thereof is . . . requiring . . . any . . . person . . . to cease doing business with any other person." Douds (P) argued Ebasco and Project were "doing business."

**ISSUE:** Does the term "doing business" include the situation where a struck employer subcontracts its work to another employer in order to keep the struck business going during the work stoppage?

**HOLDING AND DECISION:** (Rifkind, J.) No. The term "doing business" does not include the situation where a struck employer subcontracts its work to another employer in order to keep the struck business going during the work stoppage. As "doing business" was not defined in the Act, its meaning must be found by examining the legislative history to discover the mischief which Congress intended to remedy. Congress sought to outlaw secondary boycotts. Here, there was no secondary boycott since Project had a strong interest in the dispute between Ebasco and the MFA (D). Project's employees did work, which, but for

the strike by the MFA (D), would have been performed by Ebasco. "The economic effect upon Ebasco's employees was precisely that which would flow from Ebasco's hiring strikebreakers to work on its own premises." The MFA (D) encouraging Project's employees to strike was not different in kind from its encouraging Ebasco employees to strike. The MFA (D), by encouraging a strike at Project, did not extend itself to an area remote from the immediate dispute "but to one intimately and indeed inextricably united to it." Further, Ebasco's prescribing in its agreement with Project that it was not the employer of Project's people; (1) showed a realization of doubts to their respective capacities, and (2) need not be taken as conclusive, as the law can examine the reality relevant to the purposes of the particular statute. Injunction denied.

▶ **ANALYSIS**

While "doing business" is not defined by the NLRA, note that the case above does not provide a definition of the term either. Rather, the case provides an example of a situation which is not included in the meaning of "doing business." However, an inference arises from the decision that "doing business" covers an area of arms-length transactions which do not go to the heart of the labor dispute. Such transactions would probably include the providing of office equipment to a struck company or supplying utilities to such a company. Picketing of the provider in such cases would appear to be a proscribed secondary boycott.

■==■

## Quicknotes

**BOYCOTT** A concerted effort to refrain from doing business with a particular person or entity, usually to achieve a particular result.

**SUBCONTRACTOR** A contractor who enters into an agreement with a principal contractor, or other subcontractor, to perform all or a part of a contract.

■==■

# Local 761, International Union of Electrical, Radio and Mach. Workers v. NLRB

Union (D) v. Labor board (P)

366 U.S. 667 (1961).

**NATURE OF CASE:** Appeal from court of appeals enforcement of NLRB finding of a union unfair labor practice.

**FACT SUMMARY:** General Electric Corp. (GE), fearful of becoming embroiled in the labor controversies of its independent contractors, set aside a separate plant gate for their sole use; the Union (D), on strike against GE, picketed this gate.

---

### 🏛 RULE OF LAW
Picketing at gates specifically set aside for egress or ingress by secondary employers does not violate § 8(b)(4)(A) of the NLRA if either the employees of the secondary employer engage in work deemed essential to the customary operations of the primary employer, or if such work is partially related to the operations of the primary employer.

---

**FACTS:** Section 8(b)(4)(A) of the NLRA makes it an unfair labor practice for a labor organization: "to engage in, or to induce or encourage the employees of any employer to engage in, a strike or a concerted refusal in the course of their employment to use, manufacture, process, transport, or otherwise handle or work on any goods, articles, materials or commodities or to perform any services, where an object thereof is: forcing or requiring . . . any employer or other person . . . to cease doing business with any other person." A proviso to the section provides that "nothing contained in this clause (B) shall be construed to make unlawful, where not otherwise unlawful, any primary strike or primary picketing." General Electric Corp. (GE) operated a large manufacturing plant outside Louisville, Kentucky. A large drainage ditch made ingress or egress impossible except over five roadways across culverts, designated as gates. Because GE wished to insulate it from the frequent labor disputes of independent contractors, a separate gate was clearly designated for their sole use. GE employees were told to use other gates. The independent contractors performed a great variety of work for GE, including maintenance, construction work on buildings, installation and repair of ventilation and heating equipment, etc. During a strike with GE (D), the Union (D) established a picket line across the entrances to all the gates, including Gate 3-A. The picket signs announced, "Local 761 on strike/GE unfair." As a result of this picketing, almost all of the employees of independent contractors refused to enter the plant. The NLRB (P) held that the picketing violated § 8(b)(4)(A), finding that an object of the picketing was to encourage the independent contractor employees to engage in a concerted refusal to perform services for their employers in order to bring pressure on GE. The court of appeals granted enforcement of the Board's (P) cease and desist order, and the Union (D) appealed.

**ISSUE:** Does § 8(b)(4)(A) always prohibit picketing at gates set aside by the primary employer for the sole and separate use of independent contractors?

**HOLDING AND DECISION:** (Frankfurter, J.) No. Section 8(b)(4)(A) does not outlaw all so-called secondary boycotts. The section does not speak in general terms, but rather describes and condemns specific union conduct directed to specific objectives. Picketing which induces secondary employees to respect a picket line is not the equivalent of picketing, which has an object of inducing those employees to engage in concerted conduct against their employer in order to force him to refuse to deal with the struck employer. Admittedly, the line of distinction is a fine one to draw. A strike, by its nature, inconveniences those who customarily do business with the struck employer, and any accompanying picketing of the employer's premises is necessarily designed to induce and encourage third persons to cease doing business with the picketed employer. In a situation where two employers perform work on a common site, but use separate gates, the key to the problem is found in the type of work that is being performed by those who use the separate entrance. Picketing is unlawful when directed against the secondary employer where the independent workers were performing tasks completely unconnected to the normal operations of the struck employer, such as construction on his buildings. On the other hand, picketing is lawful where the secondary employer, although using a separate gate, is performing work which "aids" the primary employer. Such picketing is then protected by the proviso to § 8(b)(4). Thus, secondary employers who either perform essential work for a struck employer, or perform "mixed" work which more than unsubstantially benefits the struck employer, may not invoke § 8(b)(4)(A) to ban the picketing at the separate gate. Since the Board (D) failed to consider the nature of the independent contractor's work here, the cause is reversed and remanded.

---

### ▶ ANALYSIS

In *United Steelworkers v. NLRB*, 289 F.2d 591, 595 (2nd Cir. 1961), the court laid down the converse rule of the present

*Continued on next page.*

decision. Picketing at separate gates used by employees of secondary employers is prohibited "(if) a separate gate (is) marked and set apart from other gates; the work done by the men who use the gate (is) unrelated to the normal operations of the employer, and the work (is) of a kind that would not, if done when the plant were engaged in its regular operations, necessitate curtailing those operations."

■■■

## Quicknotes

**CEASE AND DESIST ORDER** An order from a court or administrative agency prohibiting a person or business from continuing a particular course of conduct.

**INDEPENDENT CONTRACTOR** A party undertaking a particular assignment for another who retains control over the manner in which it is executed.

**NLRA (NATIONAL LABOR RELATIONS ACT)** Guarantees employees the right to engage in collective bargaining, and regulates labor unions.

**NLRB (NATIONAL LABOR RELATIONS BOARD)** An agency established pursuant to the National Labor Relations Act for the purpose of prohibiting unfair labor practices by employers and unions.

**UNFAIR LABOR PRACTICE** Conduct by labor unions and employers, which is proscribed by the National Labor Relations Act.

■■■

# NLRB v. Fruit & Vegetable Packers & Warehousemen, Local 760 (Tree Fruits)

## Labor board (P) v. Union (D)

377 U.S. 58 (1964).

**NATURE OF CASE:** Appeal from an order setting aside an NLRB finding of an NLRA § 8(b)(4)(ii)(B) violation.

**FACT SUMMARY:** Local 760 (D), in a dispute with growers of Washington State apples, picketed several Safeway supermarket stores for the purpose of discouraging customers from buying Washington State apples.

### 🏛 RULE OF LAW
Secondary picketing of retail stores, limited to an appeal to the customers of said stores not to buy the products of certain firms against which the picketers are on strike, is not violative of NLRA § 8(b)(4)(ii)(B).

**FACTS:** After Local 760 (D) went on strike against the growers of Washington State apples, it began picketing Safeway supermarket stores for the purpose of discouraging Safeway customers from purchasing Washington State apples. The picketers made clear that they were not interfering with Safeway operations or discouraging its customers, employees, or deliveries from entering the stores and no such interference occurred. A complaint issued alleging that Local 760 (D) violated § 8(b)(4)(ii)(B) by conducting a secondary boycott. The court of appeals set aside an NLRB (P) order to that effect holding that Safeway could not have been "coerced" unless the picketing had a substantial economic impact on business satisfied by affirmative proof of such impact. The NLRB (P) appealed.

**ISSUE:** Is secondary picketing of retail stores, limited to an appeal to the customers of said stores not to buy the products of certain firms against which the picketers are on strike, violative of § 8(b)(4)(ii)(B)?

**HOLDING AND DECISION:** (Brennan, J.) No. Secondary picketing of retail stores, limited to an appeal to the customers of said stores not to buy the products of certain firms against which the picketers are on strike, is not violative of NLRA § 8(b)(4)(ii)(B). The Court has recognized Congress's purpose of consistently refusing to prohibit peaceful picketing except where used to achieve specific ends which experience has shown to be undesirable and will not ascribe to Congress this purpose unless "there is the clearest indication in the legislative history." Upon examination of that history, that purpose has not been shown. There appears to be no bar on a secondary boycott aimed at the primary employer's goods sold by the secondary employer when the public is not asked to withhold its patronage from the secondary employer. A complete boycott of the secondary employer would go beyond the goods of the primary employer and would clearly be illegal. Here, Safeway was not "threatened, restrained, or coerced." The fact that Safeway's sale of apples may have dropped was not grounds in itself for finding an illegal secondary boycott. Order of the court of appeals vacated, and remanded to set aside the NLRB's (P) order.

**CONCURRENCE:** (Black, J.) Congress intended to forbid striking employees of one business from picketing the premises of a neutral business where the purpose of the picketing is to persuade customers of the neutral business not to buy goods supplied by the Safeway employer. The Act, so construed, abridges freedom of speech in violation of the First Amendment. The law only bans picketing when the picketers have a particular view.

**DISSENT:** (Harlan, J.) While the Act is properly construed by J. Black, it does not violate the First Amendment. Here, the picketing, while directed toward one product, can only discourage people from entering the store either out of social or economic conviction or because they wish to avoid picket lines. Where the neutral retailer is primarily dependent upon one product, such as gasoline, to picket the brand of gasoline would be the equivalent of asking not to patronize the gas station. Moreover, the legislative history properly interpreted did not support the majority view. The First Amendment was not violated as other avenues of communication were left open.

### ▶ ANALYSIS

"When consumer picketing is employed only to persuade customers not to buy the struck product, the union's appeal is closely confined to the primary dispute. The site of the appeal is expanded to include the premises of the secondary employer, but if the appeal succeeds, the secondary employers' purchases from the struck firms are decreased only because the public has diminished its purchases of the struck product. On the other hand, when consumer picketing is employed to persuade customers not to trade at all with the secondary employer, the latter stops buying the struck product, not because of falling demand, but in response to pressure designed to inflict injury on his business generally. In such case, the union does more than merely follow the struck product it creates a separate dispute with the secondary employer."

■=■

*Continued on next page.*

# *Quicknotes*

**FIRST AMENDMENT**  Prohibits Congress from enacting any law respecting an establishment of religion, prohibiting the free exercise of religion, abridging freedom of speech or the press, the right of peaceful assembly and the right to petition for a redress of grievances.

**NLRA (NATIONAL LABOR RELATIONS ACT)**  Guarantees employees the right to engage in collective bargaining, and regulates labor unions.

**NLRB (NATIONAL LABOR RELATIONS BOARD)**  An agency established pursuant to the National Labor Relations Act for the purpose of prohibiting unfair labor practices by employers and unions.

# National Woodwork Mfr's Ass'n v. NLRB

## Union (P) v. Labor board (D)

386 U.S. 612 (1967).

**NATURE OF CASE:** Appeal from finding of NLRB determination of a § 8(b)(4)(B) violation.

**FACT SUMMARY:** The NLRB (D) determined that a contract provision by which a general contractor agreed not to use prefitted doors because it was traditional for the carpenters to fit the doors themselves at the jobsite was not a secondary boycott of prefitted doors, but the court of appeals reversed the NLRB's (D) finding.

## 🏛 RULE OF LAW
Where a boycott is used as a shield to preserve customary jobs, rather than as a sword to gather new jobs, it is not violative of the § 8(b)(4)(B) proscription against secondary boycotts.

**FACTS:** Frouge, a general contractor which had a collective bargaining agreement with the Carpenters' International Union, was bound by a provision that prohibited it from using prefitted doors in its construction projects. The project in question required 3,600 doors, and it was traditional for union carpenters to fit the doors at the jobsite. Frouge ordered 3,600 prefitted doors from a member of National Woodwork Mfr's Ass'n (National) (P), but when the carpenters refused to hang the doors, Frouge withdrew them and supplied unfitted doors. National (P) argued that the contract provision violated § 8(e) by being an agreement to cease or refrain from handling the products of any other employer and, by enforcing the agreement, violated § 8(b)(4)(B) which prohibits secondary boycotts. The NLRB (D) found no violations of the act; the court of appeals reversed, and the NLRB (D) appealed.

**ISSUE:** Where a boycott is used as a shield to preserve customary jobs, rather than as a sword to gather new jobs, is it violative of the § 8(b)(4)(B) proscription against secondary boycotts?

**HOLDING AND DECISION:** (Brennan, J.) No. Where a boycott is used as a shield to preserve customary jobs, rather than as a sword to gather new jobs, it is not violative of the § 8(b)(4)(B) proscription against secondary boycotts. That Congress meant §§ 8(e) and 8(b)(4)(B) to prohibit only "secondary" objectives appears clearly from the legislative history. "Although the language of § 8(e) is sweeping, it closely tracks that of § 8(b)(4)(A) and just as the latter and its successor § 8(b)(4)(B) did not reach employees' activity to pressure their employer to preserve for themselves work traditionally done by them, § 8(e) does not prohibit agreements made and maintained for that purpose." Moreover, in *Fibreboard Corp. v. NLRB*, 379 U.S. 203, (1964), work preservation clauses were implicitly recognized because bargaining on the subject

was found to be made mandatory by § 8(a)(5) as it concerns "terms and conditions of employment." Here, it appeared that the union was seeking to preserve customary jobs. Thus, it did not violate § 8(e). Similarly, the union did not violate § 8(b)(4)(B) because it refused to hang prefabricated doors whether or not they were union made or even if made by its own members. Accordingly, it appeared that the union sought solely to preserve jobs. Reversed.

**DISSENT:** (Stewart, J.) Section 8(b)(4) is not limited to boycotts that have as their only purpose the forcing of any person to cease using the products of another, it is sufficient if that result is "an object" of the boycott. Here, preventing Frouge from using the prefitted doors was an object of the union's conduct. Product boycotts for work preservation purposes have consistently been regarded by the courts, and by the Congress that passed the Taft-Hartley Act, as a proscribed secondary boycott.

## ▶ ANALYSIS

The student should note that a Board or court finding that subcontracting is a "term or condition of employment" does not necessarily require an employer to bargain first with a union to no avail before proceeding with a decision to subcontract. For example, if the contract contained a provision giving management the right to subcontract, the union would be most likely held to have waived its statutory right to require bargaining by the employee. Any disputes over the meaning of such a provision would have to be settled by an arbitrator.

■=■

## Quicknotes

**ARBITRATION** An agreement to have a dispute heard and decided by a neutral third party, rather than through legal proceedings.

**NLRA (NATIONAL LABOR RELATIONS ACT)** Guarantees employees the right to engage in collective bargaining, and regulates labor unions.

**NLRB (NATIONAL LABOR RELATIONS BOARD)** An agency established pursuant to the National Labor Relations Act for the purpose of prohibiting unfair labor practices by employers and unions.

**TAFT-HARTLEY ACT** An amendment to the National Labor Relations Act, imposing limitations on unions and safeguarding the rights of employers.

■=■

# Meat & Highway Drivers, Local Union No. 710 v. NLRB

## Union (D) v. Labor board (P)

335 F.2d 709 (D.C. Cir. 1964).

**NATURE OF CASE:** Appeal from an NLRB decision finding violations of NLRA §§ 8(e) and 8(b)(4)(A) and (B).

**FACT SUMMARY:** The drivers (D), whose members were employed by various Chicago area meatpackers, sought in their new contract to recover jobs lost when the meatpacking companies moved their operations outside of Chicago.

---

### 🏛 RULE OF LAW
If jobs are fairly claimable by a bargaining unit, they may be protected by provision for, and implementation of, no subcontracting or union standards clauses in the bargaining agreements without violating either § 8(e) or § 8(b)(4)(A) or (B).

---

**FACTS:** For about 20 years, Chicago Meat Packers had agreed with drivers (D) that meat deliveries by truck within the Chicago area would be made directly by the packers, using their own equipment driven by their own employees represented by Local 710 (D). Meat distribution practices changed drastically when the major packers moved their operations outside of Chicago. Drivers employed by the packers continued to make deliveries from the remaining plant facilities in Chicago to customers within a 50-mile radius, but deliveries to customers within the same area were increasingly being made by over-the-road drivers whose runs originated from the packers' facilities outside Chicago. During contract negotiations, drivers (D) sought to recover the large number of jobs lost by these changes. The new contract contained: (1) a work allocation clause which required all deliveries in Chicago, whether from within the city or from out-of-state, to be made by local employees covered by the agreement; (2) a union standards' subcontracting clause which required that when subcontracting was necessary, it must be given to a company whose pay and benefits matched or exceeded drivers' members' pay and benefits; and (3) a union signatory clause which required that subcontracting, when necessary, for deliveries within a 50-mile radius of Chicago be with companies employing members of Local 710, drivers (D). The NLRB (P) found these clauses to be violative of NLRA § 8(e), which in part makes it an unfair labor practice for any labor organization and any employer to enter into any contract or agreement whereby the employer shall not handle, sell, transport, or otherwise deal in any products of any other employer, and of § 8(b)(4)(A) and (B) by the economic action taken to obtain the clauses. Drivers (D) appealed.

**ISSUE:** If jobs are fairly claimable by a bargaining unit, may they be protected by provision for, and implementation of, no subcontracting or union standards clauses in the bargaining agreements without violating either § 8(e) or § 8(b)(4)(A) or (B)?

**HOLDING AND DECISION:** (Wright, J.) Yes. If jobs are fairly claimable by a bargaining unit, they may be protected by provision for, and implementation of, no subcontracting or union standards clauses in the bargaining agreements without violating either § 8(e) or § 8(b)(4)(A) or (B). As for the work allocation clause, delivery in the Chicago area, irrespective of the shipment's origin, was work fairly claimable by Local 710, drivers (D). The work was of a type which the members of the bargaining unit had the skills and experience to do. Further, the work was not being newly acquired, but was being recaptured after loss of jobs caused by the packers moving out of the city. As for a union standards clause, generally its purpose is to protect unit work by partially deterring the employer from subcontracting to employers who pay less than union scale, and while it is not necessary to assume that the employer would use such a tactic, it is sufficient that a union could fear it and seek to prevent it. While the NLRB (P) believed that the Local 710's (D) purpose for the clause was to aid unions generally rather than its own members, which is an invalid secondary purpose, such a finding on the part of the union alone is insufficient to find a § 8(e) violation. Section 8(e) requires a finding that both the union and employer agreed to a secondary object. As for the union signatory clause, while the work allocations features were valid, the provision requiring or encouraging a boycott of companies lacking union contracts violated § 8(e). By deleting the void portion, the agreement could be kept closely within the parties' intentions. Reversed in part.

---

### ▶ ANALYSIS

Note that activities and agreements which directly protect fairly claimable jobs are of primary, and hence, valid purpose under the act. If such activities and agreements have incidental secondary effects, they do not become invalid as a result thereof. The "cease doing business" language found in § 8(e) cannot be literally construed because all subcontracting clauses have inherent in them refusal to deal with at least some contractors. In regards to work standards clauses, the Board had traditionally taken the position distinguishing clauses which regulated "who" may receive subcontracting work as secondary, while only clauses which regulated "when" subcontracting could occur as primary. The courts have uniformly rejected that view.

---

*Continued on next page.*

## *Quicknotes*

**ARBITRATION**  An agreement to have a dispute heard and decided by a neutral third party, rather than through legal proceedings.

**CEASE AND DESIST ORDER**  An order from a court or administrative agency prohibiting a person or business from continuing a particular course of conduct.

**NLRA (NATIONAL LABOR RELATIONS ACT)**  Guarantees employees the right to engage in collective bargaining, and regulates labor unions.

**NLRB (NATIONAL LABOR RELATIONS BOARD)**  An agency established pursuant to the National Labor Relations Act for the purpose of prohibiting unfair labor practices by employers and unions.

# NLRB v. Radio and Television Broadcast Engineers Union, Local 1212

## Labor board (P) v. Union (D)

364 U.S. 573 (1961).

**NATURE OF CASE:** Appeal by NLRB from court of appeals' refusal to enforce its order involving an unfair labor practice on part of union.

**FACT SUMMARY:** When an employer assigned certain work to one group of employees represented by one union rather than to those represented by another, the competing union (D) called for a work stoppage; the NLRB (P), without deciding the merits of the dispute, issued a cease and desist order against the competing union (D).

### RULE OF LAW
Section 10(k) of the NLRA not only authorizes the NLRB to hear unfair labor practice charges arising from jurisdictional disputes, but also to determine the merits of such disputes.

**FACTS:** Section 8(b)(4)(D) of the NLRA makes it an unfair labor practice for a labor union to induce a strike or a concerted refusal to work in order to compel an employer to assign particular work to employees represented by it rather than to employees represented by another union, unless the employer's assignment is in violation of "an order or certification of the Board determining the bargaining representative for employees performing such work." Section 10(k) authorizes the Board to direct dismissal of unfair labor practice charges upon voluntary adjustment of jurisdictional disputes; where no voluntary adjustment is made, the Board is empowered and directed to "hear and determine the dispute out of which such unfair labor practice shall have arisen." Both the technicians' union (D) and the stage employees' union had collective bargaining agreements in force with the Columbia Broadcasting System (CBS). The two unions carried on a protracted dispute over the proper assignment of "remote lighting" work to one or the other group of employees. CBS consistently refused to make a specific allocation of this work, choosing instead to divide it between the two unions according to criteria improvised apparently for the sole purpose of maintaining peace between the two. When CBS assigned the lighting work for a major telecast to the stage employees, the technicians' union (D) called a work stoppage. CBS filed unfair labor practice charges with the NLRB (P), which found that the technicians' union (D) had violated § 8(b)(4)(D). The Board (P) simply held that the technicians' union was not entitled to have the work assigned to its members because it had no right to it under either an outstanding Board order or certification or a collective bargaining agreement. The Board (P) refused to

consider other criteria, or to settle the dispute. When the technicians' union refused to comply with this decision, the Board (P) issued a cease and desist order directed at the strike. The court of appeals refused to enforce this order, and the Board (P) appealed.

**ISSUE:** Does § 10(k) require the NLRB to decide jurisdictional disputes on their merits?

**HOLDING AND DECISION:** (Black, J.) Yes. Section 10(k) requires the Board to adjudicate the merits of jurisdictional disputes fully and to make a final determination as to which of two competing unions is entitled to do the disputed work. The Board may base its determination on factors deemed important in arbitration proceedings, such as the nature of the work, the practices and customs of this and other employers and of these and other unions, and upon other factors it deems relevant. A narrower determination which looks only at prior Board orders and certifications or a collective bargaining contract would leave the broader problem of work assignments in the hands of the employer. Thus, all that would be accomplished would be a restoration of the preexisting situation with the likelihood of jurisdictional strikes still imminent. The employer would be unable to enjoy the stability of either collective bargaining agreement, not because he refuses to satisfy the unions, but because the situation is such that he cannot satisfy them. As for the contention that Congress, in considering § 10(k), eliminated a provision authorizing the Board to appoint an arbitrator, decided against the compulsory determination of jurisdictional disputes, the contrary conclusion is more likely. Section 10(k) was clearly designed to get rid of what were deemed the bad consequences of jurisdictional disputes. Requiring the Board to hear and decide jurisdictional disputes will not seriously interfere with the right of an employer to make work assignments since the employer is the very party most apt to be injured by a failure of the Board to make a binding, and conclusive, determination that he is unable to make. Finally, leaving the resolution of these disputes to the Board, in light of the Board's experience, and knowledge of arbitration standards, will not impose an undue burden on it. Accordingly, the Board (P) in the present case should have decided which of the two competing unions here was entitled to the "remote lighting" work. Affirmed.

*Continued on next page.*

## ▶ *ANALYSIS*

Section 10(k) provides for a dismissal of the § 8(b)(4)(D) charge if, within 10 days after the charge is filed with the Board, the parties reach a voluntary settlement. Both unions, and the employer must concur in this settlement. Many industry wide arbitration panels have been established to hear jurisdictional disputes. However, where the employer is not obligated to accept the arbitration decision, a union is not bound to accept the private settlement reached.

■■■

## *Quicknotes*

**ARBITRATION**   An agreement to have a dispute heard and decided by a neutral third party, rather than through legal proceedings.

**CEASE AND DESIST ORDER**   An order from a court or administrative agency prohibiting a person or business from continuing a particular course of conduct.

**COLLECTIVE BARGAINING**   Negotiations between an employer and employee that are mediated by a specified third party.

**NLRA (NATIONAL LABOR RELATIONS ACT)**   Guarantees employees the right to engage in collective bargaining, and regulates labor unions.

**NLRB (NATIONAL LABOR RELATIONS BOARD)**   An agency established pursuant to the National Labor Relations Act for the purpose of prohibiting unfair labor practices by employers and unions.

■■■

# NLRB v. Gamble Enterprises, Inc.

Labor board (D) v. Movie theatre owner (P)

345 U.S. 117 (1953).

**NATURE OF CASE:** Appeal from reversal of an NLRB decision finding no NLRA § 8(b)(6) violation.

**FACT SUMMARY:** Gamble Enterprises, Inc. (P), owner of a movie theater that was a former vaudeville house, claimed that the musicians union violated § 8(b)(6) by refusing to agree to performances by traveling bands if local musicians were not given an equal opportunity to perform.

## 🏛 RULE OF LAW
Where a union in good faith makes a proposal that contemplates the performance of actual services rather than mere "stand-by" pay, it does not violate NLRA § 8(b)(6).

**FACTS:** Gamble Enterprises, Inc. (Gamble) (P), owner of a chain of theaters, employed small pit orchestras in each of its theaters during the days of vaudeville. In 1940, this practice was stopped. At the theater in question, the Palace, located in Akron, Ohio, Gamble (P) began showing pictures with occasional appearances by traveling bands. Between 1940 and 1947, the local musicians, no longer regularly employed, were paid a sum equal to the minimum union wages for engagements similar to those played by traveling bands when traveling bands played the Palace, even though the local musicians did not perform. In 1947, § 8(b)(6), amongst other Taft-Hartley Act provisions, became law. That section prohibited a union from causing or attempting to cause an employer to pay for the services which are not performed or not to be performed. Subsequently, the musicians union local attempted to negotiate a contract with Gamble (P) by which local musicians would perform when traveling musicians played the Palace or where local musicians could put on an equal number of performances to those given by traveling bands. Gamble (P) filed unfair practice charges with the NLRB (D) which found no § 8(b)(6) violation. The court of appeals reversed, and the NLRB (D) appealed.

**ISSUE:** Where a union in good faith makes a proposal that contemplates the performance of actual services rather than mere "stand-by" pay, does it violate NLRA § 8(b)(6)?

**HOLDING AND DECISION:** (Burton, J.) No. Where a union in good faith makes a proposal that contemplates the performance of actual services rather than mere "stand-by" pay, it does not violate § 8(b)(6), Since the implementation of that section, the union neither requested nor received anymore "stand-by" payments for which no services were rendered. The union offered various suggestions as to how the local musicians could earn their pay. When an employer receives a bona fide offer of competent performance of relevant services, it remains for the employer, through free and fair negotiation, to determine whether such offer shall be accepted and what compensation shall be made for the work done. Reversed and remanded.

**DISSENT:** (Jackson, J.) Before implementation of § 8(b)(6), the union was compelling the theater to pay for no work. When this was forbidden, it sought to accomplish the same result by compelling it to pay for useless and unwanted work. "Such subterfuge should not be condoned."

## ▶ ANALYSIS

Employee practices which create employment by "unnecessarily maintaining or increasing the number of employees used, or the amount of time required to perform a job is termed "featherbedding.'" Such practices are justified by employees for reasons of job security and minimum standards of health and safety. Most common law courts found such practices economically wasteful and without justification. The legislative history of Taft-Hartley clearly shows that unions may oppose introduction of labor saving machinery and can press for make-work devices, but they cannot seek payment in return for no exchange of services.

■■■

## *Quicknotes*

**NLRA (NATIONAL LABOR RELATIONS ACT)** Guarantees employees the right to engage in collective bargaining, and regulates labor unions.

**NLRB (NATIONAL LABOR RELATIONS BOARD)** An agency established pursuant to the National Labor Relations Act for the purpose of prohibiting unfair labor practices by employers and unions.

**TAFT-HARTLEY ACT** An amendment to the National Labor Relations Act, imposing limitations on unions and safeguarding the rights of employers.

■■■

# Administration of the Collective Agreement

## *Quick Reference Rules of Law*

# Textile Workers Union v. Lincoln Mills of Alabama

## Union (P) v. Employer (D)

353 U.S. 448 (1957).

**NATURE OF CASE:** Action in federal district courts, pursuant to § 301 of the Taft-Hartley Act, for enforcement of collective bargaining agreement to arbitrate.

**FACT SUMMARY:** The district court concluded that not only did it have jurisdiction over a suit by the Textile Workers Union (Union) (P) to enforce a collective bargaining agreement to arbitrate, but also ordered Lincoln Mills of Alabama (D) to arbitrate the dispute with the Union (P).

### 🏛 RULE OF LAW
Congress, by enacting § 301 of the Taft-Hartley Act, not only gave federal district courts jurisdiction in controversies involving labor organizations in industries affecting commerce, but also authorized federal courts to fashion a body of federal law for the enforcement of these collective bargaining agreements, including agreements to arbitrate.

**FACTS:** Section 301(a) of the Labor Management Relations (Taft-Hartley) Act of 1947 provides that a federal district court has jurisdiction over actions between an employer and a labor organization, or between two unions, representing employees in an industry which affects commerce, regardless of diversity of citizenship, or the amount in controversy. Section 301 (b) makes it possible, unlike at common law, for a union, representing employees in an industry affecting commerce, to sue and be sued as an entity in the federal courts. Lincoln Mills of Alabama (Lincoln Mills) (D) entered into a collective bargaining agreement with the Textile Workers Union (Union) (P), which prohibited strikes or work stoppage, and also provided for arbitration in the event of irreconcilable disputes. During one such contract dispute, the Union (P) requested arbitration and Lincoln Mills (D) refused. Thereupon, the Union (P) brought an action in a federal district court pursuant to § 301. The district court, after concluding that it had jurisdiction, ordered Lincoln Mills (D) to arbitrate. The circuit court reversed, holding that § 301 confers jurisdiction only on federal courts, and does not empower such courts to fashion remedies, including injunctive relief, from federal law. The Union (P) appealed.

**ISSUE:** Does § 301 authorize federal courts to create a body of substantive law to enforce promises to arbitrate grievances under collective bargaining agreements?

**HOLDING AND DECISION:** (Douglas, J.) Yes. A careful review of the legislative history of the Taft-Hartley Act indicates that §§ 301(a) and (b), when read together, placed sanctions behind agreements to arbitrate grievance disputes and, therefore, by implication rejected the common-law rule against enforcement of executory agreements to arbitrate.

Congress, interested in stabilizing industrial relations, sought, by means of the Taft-Hartley Act, to promote collective bargaining that ended with agreements not to strike. To this end, collective bargaining contracts were made equally binding and enforceable on both parties. Statutory recognition of the collective agreement as a valid, binding and enforceable contract is a logical and necessary step. An agreement to arbitrate grievance disputes is the quid pro quo for an agreement not to strike. Thus, § 301 does more than confer jurisdiction on federal courts over labor organizations. It also expresses a federal policy that federal courts should enforce these agreements on behalf of or against labor organizations. The substantive law to be applied in these suits is federal law which the courts must fashion from the policy of our national labor laws. State law may be resorted to in order to find the rule that will best effectuate federal policy. However, any state law applied will be absorbed as federal law and will not be an independent source of private rights. Congress has the power under the Commerce Clause to fashion federal law where federal rights are concerned. Finally, nothing in the Norris-LaGuardia Act, which prescribes stiff procedural requirements for issuing an injunction in a labor dispute, restricts § 301(a) to damage suits. The Norris-LaGuardia Act did not list the failure to arbitrate as an act, particularly subject to abuse of the power to enjoin, failing within its protective provisions. Reversed.

**CONCURRENCE:** (Burton, J.) The district court had jurisdiction over the action since it involved an obligation running to a union and not uniquely personal rights of employees sought to be enforced by a union. The court, therefore, had the power to fashion an appropriate federal remedy. However, this is not to say that, absent the necessary involvement of some federal rights, the substantive law to be applied in a § 301 suit is federal law.

### ▶ ANALYSIS

State statutes of limitations must be referred to by a federal court entertaining a § 301 suit. Section 301 reaches not only collective bargaining agreements, but all "contracts," including strike settlements, and agreements negotiated by minority unions. Although § 301 may not be used as a vehicle by a union seeking to enforce the "personal claims" of its members, some federal cases have permitted unions to secure wages for employees which are owed them under an automatic cost-of-living pay raise provision, and to protect the claims of employees to distribution of a labor-management pension fund.

**■══■**

*Continued on next page.*

## *Quicknotes*

**ARBITRATION** An agreement to have a dispute heard and decided by a neutral third party, rather than through legal proceedings.

**TAFT-HARTLEY ACT** An amendment to the National Labor Relations Act, imposing limitations on unions and safeguarding the rights of employers.

■≡■

# United Steelworkers of America v. American Mfg. Co.

## Union (P) v. Employer (D)

363 U.S. 564 (1960).

**NATURE OF CASE:** Appeal from denial of an order to compel arbitration of a grievance.

**FACT SUMMARY:** The United Steelworkers of America (P) sought to compel arbitration of a grievance under its contract with the employer, American Mfg. Co. (D), which did not take back an employee by virtue of his seniority after he was partially disabled and paid a settlement.

### 🏛 RULE OF LAW
Under a contract providing for compulsory arbitration, all grievances must go to arbitration no matter how frivolous or meritless they may appear to a court.

**FACTS:** United Steelworkers of America (Steelworkers) (P) and American Mfg. Co. (American) (D), the employer, had a contract that provided for compulsory arbitration. The Steelworkers (P) filed a grievance on behalf of an employee who was partially disabled as the result of an on-the-job injury. American (D) refused to take the employee back on the basis of his seniority because he had accepted a settlement on the basis of his permanent partial disability. The Steelworkers (P) sought an order in district court to compel arbitration of the dispute after American (D) refused to hear the grievance. The district court granted summary judgment to American (D) on the ground that the employee was estopped to claim any seniority rights after having accepted a settlement. The court of appeals affirmed but on the ground that the grievance was frivolous and "patently baseless." The Steelworkers (P) appealed.

**ISSUE:** Under a contract which provides for compulsory arbitration, must all grievances go to arbitration no matter how frivolous or meritless they may appear to a court?

**HOLDING AND DECISION:** (Douglas, J.) Yes. Under a contract providing for compulsory arbitration, all grievances must go to arbitration no matter how frivolous or meritless they may appear to a court. National labor policy, which encourages arbitration of labor disputes, can be effectuated only if the means chosen by the parties for settlement of their differences under a collective bargaining agreement is given full effect. Here, the collective agreement requires arbitration of even those claims that courts might be unwilling to entertain. The agreement was to submit all grievances to arbitration, not just those that were meritorious. Arbitration is a stabilizing influence only as it serves as a vehicle for handling every and all disputes that arise under the agreement. Whether the moving party is right or wrong is a question of contract interpretation for the arbitrator. Reversed.

## ▶ ANALYSIS

Justices Brennan, Harlan, and Frankfurter concurred with the majority decision. They argued that a different analysis process is required when an arbitration promise excludes a particular area from arbitration. They concluded that there should be a strong general presumption in favor of arbitrability in such cases.

■■■

## Quicknotes

**ARBITRATION** An agreement to have a dispute heard and decided by a neutral third party, rather than through legal proceedings.

■■■

# United Steelworkers of America v. Warrior & Gulf Navigation Co.

Union (P) v. Employer (D)

363 U.S. 574 (1960).

**NATURE OF CASE:** Action by union under § 301 of the Taft-Hartley Act to compel an employer to submit an alleged contract dispute to arbitration.

**FACT SUMMARY:** A collective bargaining agreement provided for arbitration of all contract disputes except those which are "strictly a function of management." When the employer (D) refused to submit to arbitration the Union's (P) grievance over its contracting out work, the Union (P) brought suit.

> ## 🏛 RULE OF LAW
> In the absence of any express provision excluding a particular grievance from arbitration, only the most forceful evidence of a purpose to exclude the claim from arbitration can prevail, particularly where the contract contains a "no strike" clause, the exclusion clause is vague, and the arbitration clause quite broad.

**FACTS:** Warrior & Gulf Navigation Co. (D) entered into a collective bargaining agreement with the Union (P), which had both a "no strike" and a "no lockout" provision. The contract provided for a grievance procedure, culminating in arbitration, to resolve disputes "as to the meaning and application of the provisions of this Agreement." A separate clause provided that "matters which are strictly a function of management shall not be subject to arbitration." Warrior & Gulf (D) laid off some employees as a result of its contracting out maintenance work, previously done by its employees to other companies. The latter used Warrior & Gulf's (D) supervisors to lay out the work and hired some of the laid-off employees of Warrior & Gulf (D) at reduced wages. The Union (P), claiming that Warrior & Gulf (D) was in violation of the contract by inducing a partial lockout, demanded that the matter be submitted to arbitration. When Warrior & Gulf (D), relying on the "strictly a function of management" clause refused, the Union (P) commenced a suit under § 301 of the Taft-Hartley Act to compel arbitration. From judgment for Warrior & Gulf (D), the Union (P) appealed.

**ISSUE:** Does an arbitration clause that covers disputes over the "meaning and application" of the agreement's provisions require arbitration of any dispute arising under the contract in the absence of an express provision withdrawing the dispute from arbitration?

**HOLDING AND DECISION:** (Douglas, J.) Yes. The present federal policy is to promote industrial stabilization through the collective bargaining agreement. A major factor in achieving industrial peace is the inclusion of a provision for arbitration of grievances in the collective bargaining agreement. A court must be mindful that not all the myriad and complex disputes which may arise in an industrial plant can be explicitly covered in a contract document of 15 or even 50 pages. There must be a "common law of the shop" which implements and furnishes the context of the agreement. Arbitration is the means of solving the unforeseeable by providing for the solution of disputes not expressly covered in a way which will generally accord with the variant needs and desires of the parties. Apart from matters that the parties specifically exclude, all of the questions on which the parties disagree must, therefore, come within the scope of the grievance and arbitration provisions of the collective agreement. The parties expect the arbitrator's judgment of a particular grievance will reflect not only what the contract says, but insofar as the agreement permits, such factors as the effect upon productivity of a particular result, its consequence to the morale of the shop, and his judgment whether tensions will be heightened or diminished. While Congress has, by § 301, assigned the courts the duty of determining whether the reluctant party has breached his promise to arbitrate, doubts should be resolved in favor of coverage. In the present case, the language "strictly a function of management" might be thought to refer to any practice of management in which, under particular circumstances prescribed by the agreement, it is permitted to indulge. However, this exception would swallow up the arbitration clause. Accordingly, the phrase must be interpreted as referring only to that over which the contract gives management complete control and unfettered discretion. Contracting out is usually a matter for arbitration, which should be ordered. Reversed.

**CONCURRENCE:** (Brennan, J.) A court should be free to examine into the merits of a dispute where the arbitration clause is very narrow, or the exclusion clause is quite specific, for the inference might then be permissible that the parties had manifested a greater interest in confining the arbitrator. Furthermore, an arbitration clause is not necessarily the quid pro quo of a no-strike clause.

**DISSENT:** (Whittaker, J.) Nothing in the contract indicated that Warrior and Gulf (D) signified its willingness to submit to arbitrators whether it must cease contracting out work. By their conduct over the years, the parties interpreted the contracting out of major work to be strictly a function of management. While the Steelworkers (P) for many years repeatedly tried to induce Warrior and Gulf (D) to agree to a covenant prohibiting the contracting out of work, it was never successful.

## ▶ ANALYSIS

In answer to Brennan's concurrence, the Supreme Court had earlier stated, in *United Steelworkers v. American Mfg.*

*Continued on next page.*

*Co.*, 363 U.S. 564 (1960): "The function of the court is very limited when the parties have agreed to submit all questions of contract interpretation to the arbitrator. It is confined to ascertain whether the party seeking arbitration is making a claim which on its face is governed by the contract. Whether the moving party is right or wrong is a question of contract interpretation for the arbitrator ... The courts, therefore, have no business weighing the merits of the grievance ... The processing of even frivolous claims may have therapeutic values of which those who are not a part of the plant environment may be quite unaware."

■══■

## Quicknotes

**ARBITRATION** An agreement to have a dispute heard and decided by a neutral third party, rather than through legal proceedings.

**TAFT-HARTLEY ACT** An amendment to the National Labor Relations Act, imposing limitations on unions and safeguarding the rights of employers.

■══■

# Litton Financial Printing Div. v. NLRB

## Employer (D) v. Agency (P)

501 U.S. 190 (1991).

**NATURE OF CASE:** Appeal from order of employer duty to bargain and arbitrate in an unfair labor practice action.

**FACT SUMMARY:** When Litton Financial Printing Div. (Litton) (D) refused to submit to the union grievance and arbitration procedure concerning employee layoffs on the ground that it was not a right arising under the then-expired union contract, the NLRB (P) ruled that Litton (D), although having committed an unfair labor practice, only had a duty to bargain about the layoffs in new contract negotiations.

## RULE OF LAW
A postexpiration grievance arises under the contract only where (1) it involves facts and occurrences that arose before expiration, (2) an action taken after expiration infringes a right that accrued or vested under the agreement, or (3) under normal principles of contract interpretation, the disputed contractual right survives expiration of the remainder of the agreement.

**FACTS:** Litton Financial Printing Div. (Litton) (D) and the Printing Specialties & Paper Products Union No. 777 had a collective bargaining agreement that expired on October 3, 1979. Section 19 contained a broad arbitration provision, and § 21 then set forth a two-step grievance procedure, at the conclusion of which, if a grievance could not be resolved, the matter could be submitted for binding arbitration. Shortly before this agreement was to expire, one employee sought an election to decertify the union. Although the union won the election (by one vote), it was not (re)certified by the Board (P) until nearly a year later due to postelection legal maneuvering, and no negotiations on a new agreement took place during this time. To test the certification order, Litton (D) refused to bargain with the union, and in a separate case was found by the Board (P) to have committed an unfair labor practice. Meanwhile, Litton (D) decided to eliminate a portion of its operation and by early September 1980 had laid off 10 employees who worked either primarily or exclusively in the eliminated division. Six of those laid off were among the 11 most senior employees in the plant. Litton (D) refused to submit to the grievance and arbitration procedure and instead offered to negotiate over the layoffs. The NLRB (P) found that Litton (D) committed an unfair labor practice under NLRA §§ 8(a)(1) and (5), by refusing to bargain, by unilaterally repudiating the grievance procedure, and by repudiating any duty to arbitrate after contract expiration. The NLRB (P) ordered Litton (D) to bargain but did not order it to arbitrate, concluding that the grievances did not "arise under" the expired contract. The court of

appeals upheld the NLRB's (P) order regarding Litton's (D) duty to bargain about the layoffs but ordered Litton (D) also to arbitrate, holding that because under the old contract layoffs were to be determined on length of continuous service if other things such as aptitude and ability were equal, the layoffs did arise under the contract. The Supreme Court accepted review limited to the question of layoff arbitrability.

**ISSUE:** Does a postexpiration grievance arise under the contract only where (1) it involves facts and occurrences that arose before expiration, (2) an action taken after expiration infringes a right that accrued or vested under the agreement, or (3) under normal principles of contract interpretation, the disputed contractual right survives expiration of the remainder of the agreement?

**HOLDING AND DECISION:** (Kennedy, J.) Yes. A postexpiration grievance arises under the contract only where (1) it involves facts and occurrences that arose before expiration, (2) an action taken after expiration infringes a right that accrued or vested under the agreement, or (3) under normal principles of contract interpretation, the disputed contractual right survives expiration of the remainder of the agreement. *Nolde Bros. v. Bakery Workers*, 430 U.S. 243 (1977), established a presumption that the duty to arbitrate disputes arising under an agreement outlasts the date of expiration. The unlimited arbitration clause in the agreement in the instant case places it within the precise rationale of Nolde Bros. However, the layoffs in the present case took place almost one year after the agreement had expired and could be arbitrable only if they involved rights that accrued or vested under the agreement, or rights that carried over after expiration of the agreement. The order of layoffs was to be determined primarily with reference to "other factors such as aptitude and ability." Only where all such factors were equal was the employer required to look to seniority. The important point is that factors such as aptitude and ability do not remain constant but change over time. Thus, they cannot be said to vest or accrue or be understood as a form of deferred compensation. Therefore, the layoff provision here cannot be said to have created a right that vested or accrued during the term of the agreement or a contractual obligation that carried over after expiration. Reversed (to the extent the court of appeals failed to enforce the order in its entirety) and remanded.

**DISSENT:** (Marshall, J.) The majority mischaracterized the decision of Nolde Bros., which states a broad, rebuttable presumption in favor of arbitration applying to all posttermination disputes arising under an expired agreement. Had the majority left this issue to the arbitrator to decide, as

*Continued on next page.*

Nolde requires, the arbitrator would have had the benefit of an evidentiary hearing on the contractual question and the opportunity to explore Litton's (D) postexpiration seniority practices.

**DISSENT:** (Stevens, J.) The Court erred in reaching the merits of the issue as to whether the posttermination grievances in this case "arose under" the expired agreement rather than submitting it to an arbitrator pursuant to the broad agreement of the parties to submit to arbitration any dispute regarding contract construction.

## ▶ *ANALYSIS*

The Court explained that NLRA §§ 8(a)(5) and 8(d) require an employer to bargain "in good faith with respect to wages, hours, and other terms and conditions of employment." The Court granted review due to substantial disagreement as to the proper application of its decision in *Nolde Bros.*, 430 U.S. 243 (1977), explaining that the dispute in that case over the employer's refusal to pay severance wages called for in its agreement with the union, while arising after the expiration of the collective-bargaining contract, clearly arose under that contract. In further elaboration, the Court acknowledged that "the arbitration duty is a creature of the collective-bargaining agreement" and that the matter of arbitrability must be determined by reference to the agreement, rather than by compulsion of law.

■══■

## *Quicknotes*

**ARBITRATION** An agreement to have a dispute heard and decided by a neutral third party, rather than through legal proceedings.

**COLLECTIVE BARGAINING** Negotiations between an employer and employee that are mediated by a specified third party.

**NLRA (NATIONAL LABOR RELATIONS ACT)** Guarantees employees the right to engage in collective bargaining, and regulates labor unions.

**NLRB (NATIONAL LABOR RELATIONS BOARD)** An agency established pursuant to the National Labor Relations Act for the purpose of prohibiting unfair labor practices by employers and unions.

■══■

# United Steelworkers of America v. Enterprise Wheel & Car Corp.

## Union (P) v. Employer (D)

### 363 U.S. 593 (1960).

**NATURE OF CASE:** Action by the union to enforce arbitrator's award.

**FACT SUMMARY:** The court of appeals reversed the district court's enforcement of an arbitrator's award because arbitrator failed to indicate how he arrived at the conclusion that the collective bargaining agreement's expiration did not bar certain remedies.

## 🏛 RULE OF LAW
A mere ambiguity in the opinion accompanying an arbitration award, which permits the inference that the arbitrator may have exceeded his authority, is not a reason for a court to refuse to enforce the award.

**FACTS:** A collective bargaining agreement between the Union (P) and Enterprise Wheel & Car Corp. (Enterprise) (D) provided that all differences "as to the meaning and application" of the agreement should be submitted to arbitration which "shall be final and binding on the parties." In the event the arbitrator determined that an employee had been unjustly discharged or suspended, "the company shall reinstate the employee and pay full compensation at the employee's regular rate of pay for the time lost." Finally, the agreement also provided: "It is understood and agreed that neither party will institute civil suits or legal proceedings against the other for alleged violations of any of the provisions of this labor contract." Enterprise (D) discharged a group of employees who had left their jobs in protest against the discharge of one employee. The Union (P) filed a grievance, and when Enterprise (D) refused to arbitrate, the district court ordered arbitration. Before arbitration could begin, the collective bargaining agreement expired, although the Union (P) continued to represent the workers. The arbitrator, summarily rejecting the contention that the agreement's expiration barred reinstatement of the employees, found that the employee's discharge, in spite of their improper conduct, was unjustified, ordered reinstatement with backpay, minus pay for a justified 10-day suspension and such sums as these employees received from other employment. When Enterprise (D) refused to comply with the award, the district court ordered enforcement. The court of appeals, although holding that the district court had jurisdiction to enforce the award, found that the failure of the award to specify the amounts to be deducted from the back pay rendered the award unenforceable. This defect, it agreed, could be remedied by further arbitration. However, the court also held that the expiration of the agreement rendered all subsequent awards or arbitration orders unenforceable. The Union (P) appealed.

**ISSUE:** May a court refuse to enforce an arbitration award merely because it disagrees with the arbitrator's construction of the collective bargaining agreement?

**HOLDING AND DECISION:** (Douglas, J.) No. On the one hand, since an arbitrator is confined to interpretation and application of the collective bargaining agreement, a court may refuse to enforce an award when the arbitrator's opinion manifests an infidelity to this obligation. On the other hand, a mere ambiguity in the opinion accompanying an award, which permits the inference that the arbitrator may have exceeded his authority, is not a reason for refusing to enforce an award. Arbitrators are under no obligation to explain their reasoning to a court. To hold otherwise would encourage arbitrators to play it safe by writing no supporting opinions. This would be undesirable since a well-reasoned opinion tends to engender confidence and aids in clarifying the underlying agreement. Here, the arbitrator's opinion is ambiguous because it is unclear whether the arbitrator looked to enacted legislation (in which case he exceeded his authority) or the agreement itself in concluding that the agreement's expiration did not bar reinstatement and back pay. Nonetheless, since it is not manifestly apparent that he went beyond his submission, courts should refrain from reviewing the merits of his award. Otherwise, the essential element of finality in the arbitration process would be eroded. The parties here had bargained for the arbitrator's construction, and must abide by it. Accordingly, only that portion of the court of appeals decision which called for further arbitration is affirmed. In all other respects, it is reversed.

## ▶ ANALYSIS

Most collective bargaining agreements provide that before arbitration can be reached, a party must follow a stipulated grievance procedure. This usually entails a step-by-step submission of a complaint from lower echelon management personnel, i.e., foremen and on-line supervisors, on up the corporate ladder. However, once this process has been exhausted without the aggrieved party obtaining satisfaction, arbitration is compulsory upon request. Agreements vary as to whether a permanent arbitrator is to be designated, or a new one picked for each dispute. A common arbitration panel consists of one arbitrator chosen by management, one by labor, and the third mutually selected by the parties. Arbitrators may also be available in pools maintained by certain federal and private agencies.

■=■

## Quicknotes

**ARBITRATION** An agreement to have a dispute heard and decided by a neutral third party, rather than through legal proceedings.

■=■

# Eastern Associated Coal Corp. v. United Mine Workers, District 17

## Employer (P) v. Labor union (D)

531 U.S. 57 (2000).

**NATURE OF CASE:** Review of affirmation of order to enforce arbitration award for employee reinstatement.

**FACT SUMMARY:** Eastern Associated Coal Corp. (Eastern) (P) claimed that an arbitration award was unenforceable because it contravened public policy.

## 🏛 RULE OF LAW
A labor-management agreement that does not violate any law or regulation may be enforced by a court.

**FACTS:** Eastern Associated Coal Corp. (Eastern) (P) and the United Mine Workers, District 17 (UMW) (D) had an arbitration clause in their collective bargaining contract specifying that Eastern (P) had to prove "just cause" before discharging an employee. A truck driver who had twice tested positive for marijuana was ordered to be conditionally reinstated by the arbitrator, after providing evidence he had been a loyal employee for seventeen years. Eastern (P) claimed the reinstatement was against public policy forbidding operation of dangerous machinery by workers who had tested positive for drugs, and sought to have the order vacated. The district court held that the conditional reinstatement did not violate that policy and ordered that the arbitrator's award be enforced. The appeals court affirmed. The Supreme Court granted certiorari to settle a split in the circuits on this issue.

**ISSUE:** May a labor-management agreement that does not violate any law or regulation be enforced by a court?

**HOLDING AND DECISION:** (Breyer, J.) Yes. A labor-management agreement that does not violate any law or regulation may be enforced by a court. The arbitrator's award was consistent with the Department of Transportation's rules requiring rehabilitation before full reinstatement. The award did not violate any provision of any law or regulation. Affirmed.

**CONCURRENCE:** (Scalia, J.) An arbitration award that violated public policy would also conflict with positive law.

## ▶ ANALYSIS

The dissent disagreed with the majority's statement that the public policy exception could be invoked in circumstances that did not involve a conflict with positive law. Such a public policy must be explicit, well-defined, dominant, and ascertained by reference to the laws and legal precedents. The dissent argued that such a public policy, identified in that manner, would necessarily also conflict with positive law.

## Quicknotes

**ARBITRATION** An agreement to have a dispute heard and decided by a neutral third party, rather than through legal proceedings.

**COLLECTIVE BARGAINING** Negotiations between an employer and employee that are mediated by a specified third party.

**PUBLIC POLICY** Policy administered by the state with respect to the health, safety and morals of its people in accordance with common notions of fairness and decency.

# Boys Markets, Inc. v. Retail Clerks Union, Local 770

### Employer (P) v. Union (D)

### 398 U.S. 235 (1970).

**NATURE OF CASE:** Action by employer in state and federal courts for an injunction to enjoin union strike.

**FACT SUMMARY:** Although a collective bargaining agreement contained a "no-strike clause," and provided for compulsory arbitration of all contract disputes, the Union (D) went on strike without submitting its dispute to arbitration; the district court enjoined the strike's continuance.

## 🏛 RULE OF LAW
The anti-injunction provisions of the Norris-LaGuardia Act do not preclude a federal district court from enjoining a strike in breach of a no-strike obligation under a collective bargaining agreement which calls for binding and final arbitration of all contract disputes.

**FACTS:** The Union (D) and Boys Markets, Inc. (P) entered a collective bargaining agreement which provided that all disputes as to the contract's interpretation or application shall be settled by arbitration. The agreement also contained an express "no-strike" clause. When the Union (D) called for a strike over a work assignment dispute and refused to submit the matter to arbitration, Boys Markets (P) sought injunctive relief in a California state court. The state court issued a temporary restraining order and a show cause order, whereupon, the Union (D) removed the case to a federal district court. The district court refused to grant the Union's (D) motion to suppress the state court's temporary restraining order, and instead issued its own injunction and order for arbitration. The Union (D) appealed, arguing that the district court's ruling was contrary to *Sinclair Refining v. Atkinson*, 370 U.S. 195 (1962). In that case, the Supreme Court held that, because § 4 of the Norris-LaGuardia Act restrains federal courts from issuing injunctions in labor disputes, a federal court has the authority to award only damages when a union violates a "no-strike" clause notwithstanding that the collective bargaining agreement calls for compulsory arbitration of all contract disputes.

**ISSUE:** Should *Sinclair* be overruled?

**HOLDING AND DECISION:** (Brennan, J.) Yes. In light of decisions rendered subsequent to *Sinclair*, it has become clear that the *Sinclair* decision does not further, but rather frustrates, realization of an important goal of our national labor policy. In *Avco Corp. v. Aero Lodge No. 735*, 390 U.S. 557 (1968), the Court held that § 301(a) suits initially brought in state courts may be removed to the designated federal forum under the federal question removal jurisdiction provision. The Court, however, expressly left open the question of whether state courts are bound by the anti-injunctive proscriptions of the Norris-LaGuardia Act.

Thus, *Avco* and *Sinclair* together have the effect of promoting forum-shopping and maneuvering from one court to another with respect to an important remedial device—the injunction. This subverts the purpose of the removal device; it certainly was never intended to foreclose completely in federal courts remedies otherwise available in the state courts. Moreover, the effectiveness of arbitration agreements would be greatly reduced if injunctive relief were withheld. In such decisions as *Textile Workers Union v. Lincoln Mills of Alabama*, 353 U.S. 448 (1957), the Steelworkers Trilogy, and *Teamsters Local 174 v. Lucas Flour Co.*, 369 U.S. 95 (1962), the Court has noted the importance that Congress has attached generally to arbitration. The Norris-LaGuardia Act, enacted in 1932, was designed to protect the nascent labor movement. Since then, as § 301 indicates, congressional emphasis has shifted to the encouragement of collective bargaining and to administrative techniques for the peaceful resolution of industrial disputes. Since the danger of federal court intervention has been largely attenuated, *Sinclair* is overruled. Reversed and remanded.

**CONCURRENCE:** (Stewart, J.) *Sinclair* was improperly decided. "Wisdom too often never comes, and so one ought not to reject it merely because it comes late." (Justic Frankfurter dissenting in *Henslee v. Union Planters Bank*, 335 U.S. 595 (1949).

**DISSENT:** (Black, J.) Section 301(a) says nothing at all about granting injunctions. Nothing in its legislative history indicates that Congress meant to impair in any way Norris-LaGuardia's explicit prohibition against injunctions in labor disputes. Any changing of laws, especially in this sensitive area involving antagonistic political and economic interests, is for Congress, and not this court, to make.

**DISSENT:** (White, J.) The reasons supporting *Sinclair* must prevail.

## ▶ ANALYSIS

As the Court itself notes in *Boys Market*, an employer who seeks an injunction against concerted union activity must himself agree to accept arbitration. Furthermore, no injunction will issue unless an employer proves the following: (1) the existence of a mandatory clause in the collective bargaining agreement calling for arbitration, or some other suitable means for settling grievances; and (2) the likelihood of harm to the employer were no injunction to issue, balanced against the hardship an injunction will impose on the union. Thus, in the absence of a mandatory grievance procedure, a

*Continued on next page.*

federal court would be powerless to enjoin a union from violating a "no-strike" provision.

∎══∎

## Quicknotes

**FEDERAL QUESTION**  The authority of the federal courts to hear and determine in the first instance matters pertaining to the federal Constitution, federal law, or treaties of the United States.

**INJUNCTION**  A court order requiring a person to do or prohibiting that person from doing a specific act.

**REMOVAL**  Petition by a defendant to move the case to another court.

∎══∎

# Olin Corp.

## Union (P) v. Employer (D)

268 NLRB 573 (1984).

**NATURE OF CASE:** NLRB review of administrative law judge's refusal to defer to arbitrator's decision against union.

**FACT SUMMARY:** Despite a collective bargaining agreement no-strike clause, the Union (P) staged a "sick-out." The president of the Union (P) participated, and was subsequently discharged by Olin Corp. (D) for violating the agreement. The administrative law judge refused to defer to an arbitrator's decision against the Union (P).

---

**RULE OF LAW**

An arbitrator has adequately considered an unfair labor practice if (1) the contractual issue is factually parallel to the unfair labor practice issue, and (2) the arbitrator was presented generally with the facts relevant to resolving the unfair labor practice.

---

**FACTS:** The collective bargaining agreement between Olin Corp. (D) and the Union (P) contained a no-strike/no-lockout provision. Nevertheless, after Olin (D) suspended two pipe-fitters who refused to do work they considered to be more appropriate to millwrights, 43 employees staged a "sick out." Employee Salvatore B. Spatorico, president of the Union (P) at the time, was fired for threatening, participating in, and failing to prevent the sick out. The arbitrator was presented with the contractual issue as well as an unfair labor practice issue, which both arose from the same set of facts—Spatorico's discharge for his part in the sickout. After a hearing on Spatorico's grievance, the arbitrator found that Spatorico's conduct breached his obligations under the no-strike clause of the collective bargaining agreement, finding also that Union (P) officers implicitly have an affirmative duty not to cause strikes that are in violation of such clauses, and to try to stop them when they occur. The arbitrator also found no evidence that the employer discharged Spatorico for legitimate union activities, and that the Olin (D), therefore, did not commit an unfair labor practice. An administrative law judge declined to defer to the arbitrator's award, finding that the arbitrator did not seriously consider the unfair labor practice issue, but nevertheless agreed with the arbitrator on the merits.

**ISSUE:** Has an arbitrator adequately considered an unfair labor practice if (1) the contractual issue is factually parallel to the unfair labor practice issue, and (2) the arbitrator was presented generally with the facts relevant to resolving the unfair labor practice?

**HOLDING AND DECISION:** [Member not stated in casebook excerpt.] Yes. An arbitrator has adequately considered an unfair labor practice if (1) the contractual issue is factually parallel to the unfair labor practice issue,

and (2) the arbitrator was presented generally with the facts relevant to resolving the unfair labor practice. The contractual and statutory issues were factually parallel. The factual questions the arbitrator considered were whether there was a sickout and whether Spatorico caused, participated in, or failed to try to stop the sick out, which was his obligation under the agreement. These questions are the same as those that the NLRB would consider in a decision on the statutory question of whether the agreement clearly and unmistakably proscribed Spatorico's conduct. Second, the arbitrator was presented with the facts relevant to resolving the unfair labor practice. The General Counsel did not show that the arbitrator was lacking any evidence relevant to the determination of the nature of the obligations imposed by the no-strike clause, and to the determination of the causal connection between that clause and Spatorico's conduct. The evidence before the arbitrator was essentially the same evidence necessary for determination of the merits of the unfair labor practice charge. Finally, the arbitrator's award is not clearly repugnant to the purposes and policies of the NLRA. A union can waive the rights of its officials, and in this case, the arbitrator construed the agreement as a waiver of the union officers' right to strike. Arbitration award sustained.

**DISSENT IN PART:** (Zimmerman, Member) Deferral to the arbitrator's award was appropriate in this case, but revising the law was not necessary to effect deferral. The new standard of deference adopted by the NLRB expands the deferral policy beyond permissible statutory bounds, because it causes the NLRB to abstain from enforcing federal labor policy. In addition, judicial precedent holds that the NLRB has no authority to defer if it does not have some affirmative proof that an unfair labor practice issue was presented to and considered by an arbitrator. Third, the party seeking to have the NLRB reject deferral is now required to show that the new standard has not been met, which is unfair. No change in the law was necessary to justify NLRB deferral to the arbitration award here.

---

**ANALYSIS**

The *Olin* guidelines continue to be applied by the NLRB and at least one circuit [*Utility Workers Local 246 v. NLRB*, 39 F.3d 1210 (D.C. Cir. 1994)], but other circuits have modified or rejected the guidelines, and some courts have required proof that the arbitrator expressly considered the unfair labor practice issue. See, e.g., *Ciba-Geigy Pharmaceuticals*

*Continued on next page.*

*v. NLRB*, 722 F.2d 1120 (3d Cir. 1983); *Taylor v. NLRB*, 786 F.2d 1516 (11th Cir.), *cert. denied*, 493 U.S. 891 (1986).

■══■

## Quicknotes

**ADMINISTRATIVE LAW JUDGE**  A judge who presides over administrative hearings.

**AFFIRMATIVE DUTY**  An obligation to undertake an affirmative action for the benefit of another.

**NLRA (NATIONAL LABOR RELATIONS ACT)**  Guarantees employees the right to engage in collective bargaining, and regulates labor unions.

**NLRB (NATIONAL LABOR RELATIONS BOARD)**  An agency established pursuant to the National Labor Relations Act for the purpose of prohibiting unfair labor practices by employers and unions.

**UNFAIR LABOR PRACTICE**  Conduct by labor unions and employers, which is proscribed by the National Labor Relations Act.

■══■

# United Technologies Corp.

## Union (P) v. Employer (D)

268 NLRB 557 (1984).

**NATURE OF CASE:** Review of union grievance against employer.

**FACT SUMMARY:** The Union (P) brought unfair labor practice grievance to NLRB, and the employer (D) sought to compel arbitration.

## RULE OF LAW
The NLRB should defer to the arbitration process in disputes involving individual NLRA rights.

**FACTS:** An employee, Ms. Sherfield, filed a grievance that was denied by the company's general foreman at the first step of the grievance procedure. When she and her shop steward indicated that they would proceed to the next step, the general foreman allegedly indicated that persistence might result in discipline. Sherfield and the Union (P) brought an unfair labor practice grievance, and United Technologies Corp. (D) denied the allegations. The company argued that the NLRB should defer to the arbitration procedures of the parties' collective bargaining agreement.

**ISSUE:** Should the NLRB defer to the arbitration process in disputes involving individual NLRA rights?

**HOLDING AND DECISION:** [Member not stated in casebook excerpt.] Yes. The NLRB should defer to the arbitration process in disputes involving individual NLRA rights. The NLRB broadened its deferral policies in 1971 in *Collyer Insulated Wire*, 192 N.L.R.B. 837 (1971). There, an employer allegedly violated § 8(a)(5) of the NLRA. The NLRB held that it would dismiss charges involving refusals to bargain filed before an arbitration award if the dispute was contractual in nature, the agreement called for final and binding arbitration, and a reasonable construction of the agreement would preclude a finding that the disputed conduct violated the NLRA. The NLRB retained jurisdiction, however, to revisit the charges if the arbitration does not comply with *Spielberg* requirements. The recent case, *General American Transportation Corp.*, 228 N.L.R.B. 808 (1977), held that *Collyer* did not apply to cases involving individual rights, such as alleged discrimination. In this case, the NLRB overrules *General American Transportation*, holding that *Collyer* does apply to disputes involving individual rights. Complaint dismissed with provisions.

**DISSENT:** (Zimmerman, Member) Despite federal labor law policy favoring arbitration, disputes involving individual rights are not necessarily contractual in nature, and an arbitrator's resolution of any contractual issues will not dispose of the issues concerning the conduct by the employer and/or union that allegedly infringed on the employee's individual rights. Those issues involve conduct that may be unlawfully motivated or otherwise restrains, interferes with, or coerces employees in the exercise of their guaranteed § 7 rights under NLRA. Where statutory issues are at stake, the NLRB may properly refuse to defer to arbitration, and should do so.

## ANALYSIS

This case illustrates a growing trend by the courts to unclog the dockets by seeking alternative dispute resolution forums. In the areas of law that generate an enormous number of claims each year, such as labor law, mechanisms such as arbitration are an efficient alternative to litigation. Moreover, parties to collective bargaining agreements generally agree to resolve disputes through an arbitrator, and there is an established trend among courts to honor the terms of a contract where possible.

---

## Quicknotes

**ARBITRATION** An alternative resolution process where a dispute is heard and decided by a neutral third party, rather than through legal proceedings.

**NLRA (NATIONAL LABOR RELATIONS ACT)** Guarantees employees the right to engage in collective bargaining, and regulates labor unions.

**NLRB (NATIONAL LABOR RELATIONS BOARD)** An agency established pursuant to the National Labor Relations Act for the purpose of prohibiting unfair labor practices by employers and unions.

**UNFAIR LABOR PRACTICE** Conduct by labor unions and employers, which is proscribed by the National Labor Relations Act.

# Hammontree v. NLRB

Employee (P) v. Labor board (D)

925 F.2d 1486 (en banc) (D.C. Cir. 1991).

**NATURE OF CASE:** Petition for review of an NLRB order.

**FACT SUMMARY:** Hammontree (P) challenged the NLRB's (D) order that he must exhaust his private grievance remedies before filing an unfair labor practice charge under the NLRA.

> 🏛 **RULE OF LAW**
> The NLRB may require an individual employee to exhaust contractual grievance remedies prior to the filing of an unfair labor practice charge.

**FACTS:** Hammontree (P) was a truck driver for Consolidated Freightways (CF) (D). Hammontree (P) filed a grievance regarding a violation of his seniority rights, which he won. In response, CF (D) management stopped posting departure times for all truck runs. Hammontree (P) objected to this change of working conditions, and filed a second grievance that was rejected by the first-level grievance committee, which consisted of union and management representatives. Instead of pursuing this grievance to the next level, Hammontree (P) filed an unfair labor practice charge with the NLRB (D). An adminstrative law judge ruled for Hammontree (P), but the NLRB (D) reversed, holding that Hammontree (P) needed to exhaust the full grievance procedures established under the collective bargaining agreement with CF (D). Hammontree (P) appealed.

**ISSUE:** May the NLRB require an individual employee to exhaust contractual grievance remedies prior to the filing of an unfair labor practice charge?

**HOLDING AND DECISION:** (Wald, J.) Yes. The NLRB may require an individual employee to exhaust contractual grievance remedies prior to the filing of an unfair labor practice charge. Section 10(a) of the NLRA provides that the NLRB's (D) power to prevent unfair labor practices shall not be affected by any collective bargaining agreements. This section is an affirmative grant of authority to the NLRB (D); it is not any type of limitation. Nothing in § 10(a) reflects any congressional intent to preclude the NLRB (D) from imposing an exhaustion of grievance procedure requirement. Furthermore, § 203(d) of the NLRA provides that private grievance procedures are preferred for disputes arising under a collective bargaining agreement. Finally, deferment of an employee's right to a public forum does not prevent the attainment of a fair result. In the present case, Hammontree's (P) disputed rights involved both the collective bargaining agreement and alleged unfair labor practices. As such, the NLRB (D) acted within its authority to require Hammontree (P) to exhaust all of the grievance procedures in place under the agreement. Affirmed and petition for review denied.

**CONCURRENCE:** (Edwards, J.) It is clear that a union may waive certain rights of its members and provide for private grievance procedures under a collective bargaining agreement.

**DISSENT:** (Mikva, C.J.) Deferment to the private grievance procedure in this case is unfair because it is clear that Hammontree (P) is at odds with both his union and CF (D). Since CF (D) and union management make up the grievance panel, arbitration is an empty exercise and is unfair to Hammontree (P).

## ▶ *ANALYSIS*

The majority also rejected Hammontree's (P) argument that NLRB deferment is improper when individual employee rights are at issue under *Alexander v. Gardner-Denver Co.*, 415 U.S. 36 (1974). The court found that Alexander and its progeny were only applicable to the issue of the preclusive effect of arbitration awards. But preclusion is analytically distinct from the NLRB's (D) authority to require exhaustion of arbitration remedies. NLRB deferment does not nullify an employee's rights to a public forum under the NLRA; it merely delays them.

■=■

## *Quicknotes*

**NLRA (NATIONAL LABOR RELATIONS ACT)** Guarantees employees the right to engage in collective bargaining, and regulates labor unions.

**NLRB (NATIONAL LABOR RELATIONS BOARD)** An agency established pursuant to the National Labor Relations Act for the purpose of prohibiting unfair labor practices by employers and unions.

■=■

# Jacobs Manufacturing Co.

## Union (P) v. Employer (D)

94 NLRB 1214 (1951).

**NATURE OF CASE:** NLRB review of employer's refusal to bargain.

**FACT SUMMARY:** Jacobs Manufacturing Co. (D) refused to bargain issues raised by the Union (P) pursuant to a re-opening clause in the collective bargaining agreement.

### 🏛 RULE OF LAW
Bargainable issues that have never been discussed by the parties and that are in no way treated in a collective bargaining agreement remain matters that both the union and the employer are obligated to discuss at any time.

**FACTS:** Jacobs Manufacturing Co. (Jacobs) (D) and the Union (P) entered into a collective bargaining agreement in July 1948 that contained a clause allowing re-opening of discussions about wage rates one year after execution. In July 1949, the Union (P), pursuant to the re-opening clause, submitted wage demands, but in addition, demanded that Jacobs (D) undertake the entire cost of an existing group insurance program, and that the company establish a pension plan for employees. The insurance program had been discussed during negotiations of the 1948 agreement, and the parties had agreed to increase certain benefits and costs, but the program and its changes were not mentioned in the agreement.

**ISSUE:** Do bargainable issues that have never been discussed by the parties and that are in no way treated in a collective bargaining agreement remain matters that both the union and the employer are obligated to discuss at any time?

**HOLDING AND DECISION:** [Member not stated in casebook excerpt.] Yes. Bargainable issues that have never been discussed by the parties and that are in no way treated in a collective bargaining agreement remain matters that both the union and the employer are obligated to discuss at any time. Jacobs (D) violated § 8(a)(5) of the NLRA by refusing to discuss the matter of pensions with the union. The 1948 contract was silent on the issue of pensions, and Jacobs (D) was therefore required to discuss the matter, and the limitation contained in § 8(d) of the NLRA dealing with the duty to discuss or agree to the modification of an existing bargaining contract only rejects the notion that the duty to bargain continues even with regard to those matters agreed to and embodied in the written contract. The duty to bargain implies only an obligation to discuss the matter in question in good faith, however, and does not require that either side agree.

**CONCURRENCE IN PART:** (Herzog, Chairman) Jacobs (D) is not obligated to discuss the insurance program even though it was not addressed in the collective bargaining agreement, because it was discussed in negotiations prior to execution of the agreement.

**CONCURRENCE AND DISSENT IN PART:** (Reynolds, Member) Section 8(d) imposes no obligation on either party to bargain on any matter during the term of the contract except as to express provisions of the contract may demand, such as a re-opening clause. The stability of industrial relations depends on the integrity of collective bargaining agreements.

**DISSENT IN PART:** (Murdock, Member) Jacobs (D) properly took the position that the parties were meeting pursuant to the reopening provision of the contract to discuss wage rates and that pensions and insurance were not negotiable and would not be discussed at that time.

### ▶ ANALYSIS

The majority was careful to state in its opinion that the duty to bargain implies only an obligation to discuss the issue in good faith. It does not require that an agreement be reached. The opinion therefore does not allow for issues not addressed in the collective bargaining agreement to be binding on the parties without their consent. And with that safeguard in place, it seems good policy to maintain a list of issues that remain bargainable where the collective bargaining agreement is silent, in order for the NLRB to ensure that the important issues are covered in some way, for everyone's protection.

■■■

### Quicknotes

**COLLECTIVE BARGAINING** Negotiations between an employer and employee that are mediated by a specified third party.

**NLRA (NATIONAL LABOR RELATIONS ACT)** Guarantees employees the right to engage in collective bargaining, and regulates labor unions.

**NLRB (NATIONAL LABOR RELATIONS BOARD)** An agency established pursuant to the National Labor Relations Act for the purpose of prohibiting unfair labor practices by employers and unions.

■■■

# Johnson-Bateman Co.

## Union (P) v. Employer (D)

295 NLRB 180 (1989).

**NATURE OF CASE:** NLRB review of employer's unilateral adoption of policy not covered by collective bargaining agreement.

**FACT SUMMARY:** Johnson-Bateman Co. (D) unilaterally adopted a policy requiring mandatory alcohol and drug testing of all employees injured on the job and requiring treatment, and argued it was empowered do so without consulting the union by a management-rights clause in the collective bargaining agreement.

> ### 🏛 RULE OF LAW
> A waiver of the union's right to bargain cannot be inferred from general contractual provisions.

**FACTS:** Johnson-Bateman Co. (D) unilaterally adopted a policy requiring mandatory alcohol and drug testing of all employees injured on the job and requiring treatment. The collective bargaining agreement contained a management-rights clause providing that the company retained all rights it would have in the absence of the agreement, except to the extent that they are limited by express provisions in the agreement. The Union (P) argued that the company's (D) action violated the NLRA.

**ISSUE:** Can a waiver of the union's right to bargain be inferred from general contractual provisions?

**HOLDING AND DECISION:** [Member not stated in casebook excerpt.] No. A waiver of the union's right to bargain cannot be inferred from general contractual provisions. Waiver of a statutory right must be clear and unmistakable, and generally worded management-rights clauses will not be construed as such a waiver. The management-rights clause in the agreement in this case is generally worded, makes no reference to any particular subject, and does not therefore constitute a waiver by the Union (P) of its statutory right to bargain about the company's (D) implementation of the drug/alcohol testing requirement. In addition, there is nothing in the bargaining history of the contract to show that the meaning and potential implications of the clause, or drug/alcohol testing in particular, were fully discussed. The company's (D) unilateral implementation of the requirement without providing the union (P) with notice and an opportunity to bargain violated § 8(a)(5) and (1) of the NLRA.

## ▌ANALYSIS

Courts generally hesitate to find a waiver of rights by any party unless it is expressly stated, and have generally upheld this ruling. In addition, management-rights clauses are often construed restrictively by courts unless crafted in specific terms.

◼◼

## *Quicknotes*

**COLLECTIVE BARGAINING** Negotiations between an employer and employee that are mediated by a specified third party.

**NLRA (NATIONAL LABOR RELATIONS ACT)** Guarantees employees the right to engage in collective bargaining, and regulates labor unions.

**NLRB (NATIONAL LABOR RELATIONS BOARD)** An agency established pursuant to the National Labor Relations Act for the purpose of prohibiting unfair labor practices by employers and unions.

**UNILATERAL** One-sided; involving only one person.

◼◼

# Milwaukee Spring Div. of Illinois Coil Spring Co.

## Union (P) v. Employer (D)

268 NLRB 601 (1984), *enforced sub nom., International Union, UAW v. NLRB*, 765 F.2d 175 (D.C. Cir. 1985).

**NATURE OF CASE:** Appeal of NLRB decision against union.

**FACT SUMMARY:** Illinois Coil Spring Company (D) transferred work from unionized plant to non-unionized plant to reduce labor costs without obtaining the Union's (P) consent.

### 🏛 RULE OF LAW
The transfer of work by an employer from a unionized plant to a non-unionized plant to reduce labor costs does not modify wage and benefits provisions or the recognition clause of the collective bargaining agreement with the union.

**FACTS:** Illinois Coil Spring Company (the Company) (D) told the United Auto Workers Union (P) that the higher wage rates in Milwaukee forced the Company (D) to transfer certain operations from its unionized Milwaukee Spring facility to its non-unionized McHenry Spring facility. The Company (D) made specific proposals for alternatives to relocation, including urging the Union (P) to forgo a wage increase scheduled under the labor agreement and to make other contract concessions, but the Union (P) rejected the proposals. The Company (D) then announced its relocation decision, and the Union (P) conceded it was economically motivated and not the result of anti-union animus. The Union (P) also stipulated that the company satisfied its obligation to bargain with the union over the decision.

**ISSUE:** Does the transfer of work by an employer from a unionized plant to a non-unionized plant to reduce labor costs modify wage and benefits provisions or the recognition clause of the collective bargaining agreement with the union?

**HOLDING AND DECISION:** [Member not stated in casebook excerpt.] No. The transfer of work by an employer from a unionized plant to a non-unionized plant to reduce labor costs does not modify wage and benefits provisions or the recognition clause of the collective bargaining agreement with the union. Under § 8(d) of the NLRA, the employer must obtain the union's consent before implementing a change to the collective bargaining agreement that is in effect. Here, the decision to transfer does not modify any provision of the contract. While the relocation decision was motivated by a desire to cut labor costs, it nevertheless does not modify the contract's wage and benefits provisions. The Union (P) had rejected the Company's (D) proposal to modify the wage and benefits provisions during bargaining, and after the Union (P) did not grant its consent to modify the provisions, the Company (D) abandoned the proposals and instead decided to transfer the operations to a different plant. The Company (D) did not disturb the wages and benefits at its Milwaukee facility, and therefore did not violate § 8(d). The relocation decision also did not modify the contract's recognition clause. The language in the contract that recognizes the Union (P) as the bargaining agent for Milwaukee employees does not state that the functions that the unit performs must remain in Milwaukee. In addition, the employer is not required to obtain the union's consent on a matter not contained in the body of a collective bargaining agreement even though the subject is a mandatory subject of bargaining. The employer's obligation, absent a specific provision in the contract restricting its rights, is to bargain with the union over its decisions, and that the employer did. Reversed and complaint dismissed.

**DISSENT:** (Zimmerman, Member) The Company's (D) midterm relocation decision violated § 8(d) of the NLRA because it was simply an attempt to modify the wage rate provisions in the contract. The Company (D) obligated itself to pay a certain rate to its employees, and it cannot get out of this obligation by relocating the work.

### ▶ ANALYSIS

The NLRB slightly confused its analysis by holding that, because the parties stipulated that the Company (D) bargained but could not agree, the Company (D) did not violate section 8(a)(5). If the Company (D) had the contractual right to make the relocation decision, it had no duty to bargain before making that decision.

■━■

### Quicknotes

**ANIMUS** Intention, will.

**COLLECTIVE BARGAINING** Negotiations between an employer and employee that are mediated by a specified third party.

**NLRA (NATIONAL LABOR RELATIONS ACT)** Guarantees employees the right to engage in collective bargaining, and regulates labor unions.

**NLRB (NATIONAL LABOR RELATIONS BOARD)** An agency established pursuant to the National Labor Relations Act for the purpose of prohibiting unfair labor practices by employers and unions.

■━■

# Successorship

## *Quick Reference Rules of Law*

# Fall River Dyeing & Finishing Corp. v. NLRB

## Employer (D) v. Union (P)

482 U.S 27 (1987).

**NATURE OF CASE:** Appeal from order finding unfair labor practice.

**FACT SUMMARY:** Fall River Dyeing & Finishing Corp. (D) contended it did not violate § 8 of the NLRA by failing to bargain with the union that represented the employees of the corporation from which it purchased its equipment and real property.

### 🏛 RULE OF LAW
A successor employer has a duty to bargain with the union representing the predecessor employees where a substantial and representative complement of employees remains.

**FACTS:** Fall River Dyeing & Finishing Corp. (Fall River) (D) purchased the equipment and other assets of a defunct corporation, Sterlingwale. Fall River (D) continued to operate the same as Sterlingwale, and many former employees were hired. The Union (P), which had represented the employees under Sterlingwale, demanded Fall River (D) bargain with it. Fall River (D) denied being a successor corporation. The Union (P) filed unfair labor practices charges, which were upheld by the Board (D). The court of appeals upheld the Board's (D) order, and the Supreme Court granted certiorari.

**ISSUE:** Must a successor employer bargain with the union that previously represented the employees of the predecessor corporation?

**HOLDING AND DECISION:** (Blackmun, J.) Yes. A successor employer must bargain with the union representing the predecessor corporation's employees where a substantial and representative complement of employees remains. A union enjoys a presumption of majority support for one year after certification. The successor corporation must therefore bargain with this union. In this case, the Union's (P) demand was premature as it came prior to a substantial and representative complement of employees being hired. However, the demand is properly treated as a continuing one, obligating the employer to bargain when the complement exists. As a result, the order was proper. Affirmed.

**DISSENT:** (Powell, J.) The lack of continuity of workplace and workforce indicates a lack of successorship.

### ▶ ANALYSIS

This case illustrates that a union's presumption of majority status survives a change in ownership of the employer. This is so only if the employer is found to be a successor. If it is not, there is no duty on the successor to bargain with the union. This can be a source of abuse. If a company wishes to do away with an unfavorable collective bargaining agreement, it can attempt to reorganize.

■=■

## Quicknotes

**NLRA (NATIONAL LABOR RELATIONS ACT)** Guarantees employees the right to engage in collective bargaining, and regulates labor unions.

**NLRB (NATIONAL LABOR RELATIONS BOARD)** An agency established pursuant to the National Labor Relations Act for the purpose of prohibiting unfair labor practices by employers and unions.

**UNFAIR LABOR PRACTICE** Conduct by labor unions and employers, which is proscribed by the National Labor Relations Act.

■=■

# Howard Johnson Co. v. Detroit Local Joint Executive Bd.

Buyer (D) v. Union (P)

417 U.S. 249 (1974).

**NATURE OF CASE:** Appeal from an order to arbitrate.

**FACT SUMMARY:** The court of appeals held Howard Johnson Co. (D), as a successor to an employer bound by a collective bargaining agreement, bound to arbitrate its duties under the existing agreement.

## 🏛 RULE OF LAW
A successor employer is bound by an existing collective bargaining agreement only where there is a substantial continuity of identity in the work force hired by the successor employer.

**FACTS:** Grissom owned a restaurant and motor lodge that was subject to a collective bargaining agreement. It sold its interest to Howard Johnson Co. (D), which included in its purchase documentation a denial of any acceptance of, and a refusal to be bound by, any terms of the agreement. The existing employees were discharged prior to consummation of the sale, and a new work force was hired. The Union (P) sued, contending Howard Johnson (D) was bound by the agreement to negotiate and arbitrate its duties under the agreement. The trial court held Howard Johnson (D) was not bound by the agreement, and the court of appeals reversed. The Supreme Court granted certiorari.

**ISSUE:** Is a successor employer always bound by an existing collective bargaining agreement?

**HOLDING AND DECISION:** (Marshall, J.) No. A successor employer is bound by an existing collective bargaining agreement only where there is a substantial continuity of identity in the work force hired by the successor. In this case, the entire previous work force was replaced. Thus, clearly, no continuity existed, and no requirement of arbitration can be imposed. Reversed.

**DISSENT:** (Douglas, J.) This case distorts the primary intent of labor statutes, which is to push for expedient and peaceful resolution of problems through arbitration.

## ▌ *ANALYSIS*

The Court distinguished this case from the case of *John Wiley & Sons v. Livingston*, 376 U.S. 543 (1964). In that case, a successor employer was required to submit to the arbitration clause of an existing collective bargaining agreement. The previous employer, a corporation, ceased to exist through a merger transaction. Thus, the arbitration clause was held to survive so as to avoid taking away from the remaining employees the benefit of the bargains.

---

## Quicknotes

**ARBITRATION** An agreement to have a dispute heard and decided by a neutral third party, rather than through legal proceedings.

**COLLECTIVE BARGAINING** Negotiations between an employer and employee that are mediated by a specified third party.

**MERGER** The acquisition of one company by another, after which the acquired company ceases to exist as an independent entity.

# CHAPTER 7

# Labor and the Antitrust Laws

## Quick Reference Rules of Law

# United States v. Hutcheson

## Federal government (P) v. Union (D)

312 U.S. 219 (1941).

**NATURE OF CASE:** Appeal by Government from sustaining of demurrers to indictments for criminal combination and conspiracy in violation of the Sherman Act.

**FACT SUMMARY:** Officials (D) of a Carpenters Union who called for a strike, picketing, and a boycott against an employer over a dispute relating to job assignments against another union were prosecuted for violating the Sherman Act.

> **RULE OF LAW**
> No criminal liability may be imposed, pursuant to the Sherman Act, on a union which, because of a jurisdictional dispute with another union, calls for picketing and a boycott against an employer.

**FACTS:** Both Anheuser-Busch, Inc., and its lessee, the Gaylord Container Corp., contracted for new facilities; both companies were dependent on interstate commerce for marketing their goods, as were the construction companies for their building materials. The United Brotherhood of Carpenters and Joiners of America and the International Association of Machinists represented Anheuser-Busch's employees. Although Anheuser-Busch had given the job of erecting and dismantling machinery to the machinists, officials (D) of a Carpenters Union claimed those jobs for its own members, and refused to submit the dispute to arbitration. When Anheuser-Busch rejected the Carpenters' demand, officials (D) of the Carpenters called for a strike against Anheuser-Busch, Gaylord Container, and the construction companies, and for a boycott of Anheuser-Busch beer. The officials (D) were indicted for entering into a criminal combination and conspiracy in violation of the Sherman Act. Section I of the Act provides that "every contract, combination in the form of trust or otherwise, or conspiracy, in restraint of trade or commerce among the several states, or with foreign nations, is hereby declared to be illegal." The trial court sustained the officials' (D) demurrers to the criminal complaints, and the prosecution appealed.

**ISSUE:** Is the use of conventional, peaceful activities by a union in controversy with a rival union over certain jobs a violation of the Sherman Act?

**HOLDING AND DECISION:** (Frankfurter, J.) No. The Sherman Act cannot be considered apart from two other congressional pronouncements. Section 20 of the Clayton Act of 1914 withdrew from the general interdict of the Sherman Act specifically enumerated practices of labor unions by prohibiting injunctions against them, and also relieved such practices of all illegal taint. Although some judicial cases restricted the scope of § 20 to trade union activities directed against an employer by his own employees, it was felt by critics of this view that the area of

economic conflict should best be left to economic forces and the pressure of public opinion and not subjected to the judgment of courts. The Norris-LaGuardia Act clarified the situation by establishing that the allowable area of union activity was not to be restricted to an immediate employer-employee relation. Thus, § 20 of the Clayton Act and the Norris-LaGuardia Act, when read together, protect not only conduct against an employer because of a controversy arising in the relation between employer and employee, but also conduct similarly directed, but, ultimately due, to an internecine struggle between two unions seeking the favor of the same employer. In the present case, the Carpenters attempted to get members of other unions to join with it in refusing to work, to picket, and to patronize certain goods; these activities are all protected by § 20 of the Clayton Act as interpreted in light of the Norris-LaGuardia Act. It would be strange, indeed, that although neither the Government nor Anheuser-Busch could have sought an injunction against the acts here challenged, the elaborate efforts to permit such conduct failed to prevent criminal liability punishable with imprisonment and heavy fines. Accordingly, the officials (D) in the present case may not be prosecuted under the Sherman Act for the activities their union pursued. Affirmed.

**CONCURRENCE:** (Stone, J.) As the indictment failed to charge an offense under the Sherman Act, there was no occasion to consider the impact of the Norris-LaGuardia Act on the definition of participants in the Clayton Act.

**DISSENT:** (Roberts, J.) "To attribute to Congress an intent to repeal legislation which has had a definite and well understood scope and effect for decades past, by resurrecting a rejected construction of the Clayton Act and extending a policy strictly limited by the Congress itself in the Norris-LaGuardia Act, seems . . . a usurpation by the courts of the function of Congress."

## ▌ ANALYSIS

Generally speaking, the Norris-LaGuardia Act of 1932 restricted the equitable jurisdiction of federal courts over conventional labor economic activities to only those cases where violence or fraud is involved, where enforcement of an arbitration agreement is sought, when union-employer collusion results in a restraint of interstate commerce, or where a "no-strike" clause is violated by the union. An injunction under the Act will issue only when (1) unlawful activity will take place unless enjoined; (2) irreparable and substantial

*Continued on next page.*

harm is imminent; (3) injunctive relief would ward off a greater harm against the complainant when compared to the burden which will be inflicted on the threatening party; (4) no adequate legal remedy exists; and (5) public officials who are charged under the law with protecting the complainant's property are unable or unwilling to furnish protection.

■═■

## Quicknotes

**BOYCOTT**  A concerted effort to refrain from doing business with a particular person or entity.

**CONSPIRACY**  Concerted action by two or more persons to accomplish some unlawful purpose.

**SHERMAN ACT**  Makes every contract or conspiracy in unreasonable restraint of commerce illegal.

■═■

# United Mine Workers of America v. Pennington

## Union (D) v. Employer (P)

381 U.S. 657 (1965).

**NATURE OF CASE:** Antitrust violation against a union.

**FACT SUMMARY:** A small mine operator successfully defended a suit to collect pension benefit payments by asserting that the union had conspired with several large coal companies to drive small and nonunion coal companies out of business.

## 🏛 RULE OF LAW
The exemption of labor organizations from antitrust laws does not extend to those situations where a union conspires with non-labor organizations with the intent to diminish competition in a particular industry by embodying industrywide standard requirements in a collective bargaining agreement with only one set of employers.

**FACTS:** The United Mine Workers Welfare Fund (UMW) (D) brought suit to recover unpaid welfare benefit payments from Phillips Bros. Coal Co. (P) and from Pennington (P), one of its principals. Phillips (P) cross-complained against the UMW (D) and several large coal companies, alleging that the union had conspired with the large companies to drive small and nonunion coal companies, including Phillips (P), out of business. Specifically, Phillips (P) contended that the UMW (D) had entered into agreements with the large employers to have wage rates set at a level that the smaller companies could not pay in exchange for allowing the large companies to mechanize their operations to an extent that the smaller companies could not afford to do. Also alleged was a plan whereby the UMW (D) acquiesced in a plan by the large companies to have the TVA establish minimum wage standards for all companies selling coal to the TVA. In that latter regard, it was contended that the union approached both the Secretary of Labor and TVA, in concert with the employers, to implement the minimum wage proposal. Finally, Phillips (P) contended that the UMW (D) had agreed to impose industrywide wage and benefit standards on all employers in the industry with the knowledge that smaller employers would be forced out of business. The trial court found in favor of Phillips (P) for $90,000, and held that such amount should be trebled.

**ISSUE:** Does the exemption of labor organizations from ~~trust~~ laws extend to those situations where a union con- ~~with~~ non-labor organizations with the intent to ~~diminish competition~~ in a particular industry by embodying ~~standard~~ requirements in a collective bargain- ~~ing with on~~ly one set of employers?

**HOLDING AND DECISION:** (White, J.) No. The firm legislative and judicial policy of this country is that the antitrust laws do not apply to any labor organization acting in its self interest or for the benefit of its members. This exemption does not apply, however, where the union conspires with any non-labor organizations to diminish competition in any industry. There can be no question that the UMW (D) had the right, immune from antitrust laws, to determine that it would impose a uniform set of wages and benefits on all employers in the coal industry. However, the exemption would not apply if the UMW (D) made this plan a part of a collective bargaining agreement entered into with only one set of employers. This arrangement would remove from the union the freedom to bargain with other employers in that the union could not back down from this condition even if it determined that it would be in its best interest to do so. Further, if the UMW (D) entered into any agreement with the large coal companies designed to drive the small coal companies out of business by eliminating customers, such as TVA, then this would also fall outside the antitrust exemption. The trial court erred in this instance, however, by instructing the jury that if they found that the agreement between the UMW (D) and the employers as to the setting of minimum wage standards by TVA was intended to lessen competition, then the UMW (D) was guilty of antitrust violations. The exemption from the antitrust laws extends to concerted action by unions and non-labor groups in attempting to influence public officials. If Phillips (P) can prove its allegations independent of this at the new trial, then it is entitled to prevail. The verdict of the trial court is reversed and the court of appeals affirmed.

**CONCURRENCE:** (Douglas, J.) It should be made clear that if Phillips's (P) allegations can be proved at the new trial, then it is not only the UMW (D), but the large coal companies as well that have violated the antitrust laws. It is uniquely within the power of Congress to reshape our economy, not big business and big labor.

**CONCURRENCE AND DISSENT:** (Goldberg, J.) While we agree with the reversal of the trial court judgment, we cannot concur in the reasons therefor or the instructions for a new trial. The history of the use of the antitrust laws to frustrate the progress of the collective bargaining movement in this country should be ample warning to the majority of this court not to begin carving exceptions to the legislatively mandated exemptions from those laws. It is a legitimate aim of every labor organization to attempt to raise wages and benefits in an entire industry. There can be no

*Continued on next page.*

doubt that such attempts will have an impact on employers other than the one directly involved in the primary negotiations. But to permit, even encourage, unions to so bargain on one hand while threatening antitrust charges on the other is the height of inconsistency. In order to avoid any hint of conspiracy, the unions are forced to resort to strikes rather than to peaceably reach an agreement. In any antitrust trial, the judge and jury will be asked to evaluate the merits of the terms of the contract to determine if any evil motive was present in its formulation. This is not what the policy of this country is or should be.

## ▶ ANALYSIS

At the new trial in this case, Phillips (P) was unable to prove the antitrust violations previously alleged. However, in other cases, some small coal operators were able to secure treble damage antitrust awards against the UMW (D). One of the techniques of collective bargaining in large industries that has been sanctioned by this and other cases has been the bargaining between a large union and an association of employers that results in an industrywide contract. In those situations, however, there has usually been almost total representation of all employers by the association bargaining on their behalf.

■≡■

## Quicknotes

**ANTITRUST LAW** Body of federal law prohibiting business conduct that constitutes a restraint on trade.

■≡■

# Local Union No. 189, Amalgamated Meat Cutters v. Jewel Tea Co.

## Union (D) v. Employer (P)

381 U.S. 676 (1965).

**NATURE OF CASE:** Appeal from reversal of dismissal of a complaint alleging violation of the Sherman Act.

**FACT SUMMARY:** Jewel Tea Co. (P) alleged that a collective bargaining agreement, by which various market owners agreed with Local Union No. 189 (D) to limit the sale of meat to daytime hours only, was an illegal restraint of trade.

### 🏛 RULE OF LAW
Where a contract provision is so intimately related to wages, hours, and working conditions that the union's successful attempt to obtain the provision is through bona fide arms-length bargaining in pursuit of its own labor union policies, and not at the behest of or in combination with nonlabor groups, it is exempt from the Sherman Act.

**FACTS:** Retailers of fresh meat in the Chicago area entered into contract negotiations with Local Union No. 189 (Local 189) (D) representing the butchers. Local 189 (D) proposed to limit meat sales to the hours of 9 a.m. to 6 p.m., Monday through Saturday. Jewel Tea Co. (Jewel) (P), a meat retailer, opposed the provision even though it was accepted by the other retailers, but Jewel (P) acquiesced under threat of a strike vote. Jewel (P) then brought suit alleging a violation of the Sherman Act on the ground that the provision restrained trade and limited Jewel's (P) use of its own property besides inconveniencing those who could not shop during the day. The district court found the provision to be within the labor exception to the Sherman Act and not unreasonable. The court of appeals reversed, and Local 189 (D) appealed.

**ISSUE:** Where a contract provision is so intimately related to wages, hours, and working conditions that the union's successful attempt to obtain the provision is through bona fide, arms-length bargaining in pursuit of its own labor union policies, and not at the behest of or in combination with nonlabor groups, is it exempt from the Sherman Act?

**HOLDING AND DECISION:** (White, J.) Yes. Where a contract provision is so intimately related to wages, hours, and working conditions that the union's successful ~~att~~empt to obtain the provision is through bona fide, arms-~~length~~ ~~b~~argaining in pursuit of its own labor union policies, ~~and no~~t at the behest of or in combination with nonlabor ~~groups, it is ex~~empt from the Sherman Act. The particular ~~hours of the day an~~d the particular days of the week during ~~which employees wil~~l be required to work are subjects ~~within the meaning~~ of "wages, hours, and other terms and

conditions of employment." Night sales of meat, it was shown, would require butchers in attendance so that those who are unskilled would not add to the butchers' work during the day. Further, there was a long history, running over several decades, of limited hours which showed the limitation's intimate relation to working conditions. Reversed.

**DISSENT:** (Douglas, J.) The unions can no more aid a group of businessmen to force their competitors to follow uniform store marketing hours than to force them to sell at fixed prices. Both practices take away the freedom of traders to carry on their business in their own competitive fashion.

**CONCURRENCE:** (Goldberg, J.) "Even if an independent conspiracy test were applicable to the Jewel Tea (P) situation, the simple fact is that the multi-employer bargaining conducted at arm's-length does not constitute union abetment of a business combination. It is often a self-defensive form of employer bargaining designed to match union strength."

### ▶ ANALYSIS

Judicial pronouncements regarding the reasonableness of restraints on hours of business are relatively few. Some cases appear to have viewed such restraints as tantamount to limits on hours of work and thus reasonable, even though contained in agreements amongst competitors. Thus, in *Chicago Board of Trade v. United States*, 246 U.S. 231 (1918), the Court upheld a rule of a grain exchange that had the form of a restriction on prices of transactions outside regular trading hours but was characterized by the Court as a rule to shift transactions to the regular trading hours, i.e., to limit hours of operation.

■══■

### *Quicknotes*

**SHERMAN ACT** Makes every contract or conspiracy in unreasonable restraint of commerce illegal.

■══■

# Connell Constr. Co. v. Plumbers and Steamfitters Local Union 100

## Contractor (P) v. Union (D)

421 U.S. 616 (1975).

**NATURE OF CASE:** Appeal from exemption from antitrust laws.

**FACT SUMMARY:** Plumbers Local 100 (Local 100) (D) picketed Connell's (P) construction site in order to convince Connell (P) to sign an agreement to award subcontracts only to members of Local 100 (D), and Connell (P) signed under protest and sought a declaration that the agreement was void and violative of antitrust laws.

> ## 🏛 RULE OF LAW
> An agreement outside the context of a collective bargaining relationship and not restricted to a particular job site that obligates a contractor to subcontract work only to union firms may be the basis of a federal antitrust suit.

**FACTS:** Plumbers Local 100 (Local 100) (D) secured contracts with many employers in the Dallas area for the subcontracting of work only to firms under contract with Local 100 (D). Local 100 (D) then approached Connell Constr. Co. (Connell) (P) regarding such an agreement, but Connell (P) refused to sign. Local 100 (D) picketed Connell's (P) construction site and Connell (P) thereupon signed under protest to end the picketing. Connell (P) sought a declaration that the agreement signed was void and was violative of federal antitrust laws. The district court held that the picketing was authorized under the NLRA and that the NLRA preempted state antitrust laws. The court of appeals affirmed, and Connell's (P) petition for certiorari was granted.

**ISSUE:** May an agreement, outside the context of a collective bargaining relationship and not restricted to a particular job site, that obligates a contractor to subcontract work only to union firms be the basis of a federal antitrust suit?

**HOLDING AND DECISION:** (Powell, J.) Yes. An agreement outside the context of a collective bargaining relationship and not restricted to a particular job site that obligates a contractor to subcontract work only to union firms may be the basis of a federal antitrust suit. An agreement of this sort has the potential for restraining competition in the business market in ways which would not follow naturally from elimination of competition over wages and working conditions. While there is nothing illegal about Local 100's (D) attempt to organize subcontractors, this does not make the methods employed to do so immune from federal antitrust law. The picketing, in order to compel signing of an agreement not related to the picketed job site for a legitimate purpose, may still violate antitrust laws.

Furthermore, the NLRA is not exclusive and does not pre-empt all other antitrust provisions. Therefore, all agreement, outside the context of a collective bargaining relationship and not restricted to a particular job site, obligating a contractor to subcontract work only to union firms, may be the basis of a federal antitrust suit. Reversed in part and remanded.

## ▶ ANALYSIS

While picketing is permitted by a union in trying to negotiate, the picket must be related to the job site picketed in some way and there must be a relationship between the picketers and the employer or contractors. This case shows an attempt to use the statutorily authorized picketing power (NLRA § 8[e]) in a manner which amounted to duress.

■══■

## Quicknotes

**ANTITRUST LAW** Body of federal law prohibiting business conduct that constitutes a restraint on trade.

**COLLECTIVE BARGAINING** Negotiations between an employer and employee that are mediated by a specified third party.

**DURESS** Unlawful threats or other coercive behavior by one person that causes another to commit acts that he would not otherwise do.

**NLRA (NATIONAL LABOR RELATIONS ACT)** Guarantees employees the right to engage in collective bargaining, and regulates labor unions.

■══■

# Federalism and Labor Relations

## Quick Reference Rules of Law

# San Diego Building Trades Council v. Garmon

## Union (D) v. Employer (P)

359 U.S. 236 (1959).

**NATURE OF CASE:** Action in state court for an injunction to enjoin peaceful picketing and for damages.

**FACT SUMMARY:** A state court, prior to the NLRB adjudicating the issues in a labor dispute, issued an injunction against peaceful picketing and awarded damages to the employer, even though the activity enjoined was arguably regulated by the NLRA.

## 🏛 RULE OF LAW
A state may not regulate, either in law or equity, concerted labor activity in the absence of the NLRB's clear determination that the activity is neither protected nor prohibited by federal law.

**FACTS:** The San Diego Building Trades Council (Council) (D), an uncertified union, sought from Garmon and his partner (P) a closed-shop agreement. Garmon (P) refused, claiming that his employees had not expressed an interest to join the Council (D), and that the Council (D) had not been designated as the employees' collective bargaining agent. The Council (D) then began a peaceful picket to exert pressure on Garmon's (P) customers not to patronize his business. The Council (D) contended that its sole purpose in picketing was to educate the workers and persuade them to become members. Garmon (P) commenced an action in a California state court against the Council (D) for an injunction and damages. Finding that the Council's (D) aim in picketing was to deter patronage of Garmon's (P) business, the trial court awarded Garmon (P) damages and issued an injunction. At the time the state suit began, the NLRB refused to accept jurisdiction over the dispute on the ground that the amount of interstate commerce involved was too little to extend its jurisdiction. On appeal, the California Supreme Court, noting that the NLRB had declined jurisdiction, held that under § 8(b)(2) and state law, the strike was not privileged; the court, however, conceded that "any distinction as between those laws was not thoroughly explored." The U.S. Supreme Court reversed, holding that at least with respect to equitable relief, the refusal of the NLRB to assert jurisdiction did not leave the states with power over more activities they otherwise would be preempted from regulating. However, the court remanded the case to the California Supreme Court for consideration of whether the judgment for damages would be sustained under California law. On remand the California Supreme Court set aside the injunction, but sustained the award of damages relying on general tort provisions of the state's civil code, as well as specific state labor enactments. The Council (D) appealed.

**ISSUE:** May the state regulate a concerted labor activity which is arguably protected or regulated by federal law?

**HOLDING AND DECISION:** (Frankfurter, J.) No. When it is clear, or even arguable, that the activities which a state purports to regulate are protected by § 7 of the NLRA, or constitute an unfair labor practice under § 8, due regard for the federal enactment requires that state jurisdiction must yield. Otherwise, there will be too great a danger of conflict and frustration of national purposes. Even when it is unclear whether a certain activity regulated by the states is governed by § 7 or § 8, the states, as well as the courts, must defer to the NLRB to adjudicate the issues. If the Board decides that certain conduct is protected by § 7, or prohibited by § 8, then the states are ousted of all jurisdiction. If the Board decides to the contrary, then the states may regulate, subject of course, to judicial review. However, the Board's determination, or precedent upon which the states rely, must be clear. Finally, the nature of state court relief is immaterial since an award of damages, as much as the issuance of an injunction, may constitute regulation. In the present case, since the NLRB has not adjudicated the dispute, which arguably falls within the scope of § 7 or § 8, California's jurisdiction is displaced. Nothing in the instant decision, it must be cautioned, deprives a state of the power to regulate where the activity is merely a peripheral concern of the Labor Management Relations Act (LMRA), or where the regulated conduct touches interests so deeply rooted in local feeling and responsibility that, in the absence of compelling congressional direction, Congress has not deprived the states of the power to act. Reversed.

**CONCURRENCE:** (Harlan, J.) To require a state to await Board determination before it can act may, because of unavoidable board delays, cause those injured by nonviolent conduct to be remediless. Therefore, where it is clear that the activity sought to be regulated is not protected, the Court should sustain the state court's judgment.

## ▶ ANALYSIS

The preemption doctrine recognizes a few exceptions. A state has the power to enjoin violent strike activity which, under federal labor law, would also be an unfair labor practice. Similarly, § 303 of the LMRA authorizes the filing of a state court suit to recover damages occasioned by certain prohibited strikes or boycotts. Section 301 of the LMRA provides that breach of contract suits involving collective bargaining agreements may be brought in state court. Finally, a union member may initiate a state court action against his union for breach of the latter's statutory obligation to provide him with fair representation.

■■■

*Continued on next page.*

## *Quicknotes*

**COLLECTIVE BARGAINING** Negotiations between an employer and employee that are mediated by a specified third party.

**NLRA (NATIONAL LABOR RELATIONS ACT)** Guarantees employees the right to engage in collective bargaining, and regulates labor unions.

**NLRB (NATIONAL LABOR RELATIONS BOARD)** An agency established pursuant to the National Labor Relations Act for the purpose of prohibiting unfair labor practices by employers and unions.

**PREEMPTION** Judicial preference recognizing the procedure of federal legislation over state legislation of the same subject matter.

■≡■

# Farmer v. United Brotherhood of Carpenters and Joiners, Local 25

## Injured (P) v. Union (D)

### 430 U.S. 290 (1977).

**NATURE OF CASE:** Appeal from denial of damages in an action of mental distress.

**FACT SUMMARY:** Farmer's (P) decedent claimed he was subjected to mental distress intentionally inflicted by the United Brotherhood of Carpenters (D) as a result of differences over internal policy.

## 🏛 RULE OF LAW
The NLRA does not preempt a tort action brought in state court by a union member against the union and its officials to recover damages for the intentional infliction of emotional distress.

**FACTS:** Farmer's (P) decedent, formerly a union official, alleged that he was subjected to mental distress intentionally inflicted by the United Brotherhood of Carpenters (Carpenters) (D), as a result of differences over internal policy, and was discriminated against in hiring referrals. The trial court instructed that the NLRB had no jurisdiction to award damages for mental distress and liability and therefore required "outrageous conduct." The jury then returned a verdict of $7,500 actual damages and $175,000 punitive damages against the Carpenters (D), and the trial court entered a judgment on the verdict. The state court of appeal reversed, holding that the state courts had no jurisdiction over employment relations. The state Supreme Court denied review, and the Supreme Court granted certiorari.

**ISSUE:** Does the NLRA preempt a tort action brought in state court by a union member against the union and its officials to recover damages for the intentional infliction of emotional distress?

**HOLDING AND DECISION:** (Powell, J.) No. The NLRA does not preempt a tort action brought in state court by a union member against the union and its officials to recover damages for the intentional infliction of emotional distress. Where the state has a substantial interest in regulation of the conduct at issue and that state's interest is one that does not threaten undue interference with the federal regulatory scheme, inflexible application of the preemption doctrine should not lie. Here, the state has a substantial interest in protecting its citizens from intentional infliction of emotional distress. The NLRB could not award Farmer's (P) decedent damages for this. The question of whether Farmer's (P) decedent was discriminated against in hiring referrals could cause interference with the federal scheme, but the state can adjudicate the tort action without resolving the labor dispute. State jurisdiction will lie where the tort is unrelated to employment discrimination, or a function of the way the discrimination is carried out, rather than a function of the actual discrimination itself. Since state law permits recovery only for "outrageous conduct," and not on the basis of the normal personality clashes in a union, excessive interference could result, and if the state does not award excessive damage awards, the state jurisdiction should be upheld. However, since the evidence is not sufficient to support the claim under state law, the trial court's judgment cannot be reinstated. Vacated and remanded.

## ▶ ANALYSIS

Historically, the extent of NLRB jurisdiction has not always been clear. In the pre-World War II period, the concept of federal power was a restrictive one. After the war, the NLRB would examine its power to exercise its jurisdiction on a case-by-case basis where a "small business having only local significance" was involved. (Cox at 1165.) The Eisenhower period saw an NLRB which favored restricting federal jurisdiction. However, it was soon realized that federal labor law was generally pervasive and supreme over state law.

■═■

## Quicknotes

**INTENTIONAL INFLICTION OF EMOTIONAL DISTRESS** Intentional and extreme behavior on the part of the wrongdoer with the intent to cause the victim to suffer from severe emotional distress, or with reckless indifference, resulting in the victim's suffering from severe emotional distress.

**NLRA (NATIONAL LABOR RELATIONS ACT)** Guarantees employees the right to engage in collective bargaining, and regulates labor unions.

**NLRB (NATIONAL LABOR RELATIONS BOARD)** An agency established pursuant to the National Labor Relations Act for the purpose of prohibiting unfair labor practices by employers and unions.

**PREEMPTION** Judicial preference recognizing the procedure of federal legislation over state legislation of the same subject matter.

■═■

# Lodge 76, International Ass'n of Machinists v. Wisconsin Employment Relations Comm'n

Union (D) v. State commission (P)

427 U.S. 132 (1976).

**NATURE OF CASE:** Appeal from an injunction issued under NLRA § 8(a)(3).

**FACT SUMMARY:** The Machinists (D) argued that the Commission (P) lacked authority to enjoin its refusal to work overtime on the ground that federal labor policy preempted state authority in that area of the law.

## 🏛 RULE OF LAW
Federal labor policy preempts the authority of a state labor relations board to grant an employer covered by the NLRA an order enjoining a union and its members from continuing to refuse to work overtime, pursuant to a union policy to put economic pressure on the employer in collective bargaining negotiations.

**FACTS:** After expiration of their contract, Machinists (D) and their employer entered into collective bargaining negotiations for renewal. In order to put economic pressure on the employer, the Union (D) voted to refuse to work any overtime. The employer filed a charge with the NLRB that the Union's (D) action violated NLRA § 8(a)(3). The charge was dismissed on the ground that the action complained of did not violate the NLRA. The employer then complained to the Commission (P) which held that the refusal to work overtime was not a protected activity and that it was an unfair labor practice. It enjoined such continued conduct. The Machinists' (D) appeals were rejected in the state courts. This appeal was brought to the Supreme Court on the ground rejected by the Commission (P) that federal policy preempted state authority in this area of labor law

**ISSUE:** Does federal labor policy preempt the authority of a state labor relations board to grant an employer covered by the NLRA an order enjoining a union and its members from continuing to refuse to work overtime, pursuant to a union policy to put economic pressure on the employer in collective bargaining negotiations?

**HOLDING AND DECISION:** (Brennan, J.) Yes. Federal labor policy preempts the authority of a state labor relations board to grant an employer covered by the NLRA an order enjoining a union and its members from continuing to refuse to work overtime, pursuant to a union policy to put economic pressure on the employer in collective bargaining negotiations. States are not precluded from regulating aspects of labor relations involving conduct touching interests so deeply rooted in local feeling and responsibility that it could not be inferred that Congress had deprived the states of the power to act. Preemption analysis under the NLRA has focused upon the "crucial inquiry" whether Congress intended

that the conduct involved be unregulated because it should be left "to be controlled by the free play of economic forces." In the *Briggs-Stratton* case, it was held that methods neither made a right under federal law nor did a violation of it preempt state power (*U.A.W./A.F. of L. Local 32 v. Wisconsin Emp. Rel. Bd.*, 336 U.S. 245 (1949)). But in *NLRB v. Insurance Agents' Union*, 361 U.S. 488 (1960), this view was undercut by finding that an activity was protected where Congress intended it to be unrestricted by any governmental power to regulate, if it was among the permissible economic weapons recognized by the various labor laws. Economic pressure is "part and parcel" of the collective bargaining process, and the NLRB cannot find certain economic tactics acceptable and others unacceptable without being inconsistent with that policy. "For a state to impinge on the area of labor combat designed to be free is as much an obstruction of federal labor policy as if the state were to declare picketing free for purposes or by methods which the federal act prohibits." Whether economic pressure is used by union or employer the inquiry is the same: "Whether the exercise of plenary state authority to curtail or entirely prohibit self-help would frustrate effective implementation of the Act's processes." Here, the employees' economic weakness could not justify the state's giving aid contrary to federal law. *Briggs-Stratton* is expressly overruled because the state's attempts to influence substantive terms of collective bargaining agreements are inconsistent with the federal regulatory scheme. Reversed.

**CONCURRENCE:** (Powell, J.) The states should still be permitted to apply their "neutral" laws, "state laws that are not directed toward altering the bargaining position of employers or unions but which have an incidental effect on relative bargaining strength."

**DISSENT:** (Stevens, J.) "If adherence to the rule of *Briggs-Stratton* would permit the States substantially to disrupt the balance Congress has struck between union and employer, I would readily join in overruling it. But I am not persuaded that partial strike activity is so essential to the bargaining process that the States should not be free to make it illegal."

## ▶ ANALYSIS

Another line of preemption analysis was discussed by the court but omitted by the editors. That line is based predominantly on the primary jurisdiction of the NLRB and is distinguished from that based on federal protection of the conduct in question. Cases discussing this other analysis

*Continued on next page.*

are *San Diego Unions v. Garmon*, 359 U.S. 236 (1959), and *Motor Coach Employees v. Lockridge*, 403 U.S. 274, 290-291 (1971). As for Justice Powell's concurrence, the "neutral" laws to which he referred involve torts and contracts, but not laws reflecting an accommodation of the special interests of employers, unions, or the public in areas such as employee self-organization, labor disputes and collective bargaining. In *American Radio Association v. Mobile Steamship Association*, 419 U.S. 213 (1974), the Court held (5-4) that a state court was not preempted from issuing an injunction, upon request of shippers and stevedores, against picketing of a foreign flag ship by maritime unions because the foreign flag ship was not "in commerce."

■══■

## Quicknotes

**COLLECTIVE BARGAINING** Negotiations between an employer and employee that are mediated by a specified third party.

**NLRA (NATIONAL LABOR RELATIONS ACT)** Guarantees employees the right to engage in collective bargaining, and regulates labor unions.

**NLRB (NATIONAL LABOR RELATIONS BOARD)** An agency established pursuant to the National Labor Relations Act for the purpose of prohibiting unfair labor practices by employers and unions.

**PREEMPTION** Judicial preference recognizing the procedure of federal legislation over state legislation of the same subject matter.

■══■

# Chamber of Commerce v. Brown

## Association of businesses (P) v. State (D)

554 U.S. 60 (2008).

**NATURE OF CASE:** Appeal from judgment of federal appeals court.

**FACT SUMMARY:** A California statute bans recipients of state funds from using the funds to affect union organizing. The Chamber of Commerce (P) sued California agencies (D) enforcing the law.

### 🏛 RULE OF LAW
A state statute prohibiting several classes of employers that receive state funds from using the funds to assist, promote, or deter union organizing is preempted by federal law mandating that certain zones of labor activity be unregulated.

**FACTS:** A California statute forbids certain employers that receive state funds from using those funds to assist, promote, or deter union organizing. The prohibition includes any attempt by an employer to influence the decision of its employees regarding whether to support or oppose a labor organization and whether to become a member of any labor organization. It exempts activities connected to promotion of unionization, including allowing a labor organization or its representatives access to the employer's facilities or property and negotiating a voluntary recognition agreement with a labor organization. Covered employers must certify that no state funds will be used for prohibited expenditures, and must maintain and provide records backing up their compliance. The Chamber of Commerce (P) brought this case against the California Department of Health Services (D) and its officials to enjoin enforcement of the statute. Two labor unions intervened to defend the statute's validity. The district court granted partial summary judgment in favor of the Chamber of Commerce (P), and the Ninth Circuit Court of Appeals reversed on a rehearing en banc, concluding that Congress did not intend to preclude states from imposing such restrictions on the use of their own funds.

**ISSUE:** Is a state statute prohibiting several classes of employers that receive state funds from using the funds to assist, promote, or deter union organizing preempted by federal law mandating that certain zones of labor activity be unregulated?

**HOLDING AND DECISION:** (Stevens, J.) Yes. A state statute prohibiting several classes of employers that receive state funds from using the funds to assist, promote, or deter union organizing is preempted by federal law mandating that certain zones of labor activity be unregulated. The NLRA contains no express preemption provision, but Congress implicitly mandated two types of preemption as necessary to implement federal labor policy. The first is known as *Garmon* preemption, and it precludes state interference with the

NLRB's interpretation and enforcement of the NLRA. *San Diego Building Trades Council v. Garmon*, 359 U.S. 236 (1959). The second is known as the *Machinists* preemption, and it forbids both the NLRB and states to regulate conduct that Congress intended to be unregulated in the interests of a free market. *Machinists v. Wisconsin Employment Relations Commn.*, 427 U.S. 132 (1976). The state statute at issue here regulates within a zone of market freedom, and is therefore preempted under *Machinists*. Because it is preempted under *Machinists*, whether it is preempted under *Garmon* is immaterial. The NLRB's position is that § 8 demands complete employer neutrality during organizing campaigns, because any partisan speech by the employer about unions would interfere with § 7 rights. Congress passed the Labor Management Relations Act because it was concerned that the labor-relations balance weighed too heavily in unions' favor. In so doing, Congress sought to protect free debate, and its emphasis in that area supports the preemption analysis in this case, because here, as there, Congress intends to leave noncoercive speech unregulated. The California statute represents a policy by the state of California that directly contradicts the federal labor policy laid out by Congress in the NLRA. The statute's preamble states that even noncoercive employer speech interferes with an employee's choice about whether to join or to be represented by a labor union. Congress preempted states from acting on this view by adding to the NLRA § 8(c), which provides that noncoercive speech by either unions or employers cannot be subject to NLRB regulation as an unfair labor practice, thereby establishing precisely the opposite judgment as the labor policy of the United States. Arguments against preemption are unpersuasive. First, there is no distinction between the California statute's restrictions on the use of state funds and impermissible restrictions on who may receive state funds. The premise that use and receipt could be legally different is acceptable, but the California statute's restrictions are impermissibly burdensome, even if drafted as use restrictions, because they are accompanied by compliance costs and litigation risks that are calculated to make union-related advocacy prohibitively expensive for employers that receive state funds. Second, the Ninth Circuit's reliance on special NLRA provisions allowing the NLRB to regulate non-coercive employer speech immediately before a union election is unpersuasive here. The Ninth Circuit took these provisions as an indication that Congress did not intend to leave non-coercive speech completely unregulated, and therefore did not intend to preempt state laws like the one here. The statute here reaches beyond the narrow context of election time to regulate speech that is clearly left unregulated by the NLRA. Third, three federal statutes forbidding the use of particular grant and program funds to assist, promote or deter union

*Continued on next page.*

organizing, using the exact same language as the statute here, did not suggest that Congress intended to leave non-coercive employer speech open to state regulation. The Ninth Circuit reasoned that Congress was unlikely to have intended to pre-empt California from doing something it freely did itself in other contexts. The federal statutes are tailored exceptions to otherwise applicable federal policies that did not represent congressional intent to tolerate a substantial measure of diversity in the regulation of employer speech. The court of appeals judgment reversing the summary judgment for the Chamber of Commerce (P) is reversed and remanded.

## ▶ ANALYSIS

This case brings into question labor laws in 15 states that are similar to the California statute, including "Worker Freedom" legislation that outlaws employer captive-audience speeches. It also marks another victory for federal preemption, this time over state spending restrictions that conflict with federal policy. Remember that state laws often attempt to neutralize the playing field, and even those laws are likely preempted.

■══■

## Quicknotes

**EN BANC** The hearing of a matter by all the judges of the court, rather than only the necessary quorum.

**ENJOIN** The ordering of a party to cease the conduct of a specific activity.

**NLRA (NATIONAL LABOR RELATIONS ACT)** Guarantees employees the right to engage in collective bargaining, and regulates labor unions.

**NLRB (NATIONAL LABOR RELATIONS BOARD)** An agency established pursuant to the National Labor Relations Act for the purpose of prohibiting unfair labor practices by employers and unions.

**PARTIAL SUMMARY JUDGMENT** Judgment rendered by a court in response to a motion by one of the parties, claiming that the lack of a question of material fact in respect to one of the issues warrants disposition of that issue without going to the jury.

**SUMMARY JUDGMENT** Judgment rendered by a court in response to a motion made by one of the parties, claiming that the lack of a question of material fact in respect to an issue warrants disposition of the issue without consideration by the jury.

■══■

# Local 24, International Teamsters v. Oliver

## Union (D) v. Truck driver (P)

### 358 U.S. 283 (1959).

**NATURE OF CASE:** Appeal from issuance of a permanent injunction.

**FACT SUMMARY:** Oliver (P), owner-driver of a truck, obtained a permanent injunction in state court against the Union (D) and the motor carriers (D) to keep them from preventing him from leasing his truck at a rate which would return to him an amount less than union wages.

---

### 🏛 RULE OF LAW
The goal of federal labor policy, to encourage the employer and the employees' representatives to establish, through collective bargaining, their own charter for industrial relations, would be defeated if states could limit the solutions arrived at by the parties.

---

**FACTS:** Oliver (P), owner-driver of a truck, secured employment by leasing his truck to interstate carriers which paid him for both his driving services and his truck rental. The motor carriers (D) and the Union (D) negotiated a contract by which Article XXXII regulated the minimum rental rate for trucks leased to a carrier by an owner-driver. The Union (D) sought to prevent owner-drivers from renting their trucks at a rate which after expenses would leave them with a profit less than union wages for the equivalent time worked. Oliver (P) obtained a permanent injunction against this article in state court on the ground that it violated Ohio antitrust law as a price-fixing agreement. The Union (D) and the motor carriers (D) appealed.

**ISSUE:** Would the goal of federal labor policy, to encourage the employer and the employees' representatives to establish, through collective bargaining, their own charter for industrial relations, be defeated if states could limit the solutions arrived at by the parties?

**HOLDING AND DECISION:** (Brennan, J.) Yes. The goal of federal labor policy, to encourage the employer and the employees' representatives to establish, through collective bargaining, their own charter for industrial relations, would be defeated if states could limit the solutions arrived at by the parties. Here, the point of Article XXXII was wages, not price fixing. It was designed to protect a negotiated wage scale and was not a remote and indirect approach to the subject of wages. Under § 8(d) of the Act, there is an obligation to bargain collectively with respect to wages, hours, and other terms and conditions of employment. Thus, the state antitrust law could not be applied in this area. Where federal and state laws conflict, federal law prevails. If there is to be any limitation which seeks to adjust commercial relationships, it is for Congress, not the states, to provide it. Reversed.

### ▶ ANALYSIS

By 1945, state law, whether legislatively enacted or judge-made, began to collide with federal labor law on several fronts. The Supreme Court originally left the matter to Congress to settle. When Congress failed to settle the questions, the Court began to state its determinations of the intent of Congress. By the decision above, it appears that a state may not regulate the collective bargaining process and the ultimately negotiated contract by regulating on matters of local concern including hiring discrimination, safety, hours and wages, and restraint of trade.

---

### Quicknotes

**ANTITRUST LAW** Body of federal law prohibiting business conduct that constitutes a restraint on trade.

**COLLECTIVE BARGAINING** Negotiations between an employer and employee that are mediated by a specified third party.

# Metropolitan Life Ins. Co. v. Commonwealth of Massachusetts

Insurance company (D) v. State (P)

471 U.S. 724 (1985).

**NATURE OF CASE:** Action to compel compliance with state law.

**FACT SUMMARY:** Massachusetts (P) sought to force Metropolitan Life Ins. Co. (D) and other insurance companies to comply with a state law providing for certain mandated benefits to any state resident insured under certain types of policies.

## 🏛 RULE OF LAW
Although Massachusetts' mandated benefit law does affect terms of employment, it does not limit the rights of self-organization or collective bargaining protected by federal law and is not preempted by federal labor law.

**FACTS:** Metropolitan Life Ins. Co. (Metropolitan) (D) was among many insurance companies that issued group-health policies providing hospital and surgical coverage to employers or unions having employees or members residing in Massachusetts (P). A Massachusetts (P) mandatory benefit law provided that any resident insured under a general insurance policy, accident or sickness insurance policy, or an employee heath-care plan covering hospital and surgical expenses had to be provided with specified minimum mental healthcare benefits. Massachusetts (P) brought an action to enforce the law, which Metropolitan (D) claimed covered a mandatory subject of bargaining under the NLRA and was thus preempted by such. The state courts held the law was not preempted.

**ISSUE:** Is Massachusetts' mandated benefit law preempted by federal labor law?

**HOLDING AND DECISION:** (Blackmun, J.) No. Federal labor law does not preempt the Massachusetts mandated benefit law. Mandated benefit laws do not seek to discourage or encourage employees in the promotion of their interest collectively. They are, instead, designed in part to give specific minimum protections to individual workers. It simply would not make sense to interpret federal law as requiring that workers who have chosen to join a union be penalized by preventing them from benefiting from state labor regulations imposing minimal standards on nonunion employers. Federal labor law supplements state law where, as in this case, they are compatible. It supplants state law only when state law prevents the accomplishment of the purposes of the federal act.

## ▶ ANALYSIS

Many traditional state regulations have been unsuccessfully challenged as being preempted by federal labor law. They include laws mandating employer contributions to unemployment and workmen's compensation funds, fixing mandatory state holidays, and requiring payment to employees for time spent at the polls or on jury duty.

■■■

## Quicknotes

**COLLECTIVE BARGAINING** Negotiations between an employer and employee that are mediated by a specified third party.

**NLRA (NATIONAL LABOR RELATIONS ACT)** Guarantees employees the right to engage in collective bargaining, and regulates labor unions.

**PREEMPTION** Judicial preference recognizing the procedure of federal legislation over state legislation of the same subject matter.

■■■

# Belknap, Inc. v. Hale

## Employer (D) v. Employees (P)

463 U.S. 491 (1983).

**NATURE OF CASE:** Appeal of a damage award for misrepresentation and breach of contract.

**FACT SUMMARY:** After promising workers hired during a strike that they were permanent replacements, Belknap, Inc. (D) fired them and reinstated the strikers as part of a settlement with the union.

## 🏛 RULE OF LAW
State law causes of action are not preempted by the NLRA if they concern activities of substantial state interest or were not purposely left unregulated by Congress.

**FACTS:** Belknap, Inc. (D) hired Hale (P) and others specifically promising them several times that they were permanent replacements for striking workers. During the economic strike, Belknap (D) unilaterally gave a wage increase and the union brought an unfair labor practice charge. Before the hearing, a settlement was reached calling for the reinstatement of the strikers, and Belknap (D) thereafter fired the replacements. Hale (P) brought suit in state court for breach of contract and misrepresentation and the jury awarded damages. The court of appeals rejected Belknap's (D) argument that the actions were preempted by the NLRA and affirmed the award. Belknap (D) appealed.

**ISSUE:** Are state law causes of action preempted by the NLRA if they concern activities of substantial state interest or which were not purposely left unregulated by Congress?

**HOLDING AND DECISION:** (White, J.) No. State law causes of action are not preempted by the NLRA if they concern activities of substantial state interest or which were not purposely left unregulated by Congress. In enacting the NLRA, Congress did not intend to allow employers to make unenforceable, misleading promises in order to gain bargaining advantages over striking workers. The restriction on this power caused by conditioning offers of employment to replacements on settlements which may require dismissal does not override the injury to innocent third parties who detrimentally rely on misleading offers. Further, if as in this case, the strike is adjudicated an unfair labor practice strike, the focus in the litigation would be on the strikers' rights rather than on the replacements' rights as would be the focus in the state cause of action. Therefore, the controversy presented to the NLRB would differ from that presented to the state court, and thus the state causes of action do not infringe on the NLRB's jurisdiction. Accordingly, the actions are not preempted. Affirmed.

**DISSENT:** (Brennan, J.) Subjecting employers to state law causes of action arising from settlement of labor disputes exposes them to competing state and federal regulation. The breach of contract action is preempted because if the strike is based on an unfair labor practice, federal law requires dismissal of the workers regardless of state law. The misrepresentation action is preempted because the threat of such suit inhibits an employer from using the bargaining weapon of permanent replacement granted him by federal law.

## ▶ ANALYSIS

It has been argued that allowing permanent replacements to be hired violates the NLRA as it discriminates in regard to hiring and retention on the basis of union activities. Also both the NLRA and the NLRB's interpretation thereof have traditionally treated unfair labor practice-based strikers better than economic strikers because unfair labor practices are peacefully resolved under the procedures of the Act while no such guarantee exists in economic disputes.

■=■

## Quicknotes

**BREACH OF CONTRACT** Unlawful failure by a party to perform its obligations pursuant to contract.

**MISREPRESENTATION** A statement or conduct by one party to another that constitutes a false representation of fact.

**NLRA (NATIONAL LABOR RELATIONS ACT)** Guarantees employees the right to engage in collective bargaining, and regulates labor unions.

**NLRB (NATIONAL LABOR RELATIONS BOARD)** An agency established pursuant to the National Labor Relations Act for the purpose of prohibiting unfair labor practices by employers and unions.

**PREEMPTION** Judicial preference recognizing the procedure of federal legislation over state legislation of the same subject matter.

■=■

# Lingle v. Norge Div. of Magic Chef, Inc.

## Employee (P) v. Employer (D)

486 U.S. 399 (1988).

**NATURE OF CASE:** Appeal from dismissal of retaliatory discharge action.

**FACT SUMMARY:** The court of appeals held that Lingle's (P) suit for retaliatory discharge was preempted by the procedures for grievance outlined in the collective bargaining agreement.

## 🏛 RULE OF LAW
State law causes of action are not preempted by a collective bargaining agreement unless their resolution necessarily requires an interpretation of the agreement.

**FACTS:** Lingle (P) was discharged for filing a false worker's compensation claim. She brought a state law action for retaliatory discharge against her employer Norge (D), which removed the action to federal court. Norge (D) then successfully moved to dismiss on the basis such suit was preempted by the arbitration clause of the collective bargaining agreement. The court of appeals affirmed, and the Supreme Court granted review.

**ISSUE:** Are state law causes of action preempted by collective bargaining agreements only where their resolution requires an interpretation of the agreement?

**HOLDING AND DECISION:** (Stevens, J.) Yes. State law causes of action are not preempted by collective bargaining agreement unless their resolution depends upon an interpretation of the agreement. Although an analysis of the same facts and application of the same legal standards would occur, there is no need to interpret the agreement to determine whether Lingle (P) was the victim of retaliatory discharge. Substantive rights may be adjudicated in the labor context without interpreting the collective bargaining agreement, and such has been recognized for some time. Reversed.

## ▶ ANALYSIS

Courts tend to lean over backwards to induce parties to arbitrate disputes. However, there are certain basic rights which must be allowed a judicial forum. The conflict between national labor policy, including the promotion of the integrity of collective bargaining agreements, and the rationale behind the worker's compensation system was clearly presented in this case. The right of the worker to apply for worker's compensation benefits was found, at least in this case, to override the strong pro-arbitration policy usually applied.

## Quicknotes

**PREEMPTION** Judicial preference recognizing the procedure of federal legislation over state legislation of the same subject matter.

**RETALIATORY DISCHARGE** The firing of an employee in retribution for an act committed against the employer's interests.

# The Individual and the Union

## Quick Reference Rules of Law

# Air Line Pilots Ass'n, Intern. v. O'Neill

Union (D) v. Pilots (P)

499 U.S. 65 (1991).

**NATURE OF CASE:** Appeal of reversal of summary judgment denying damages for breach of duty of adequate representation.

**FACT SUMMARY:** A class of pilots (P), including O'Neill (P), sued their union, the Air Line Pilots Association (ALPA) (D), claiming ALPA (D) settled a strike on terms worse than surrender.

## 🏛 RULE OF LAW
A union's duty of fair representation extends to contract negotiation, but a bargaining agreement is in breach of duty only if it is discriminatory, reached in bad faith, or irrational or arbitrary.

**FACTS:** Continental Airlines' pilots bid on new assignments whenever positions became vacant. Bids were accepted on a seniority basis. A strike against Continental by pilots represented by the Air Line Pilots Association (ALPA) (D) lasted two years. Continental kept operating by using non-striking pilots, replacements, and pilots who returned to work during the strike. Continental was set to accept bids for 441 future positions (the "85-5 bid"), and chose to accept bids from working pilots only. Fearing striking pilots would be shut out, ALPA (D) intensified negotiations and reached a settlement with Continental. Striking pilots desiring reinstatement would have low priority for the 85-5 bid but would regain seniority for future bids. A group of striking pilots (P) sued ALPA (D) for breach of its duty of fair representation, claiming that had they voluntarily returned to work without an agreement, Continental would have respected their priorities on the 85-5 bids. Thus, the terms of settlement were worse than terms of surrender. ALPA (D) argued that a union has no enforceable duty of adequate representation, that the duty of fair representation requires only that it act in good faith and in a nondiscriminatory manner. ALPA (D) argued that *Vaca v. Sipes*, 386 U.S. 171 (1967), the case which defined a union's duty as having three components—nondiscrimination, good faith, and nonarbitrary conduct—did not apply to contract negotiation. The district court dismissed on summary judgment. The court of appeals reversed. It applied *Vaca*, then held that a finding that the deal struck by ALPA (D) was worse than terms of surrender could alone support a judgment that ALPA (D) had acted arbitrarily and breached its duty. ALPA (D) appealed.

**ISSUE:** Does a union breach its duty of fair representation by making an unfavorable bargaining agreement which is not discriminatory, not reached in bad faith, and not irrational or arbitrary?

**HOLDING AND DECISION:** (Stevens, J.) No. A union's duty of fair representation extends to contract negotiation, but a bargaining agreement is in breach of duty only if it is discriminatory, reached in bad faith, or irrational or arbitrary. The cases which have found a union duty not to act arbitrarily involved contract administration and enforcement, but *Vaca's* tripartite standard also applies to contract negotiation. However, Congress intended judicial review of union performance to be highly deferential, recognizing the wide latitude union negotiators need to carry out their duties and the strong policy favoring peaceful settlement of labor disputes. Therefore, a court may not find a settlement arbitrary simply because it proves unfavorable to labor; to be a breach of duty the agreement must be so far outside a wide range of reasonableness as to be wholly irrational or arbitrary. A settlement is not irrational just because in retrospect it turns out to be bad. Here, viewed in light of the legal setting at the time of settlement and Continental's determined resistance to ALPA (D), it was not irrational for ALPA (D) to decide that the settlement it reached was better than surrender. Reversed and remanded.

## ▶ ANALYSIS

In *Wooddell v. International Brotherhood of Electrical Workers, Local 71*, 112 S. Ct. 494 (1992), the plaintiff sued his local for a violation of the parent union's constitution. The Court held that a union's constitution is a contract between the parent and its locals and, as a result, the plaintiff could sue the local under § 301 as a third-party beneficiary of the contract.

### Quicknotes

**THIRD-PARTY BENEFICIARY** A party who benefits from a promise made pursuant to a contract although he is not a party to the agreement.

# Vaca v. Sipes

Parties not identified.

386 U.S. 171 (1967).

**NATURE OF CASE:** Action by union member in state court alleging union had breached its duty of fair representation.

**FACT SUMMARY:** Owens (P), who had been discharged for medical reasons, sued the Union (D) in state court when the Union (D), after processing his grievance, concluded that Owens's (P) claim lacked merit and refused to take the matter to arbitration.

## 🏛 RULE OF LAW

Although a union's breach of its duty of fair representation constitutes an unfair labor practice, a state court is not thereby preempted of its jurisdiction over a union member's actions for damages where the member alleges that his union has failed to provide him with fair representation by inadequately processing his grievance.

**FACTS:** Owens (P), a long-time high blood pressure patient, returned from a half-year sick leave to resume his heavy work in a meat packing plant. The company physician disagreed with Owens's (P) doctor that he was fit to work and Owens (P) was permanently discharged. Owens's (P) Union (D) then processed a grievance through to the fourth step, just short of arbitration, as established by a collective bargaining agreement. Finally, in order to "get some better medical evidence so that we could go to arbitration," the Union (D), at its own expense, sent Owens (P) to a new doctor. The medical examination failed to support Owens's (P) position. Thereafter, the Union's (D) executive board voted not to take the grievance to arbitration. Owens (P) rejected the Union's (D) suggestion that he accept the company's offer of referral to a rehabilitation center and insisted on arbitration. When the Union (D) stood by its refusal, Owens (P) brought a class action, pursuant to § 301 of the Labor Management Relation Act (LMRA), in a Missouri state court against the officers and representatives of the Union (D), alleging that the Union (D) had "arbitrarily and capriciously" failed to take his case to arbitration. Owens (P) received a jury damage award. On appeal, the Union (D) argued that since the NLRB, in *Miranda Fuel Co.*, 140 NLRB 181 (1962), had decided that a union's breach of its statutory duty of fair representation violates § 8(b) of the NLRA, the state trial court lacked jurisdiction. The Missouri Supreme Court affirmed, holding that it had jurisdiction and that the dispositive question of the issue of liability was whether the evidence supported Owens's (P) assertion that he had been wrongfully discharged by the company, regardless of the Union's (D) good faith in reaching a contrary conclusion. The Union (D) appealed.

**ISSUE:** Does the NLRB's authority to hear complaints that arguably involve a union's breach of its duty of fair representation preempt state court jurisdiction over a union member's suit alleging that his union failed to fully process his grievance against the employer?

**HOLDING AND DECISION:** (White, J.) No. The preemption doctrine, as recognized in *Garmon* has never been rigidly applied to cases where it could fairly be inferred that Congress intended exclusive jurisdiction to lie with the NLRB. A primary justification for the doctrine, the desire not to develop conflicting rules of substantive labor relations law and to leave such developments to the administrative agency entrusted by Congress, is not applicable to cases involving alleged breaches of the union's duty of fair representation. Federal courts have long adopted the doctrine. Furthermore, determinations in these actions frequently require review of the substantive positions taken and policies pursued by a union in its contract negotiations and handling of the grievance machinery. These are not normally matters within the Board's unfair labor practice jurisdiction. Moreover, the concern of the Board is more with promoting industrial peace and the improvement of working conditions; the individual is necessarily submerged in the interests of the collective body. Finally, since an employee who alleges that his employer has violated a collective bargaining agreement may also present evidence that his union has failed to press his grievance, there is no reason why the employee cannot, in a § 301 action, sue the union directly. However, while the Missouri courts did have jurisdiction over this suit, they erred in applying the proper standard for resolving the Union's (D) duty. A breach of the statutory duty of fair representation occurs only when a union's conduct toward a member of the collective bargaining unit is arbitrary, discriminatory, or in bad faith. While a union may not arbitrarily ignore a meritorious grievance or process it in perfunctory fashion, the individual employee does not have an absolute right to have his grievance taken to arbitration regardless of the governing contract provisions. Otherwise, the union's incentive to settle grievances short of arbitration would be seriously reduced. Here, as a matter of law, the evidence does not support a verdict that the Union (D) breached its duty of fair representation. The Union (D) processed the grievance into the fourth step, attempted to gather sufficient evidence to prove Owens's (P) case, attempted to secure for Owens (P) less vigorous work at the plant, and joined in the employer's efforts to have Owens (P) rehabilitated. Only when all these efforts proved unsuccessful did the Union (D) conclude that arbitration

*Continued on next page.*

was fruitless. The Union (D) clearly acted in good faith. Reversed.

**CONCURRENCE:** (Fortas, J.) A complaint by an employee that the union has breached its duty of fair representation is subject to the exclusive jurisdiction of the NLRB. Owens (P) might have maintained a § 301 action against his employer for wrongful discharge from employment. Such an action would have clearly been, as Congress intended by enacting § 301, one to enforce a collective bargaining agreement. However, since it may be the employer who has breached the contract, the union cannot be required to pay damages. The appropriate remedy, if required, is arbitration which the Board has the authority to order. Finally, the standard of "arbitrary or bad faith conduct" involves nuances of union-employee relationships—delicate matters for the Board alone to decide.

**DISSENT:** (Black, J.) This decision, while giving the worker an ephemeral right to sue his union for breach of its duty of fair representation, creates insurmountable obstacles to block his far more valuable right to sue his employer for breach of the collective bargaining agreement. "[I]f, as the court goes on to hold, the employee cannot sue his employer for breach of contract unless his failure to exhaust contractual remedies is due to the union's breach of its duty of fair representation, then I am quite unwilling to say that the union's refusal to exhaust such remedies—however nonarbitrary—does not amount to a breach of its duty. Either the employee should be able to sue his employer for breach of contract after having attempted to exhaust his contractual remedies, or the union should have an absolute duty to exhaust contractual remedies on his behalf. The merits of an employee's grievance would thus be determined by either a jury or an arbitrator. Under today's decision, it will never be determined by either."

> ▌ *ANALYSIS*

NLRA § 9(a) provides that an individual employee may deal directly with his employer in adjusting grievances so long as such dealings are not in conflict with the collective bargaining agreement and the union is afforded the opportunity to be present at the employee-employer meeting.

■=■

## Quicknotes

**ARBITRATION** An agreement to have a dispute heard and decided by a neutral third party, rather than through legal proceedings.

**BREACH OF CONTRACT** Unlawful failure by a party to perform its obligations pursuant to contract.

**NLRA (NATIONAL LABOR RELATIONS ACT)** Guarantees employees the right to engage in collective bargaining, and regulates labor unions.

**NLRB (NATIONAL LABOR RELATIONS BOARD)** An agency established pursuant to the National Labor Relations Act

for the purpose of prohibiting unfair labor practices by employers and unions.

**WRONGFUL DISCHARGE** Unlawful termination of an individual's employment.

■=■

# Bowen v. United States Postal Service

## Employee (P) v. Employer (D)

459 U.S. 212 (1983).

**NATURE OF CASE:** Appeal of a damage award for breach of fair representation.

**FACT SUMMARY:** Bowen (P) was discharged by the United States Postal Service's (D) in violation of the collective bargaining agreement, yet the Union (D) refused to process Bowen's (P) grievance.

---

🏛 **RULE OF LAW**
A union may be held liable for damages caused by the breach of its duty of fair representation.

---

**FACTS:** The district court held that damages caused by the United States Postal Service's (Service) (D) discharge of Bowen (P) without cause and in violation of the collective bargaining agreement were increased by the Union's (D) refusal to process Bowen's (P) grievance, thereby breaching its duty of fair representation. It then allocated the total damages, back pay and benefits between the Service (D) and the Union (D). The court of appeals affirmed the award against the Service (D), but held that even though the Union (D) had breached its duty, it could not be held liable in damages. It thereby awarded Bowen (P) damages only in the amount chargeable to the Service (D) before a hypothetical date on which the dispute would have been resolved had the Union (D) not breached its duty. Bowen (P) appealed.

**ISSUE:** May a union be held liable in damages caused by the breach of its duty of fair representation?

**HOLDING AND DECISION:** (Powell, J.) Yes. A union may be held liable for damages caused by the breach of its duty of fair representation. The efficacy of the grievance procedure depends upon the union processing meritorious claims, not only to protect its membership, but to put employers on notice. It would be unjust to penalize the employer with damages caused by the union's breach of this responsibility. Therefore, the employer's liability for backpay when he has unlawfully discharged an employee should end on the date the dispute would have been resolved had the union not breached its duty of fair representation. Because the employee has a right to be made whole, the union must be held liable for damages beyond that hypothetical date. Imposing this liability provides greater incentives to unions to administer the grievance procedure to the benefit of all. Reversed and remanded.

**CONCURRENCE AND DISSENT:** (White, J.) Because union liability for damages compromises the interests of all members for the reimbursement of one, unions should be held liable only when the employer cannot pay the full damage award and the union is secondarily liable, or when the union affirmatively induces the employer's initial breach. In all other cases, traditional contract law requires the employer be held liable for all damages caused by his breach regardless of the union's contributing factor. Further, the Court's opinion holding the union liable for back pay accrued beyond the hypothetical date of resolution, exposes the union to potentially greater liability than the employer who caused the dispute because the damages will continue to accrue until final resolution, which may be excessively delayed. For these reasons, the court of appeals must be affirmed.

---

▶ **ANALYSIS**

In this case, the Court relies heavily on its decision in *Vaca v. Sipes*, 386 U.S. 171 (1967), the holding of which had been inconsistently interpreted by several courts of appeals, and this case is decided by a 5-4 majority evidencing the continued vagueness of the validity of holding unions liable in damages for breaches of the duty of fair representation. It is clear, however, that some sanction must apply to ensure the proper administration of the system of grievance resolution as this is fundamental to the policies of American labor law, while on the other hand, the individual member cannot be allowed to compromise the interests of all other members.

---

## Quicknotes

**BREACH OF CONTRACT** Unlawful failure by a party to perform its obligations pursuant to contract.

# NLRB v. General Motors Corp.

### Labor board (P) v. Employer (D)

373 U.S. 734 (1963).

**NATURE OF CASE:** Appeal by NLRB from refusal of court of appeals to enforce its finding of an employer unfair labor practice.

**FACT SUMMARY:** General Motors Corp. (D) refused to bargain with the union over the latter's proposal of an agency shop arrangement on the ground that acceding to such an agreement would constitute an unfair labor practice.

### 🏛 RULE OF LAW

The "agency shop" (under which, as a condition of employment, all employees who decline to join a union must nevertheless pay initiation fees and dues) is not an unfair labor practice.

**FACTS:** Section 8(a)(3) of the NLRA provides that it is an unfair labor practice for an employer "by discrimination in regard to hire or tenure of employment or any term or condition of employment, to encourage or discourage membership in any labor organization." A proviso to § 8(e) declares: "That nothing in this act . . . or in any other statute of the United States, shall preclude an employer from making an agreement with a labor organization . . . to require as a condition of employment membership therein, if such labor organization is the representative of the employees as provided in § 9(a). "The Taft-Hartley Act amended § 8(a)(3) by outlawing the "closed shop" (where membership in a union is required prior to hiring), and providing that expulsion from a union cannot be a ground of compulsory discharge if the worker is not delinquent in paying his initiation fees or dues. The Indiana "fight-to-work" law prohibited making union membership a condition of employment. Indiana courts held that an "agency shop" arrangement (under which all employees are required as a condition of employment to pay dues to the union and pay the union's initiation fee, but are not required to actually become union members) would not violate the state right-to-work law. The union, which had a collective bargaining agreement providing for maintenance of membership and the union shop with General Motors Corp. (D) at the latter's plant in Indiana, proposed an agency shop arrangement. Pursuant to this proposal, employees who refused to join the union would still be obligated, as a condition of employment, to pay initiation fees and dues. Such employees would not be entitled to attend union meetings, vote at meetings, or otherwise have a voice in the internal affairs of the union, but would be eligible to receive union benefits. General Motors (D), contending that the arrangement would violate the NLRA, refused to bargain with the union over its proposal. The NLRB (P) held that General Motors'

(D) refusal to bargain constituted an unfair labor practice under § 8(a)(5). When the court of appeals refused to enforce its order, the Board (P) appealed.

**ISSUE:** Is an agency shop an unfair labor practice?

**HOLDING AND DECISION:** (White, J.) No. The Taft-Hartley amendment to § 8(a)(3) was intended only to remedy the most serious abuses of compulsory union membership. As far as federal law is concerned, employers and unions could, by voluntary agreements, promote stability by eliminating "free riders." Certainly, if Congress saw fit to authorize a closed or union shop, it also intended to preserve the status of less vigorous, less compulsory contracts, such as agency shop agreements, which demand less adherence to the union. The new proviso to § 8(a)(3) prevents only utilization of union security agreements for any purpose other than to compel payment of union dues and fees. Thus, Congress recognized the validity of unions' concern about employees who receive the benefits of union representation but are unwilling to contribute their fair share of financial support to such union, and gave the unions the power to contract to meet the problem while withholding from unions the power to cause the discharge of employees for any other reason. In the present case, the agency shop proposal, by placing the option of membership in the employee while still requiring the same monetary support as does a union shop, serves, rather than violates, the desire of Congress to reduce the evils of compulsory unionism while allowing financial support for the bargaining agent. Accordingly, General Motors (D) was not excused from its duty to bargain over the proposal on the theory that its acceding to it would necessarily involve it in an unfair labor practice. Reversed and remanded.

### ▶ ANALYSIS

The original proviso to § 8(a)(3) legitimated not only union shop agreements (under which an employee must join the union within 30 days after securing employment so long as the union is the majority bargaining agent) but maintenance-of-membership clauses as well. Pursuant to this type of agreement, an employee is not required to join the union. However, existing members can renounce their membership only within a specified period after the collective bargaining agreement takes effect. New members who join the union are obligated to remain members in the union for the entire duration of the agreement.

■▬■

*Continued on next page.*

## *Quicknotes*

**NLRA (NATIONAL LABOR RELATIONS ACT)** Guarantees employees the right to engage in collective bargaining, and regulates labor unions.

**NLRB (NATIONAL LABOR RELATIONS BOARD)** An agency established pursuant to the National Labor Relations Act for the purpose of prohibiting unfair labor practices by employers and unions.

**TAFT-HARTLEY ACT** An amendment to the National Labor Relations Act, imposing limitations on unions and safeguarding the rights of employers.

■══■

# International Association of Machinists v. Street

## Union (D) v. Employees (P)

367 U.S. 740 (1961).

**NATURE OF CASE:** Action against union by its employees.

**FACT SUMMARY:** Various union members charged that their dues were being used to finance the campaigns of candidates they did not support and to express views which they were against.

## 🏛 RULE OF LAW
A union may be restrained from using dues, collected from nonunion members in a union shop, to express unpopular views or to support political candidates.

**FACTS:** Under the authority of § 2, Eleventh of the Railway Labor Act, a union was assigned as exclusive bargaining agent of all members of the class, even if the employees were not union members and were not eligible for membership. To prevent "free riders," these employees were required to pay union dues and assessments. Street (P) and other nonunion employees objected to the way in which their dues were being used. It was alleged that the funds were being expended to back political candidates and to express opinions of which these employees disapproved. Street (P) brought an action alleging that the Act was unconstitutional.

**ISSUE:** May unions use the funds received from nonunion members to back candidates and to express opinions which are opposed by such nonmembers?

**HOLDING AND DECISION:** (Brennan, J.) No. Congress could declare that interstate carrier employees must all be represented by unions which would act as exclusive bargaining agents for each class of employees. This was within Congress's Commerce Clause powers to reduce labor strife. Congress could also validly require dues to be paid by all employees receiving the benefit of such representation even if they were not union members. Congress, however, never intended that these funds be used, over the dissent of nonmembers, to finance political candidates or to express views contrary to those held by such nonmembers. Use of such funds for impermissible purposes does not render the Act unconstitutional. It merely means that where violations have occurred, an injunction or other remedial measures must be sought. The obligation to continue to pay dues is not suspended. Street (P) should seek injunctive relief preventing such expenditures. Reversed and remanded.

**CONCURRENCE:** (Douglas, J.) If an association is competent, the individual should not be forced to surrender any matters of conscience or be required to finance the promotion of causes with which he disagrees.

**DISSENT:** (Black, J.) When federal law requires that union dues are mandatory from nonmembers, the union may not engage in such conduct which would infringe on the First Amendment rights of dissenters. This injects federal compulsion into the political and ideological process. Dues should be exacted for no more than the cost of defraying actual representation expenses.

**DISSENT:** (Frankfurter, J.) Neither the text, the context, the history nor the purpose of the legislation under review admits of the restrictive interpretation advanced by the majority. Congress designed a scheme whereby the cost of securing benefits of union exertions would be equitably shared. Union members who object to the expenditure of union funds for political objectives with which they disagree are free to express themselves and should not be permitted to erroneously advance a free speech argument to bar railway unions under a union-shop agreement from expending funds in their traditional manner.

## ▶ ANALYSIS

The remedial problems in *Street* were clarified in *Railway Clerks v. Allen*, 373 U.S. 1 13 (1963). The union was deemed responsible for establishing the proportion of political to total union expenditures. If there were fluctuations in political expenditures, the union would have to seek modification of the decree. Refunds and/or reductions in future union exactions were found to be beyond the scope of *Street*.

---

## Quicknotes

**FIRST AMENDMENT** Prohibits Congress from enacting any law respecting an establishment of religion, prohibiting the free exercise of religion, abridging freedom of speech or the press, the right of peaceful assembly and the right to petition for a redress of grievances.

**INJUNCTION** A court order requiring a person to do or prohibiting that person from doing a specific act.

---

# Marquez v. Screen Actors Guild, Inc.

Employee (P) v. Labor union (D)

525 U.S. 33 (1998).

**NATURE OF CASE:** Appeal from judgment for defendant in employee suit against a union.

**FACT SUMMARY:** Marquez (P) alleged that her union, the Screen Actors Guild (SAG) (D), had breached its duty to her by negotiating a misleading union security clause in its agreement with employers.

## 🏛 RULE OF LAW
A union breaches its duty of fair representation when its conduct toward a member of the bargaining unit was arbitrary, discriminatory, or in bad faith.

**FACTS:** A film production company had signed a collective bargaining agreement with the Screen Actors Guild (SAG) (D), making SAG (D) the exclusive bargaining agent for the performers the company hired for its productions. This agreement contained a standard union security clause, providing that any performer who worked under the agreement must be a member in good standing of the union. Marquez (P), a part-time actress who had been hired for a one-line role in an episode of a television series, failed to pay the required union fees by the day before her part was to be filmed, and another actress was hired to fill the part. Marquez (P) sued, alleging that the union breached its duty of fair representation when it negotiated a union security clause inconsistent with the statute, and that the 30-day grace period provision of the union security clause was misleading, since a new grace period should be required for each employment relationship. The court of appeals rejected Marquez's (P) argument that the union had breached its duty of fair representation, and refused to exercise jurisdiction over Marquez's (P) challenge to the 30-day grace period requirement, since the NLRB had jurisdiction over such claims. Marquez (P) appealed. The Supreme Court granted certiorari.

**ISSUE:** Does a union breach its duty of fair representation when its conduct toward a member of the bargaining unit was arbitrary, discriminatory, or in bad faith?

**HOLDING AND DECISION:** (O'Connor, J.) Yes. A union breaches its duty of fair representation when its conduct toward a member of the bargaining unit was arbitrary, discriminatory, or in bad faith. Marquez (P) did not claim that SAG's (D) negotiations of the union security clause were discriminatory. A union's conduct can be classified as arbitrary only when it is irrational. SAG's (D) negotiation of a union security clause with language derived from the NLRA authorizing such a clause is far from arbitrary. It is difficult to conclude that a union acts in bad faith by notifying workers of their rights through more

effective means of communication. The union's conduct in negotiating a union security clause that tracked the statutory language cannot be said to have been either arbitrary or in bad faith. Affirmed.

**CONCURRENCE:** (Kennedy, J.) The negotiation of a security clause containing language requiring membership, without further definition, does not necessarily, or in all circumstances, violate the union's duty of fair representation. Affirmed.

## ▶ ANALYSIS

The dissent explained that there was no basis in the court's holding in this case for an inference that inclusion of the statutory language was somehow a defense to allegations of violation of the fair-representation duty. In cases alleging such a violation where facts in addition to the bare language of the contract have been adduced to show the violation, inclusion of such language would not be a valid defense. A security clause requiring membership in a union has been interpreted to mean only that a member must pay union dues necessary to support the union's activities as the employee's exclusive bargaining representative.

■=■

## Quicknotes

**BREACH** The violation of an obligation imposed pursuant to contract or law, by acting or failing to act.

**NLRA (NATIONAL LABOR RELATIONS ACT)** Guarantees employees the right to engage in collective bargaining, and regulates labor unions.

**NLRB (NATIONAL LABOR RELATIONS BOARD)** An agency established pursuant to the National Labor Relations Act for the purpose of prohibiting unfair labor practices by employers and unions.

■=■

# Local 357, International Bhd. of Teamsters v. NLRB

Union (D) v. Labor board (P)

365 U.S. 667 (1961).

**NATURE OF CASE:** Appeal from an NLRB finding of violations of NLRA §§ 8(a)(1) and (3) and 8(b)(2) and (1)(A).

**FACT SUMMARY:** An employer, upon complaint of Local 357 (D), fired an employee who failed to get his job through the union hiring hall as required by the collective bargaining agreement.

> 🏛 **RULE OF LAW**
> The only encouragement or discouragement of labor union membership that is unlawful is that which is accomplished by means of discrimination.

**FACTS:** Local 357 (D) executed a collective bargaining agreement with the California Trucking Association which provided in regards to the hiring of casual or temporary workers that they be hired on a seniority basis (most senior first) irrespective of whether the worker was a member of the union or not. It was also agreed that to find workers, employers would call Local 357 (D) or a dispatching hall designated by it, but if no workers were available, the employer could go to any other source. Slater, who ordinarily sought work through the hiring hall, circumvented the hall by getting a casual job with an employer, who had signed the union contract, without being dispatched by the hall. Slater was fired when Local 357 (D) complained to the employer. The NLRB (P) found the hiring hall illegal per se even though there was to be no discrimination and that Slater's discharge was a § 8(b)(2), (a)(1), and (a)(3) violation by the employer and a § 8(b)(2) and (b)(1)(A) violation by Local 357 (D). The court of appeals affirmed with slight modification, and this appeal followed.

**ISSUE:** Is the only encouragement or discouragement of labor union membership which is unlawful that which is accomplished by means of discrimination?

**HOLDING AND DECISION:** (Douglas, J.) Yes. Hiring halls are not necessarily illegal. An employer can contract with a union to act in the capacity of an employment agency. An employer should not be able to bind himself to reject nonunion men nor contract to accept men on a rotary-hiring basis. Thus, while hiring halls are not necessarily illegal, certain acts under them which have the effect of creating a closed shop are illegal. Section 8(a)(3) makes it an unfair labor practice for an employer to encourage or discourage union membership by discrimination. Not all encouragement of discouragement of labor union membership is unlawful; only that accomplished by means of discrimination. The test is the "true purpose" or "real motive" in hiring or firing. The NLRB (P) may infer

discrimination by drawing on its experience in factual inquiries. Discrimination cannot be inferred from the instrument's face when it specifically provides for no discrimination against casual employees because of the presence or absence of union membership. So when an employer and union enforce the agreement against union members, the court cannot say without more that either discriminates within the intent of the Act. Nothing can be inferred from the hiring hall provision except that the employer and Local 357 (D) sought casual employees through the hiring hall and required union members of which Slater was one to adhere to that system. Reversed.

**CONCURRENCE:** (Harlan, J.) "I think it was in the realm of board expertise to say that the natural and foreseeable effect of this clause is to make employees and job applicants think that union status will be favored."

**DISSENT IN PART:** (Clark, J.) Without the safeguards at issue, a contract conditioning employment solely upon union referral encourages membership in the union by that very distinction.

> ▶ **ANALYSIS**

A union using a hiring hall acts as a job referral service directing employees to employers who are offering employment. They are used most often in maritime, longshoring, and construction which typically have irregular and temporary employment opportunities. The hiring hall is paid for out of union dues with generally no cost to the employer. The arrangement is a tempting one for union officials to discriminate in favor of union members. The key issue in such cases is whether the hiring hall arrangement, as written or as practiced, works a union-induced discrimination which encourages union membership.

---

## Quicknotes

**DISCRIMINATION** Unequal treatment of a class of persons.

**NLRA (NATIONAL LABOR RELATIONS ACT)** Guarantees employees the right to engage in collective bargaining, and regulates labor unions.

**NLRB (NATIONAL LABOR RELATIONS BOARD)** An agency established pursuant to the National Labor Relations Act for the purpose of prohibiting unfair labor practices by employers and unions.

# Local 900, International Union of Electrical Workers v. NLRB (Gulton Electro-Voice, Inc.)

## Union (P) v. Labor board (D)

727 F.2d 1184 (D.C. Cir. 1984).

**NATURE OF CASE:** Cross-petitions relating to an order of the NLRB.

**FACT SUMMARY:** Local 900 (P) sought reversal of an NLRB (D) order which struck down a contract clause granting superseniority with regard to layoff and recall to the union's Financial Secretary and Recording Secretary.

### 🏛 RULE OF LAW
Superseniority with regard to layoff and recall is lawful only when extended to union officials who are involved in on-the-job contract administration, such as grievance processing.

**FACTS:** The NLRB (D) overruled prior precedent when it held invalid a contract clause granting superseniority with regard to layoff and recall to Local 900's (P) Financial Secretary and Recording Secretary. In its decision, the NLRB (D) held such superseniority is lawful only when extended to union officers who are involved in on-the-job contract administration, such as grievance processing. Neither official involved could satisfy that criteria. While the NLRB (D) sought to have its order enforced, Local 900 (P) petitioned for its reversal.

**ISSUE:** Is superseniority with regard to layoff and recall lawful only when extended to union officials who are involved in on-the-job contract administration?

**HOLDING AND DECISION:** (McGowan, J.) Yes. Since it is reasonable and supported by the record, the decision of the NLRB (D) must stand, and the principle under which it was rendered is recognized as controlling. Superseniority with regard to layoff and recall is lawful only when extended to union officers who are involved in on-the-job contract administration, such as grievance processing. Granting such superseniority to officers who are not so engaged would run counter to federal labor law. It would encourage union activism and discriminate with respect to on-the-job benefits against employees who prefer to refrain from union activity. Yet, it furthers a principle of federal labor law to encourage the continued presence of officers who are involved in contract administration because it fosters the effective administration of bargaining agreements on the plant level. Thus, the principle adopted by the NLRB (D) must be respected and its order enforced.

## ▶ ANALYSIS

Many cases challenging the granting of special employment benefits to union officials have generated vehement arguments that union members who vote for a contract granting such benefits have waived their right not to have their level of participation in union affairs subject to such influence. It has yet to work, as the courts have held such rights are not waivable.

◼══◼

## Quicknotes

**CONTRACT** An agreement pursuant to which a party agrees to act, or to forbear from acting, in exchange for performance on the part of the other party.

**NLRB (NATIONAL LABOR RELATIONS BOARD)** An agency established pursuant to the National Labor Relations Act for the purpose of prohibiting unfair labor practices by employers and unions.

◼══◼

# NLRB v. Allis-Chalmers Mfg. Co.

## Labor board (D) v. Employer (P)

388 U.S. 175 (1967).

**NATURE OF CASE:** Appeal from reversal of finding of NLRA § 8(b)(1)(A) violation.

**FACT SUMMARY:** Allis-Chalmers Mfg. Co. (P) filed unfair labor practice charges alleging that the United Auto Workers violated § 8(b)(1)(A) by fining the members who crossed picket lines and continued to work during a strike against it.

## 🏛 RULE OF LAW
It is not violative of §§ 7 and 8(b)(1)(A) for a union to fine its members for breaking a strike and to enforce the fine by obtaining a judgment in court in the amount of the fine.

**FACTS:** During a lawful strike by the United Auto Workers (UAW) against Allis-Chalmers Mfg. Co. (P), certain union members crossed picket lines and continued to work. After the strike was over, the union brought disciplinary proceedings against those members who broke the strike and fined those members from $20 to $100 a piece. Some of the fined members did not pay the fines, and the UAW obtained a judgment in the amount of the fine against one of its members in a test suit. Allis-Chalmers (P) filed unfair labor practice charges alleging a § 8(b)(1)(A) violation. The NLRB (D) dismissed the complaint. The Seventh Circuit set aside the NLRB (D) order holding that under a literal reading of §§ 7 and 8(b)(1)(A) a union member who crossed picket lines would be exercising his § 7 rights to refrain from participating in a particular concerted activity, and union fines disciplining for so refraining would therefore, "restrain or coerce" in violation of § 8(b)(1)(A). The NLRB (D) appealed.

**ISSUE:** Is it violative of §§ 7 and 8(b)(1)(A) for a union to fine its members for breaking a strike and to enforce the fine by obtaining a judgment in court in the amount of the fine?

**HOLDING AND DECISION:** (Brennan, J.) No. It is not violative of §§ 7 and 8(b)(1)(A) for a union to fine its members for breaking a strike and to enforce the fine by obtaining a judgment in court in the amount of the fine. Integral to federal labor policy has been the power of the union to protect against erosion of its status under that policy through reasonable discipline of members who violate rules and regulations governing membership. The legislative history of § 8(b)(1)(A) contains no reference to the application of its prohibitions to traditional internal union discipline in general or disciplinary fines in particular. Rather, sponsors assumed that the section was not meant to regulate union internal affairs. Section 8(b)(1) states that

nothing shall impair the right of the union to prescribe its own rules with respect to membership. It is not enough to say that § 8(b)(1)(A) allows a union to expel an offending member. Where the union is strong, it would be unreasonable to expel when a fine would be appropriate. Where the union is weak, a union might have to condone offensive conduct rather than suffer the loss of a needed member. Reversed.

**DISSENT:** (Black, J.) The real reason for the Court's opinion is its policy decision that unions, in particular weak ones, need the power that the majority has approved. It does not follow that seeking outside assistance in the courts can be within "internal union discipline." While it is proper to consult the legislative history, the Court cannot ignore the plain meaning of the section.

## ▶ ANALYSIS

The Court noted that it was suggested that reading § 8(b)(1) to allow court enforcement of fines would add a "new weapon to the union's economic arsenal" and would be inconsistent with the mood of Congress to curtail union powers. The Court eliminates the real question, not whether Congress gave to unions a new power, but whether it eliminated, without debate, a power which the unions already possessed. As for reasonableness of union fines of its members, there is no requirement that the amount of the fines be reasonable. See *NLRB v. Boeing*, 412 U.S. 67 (1973).

■=■

## Quicknotes

**JUDGMENT** A determination of the rights between the parties by a court having jurisdiction over the matter.

**NLRA (NATIONAL LABOR RELATIONS ACT)** Guarantees employees the right to engage in collective bargaining, and regulates labor unions.

**NLRB (NATIONAL LABOR RELATIONS BOARD)** An agency established pursuant to the National Labor Relations Act for the purpose of prohibiting unfair labor practices by employers and unions.

■=■

# Scofield v. NLRB

Employees (P) v. Labor board (D)

394 U.S. 423 (1969).

**NATURE OF CASE:** Appeal from NLRB finding of no violation of NLRA § 8(b)(1)(A).

**FACT SUMMARY:** Scofield (P) and other employees contended that a union rule prohibiting employees from earning more than a certain wage per day on a piecework basis violated § 8(b)(1)(A).

🏛 **RULE OF LAW**
Section 8(b)(1) allows a union to enforce a properly adopted rule which reflects a legitimate union interest, impairs no policy Congress has imbedded in the labor laws, and is reasonably enforced against union members who are free to leave the union and escape the rule.

**FACTS:** The employer paid workers on a piecework basis. As part of the collective bargaining agreement, it was agreed that there would be a ceiling on the amount of piecework pay that could be earned in a day. Any excess earnings were to be held by the employer who would pay out of the fund to employees on days when the ceiling was not reached for some reason. Employees could demand to be paid above the ceiling limit for days on which they exceeded it and the employer would pay it, but the union could fine employees who made such a demand. Scofield (P) and certain other employees, who were fined $100 and suspended from the union for demanding pay above the limit, argued that such a union rule violated § 8(b)(1)(A). The NLRB (D) and court of appeals denied their claim and they appealed.

**ISSUE:** Does § 8(b)(1) allow a union to enforce a properly adopted rule which reflects a legitimate union interest, impairs no policy Congress has imbedded in the labor laws, and is reasonably enforced against union members who are free to leave the union and escape the rule?

**HOLDING AND DECISION:** (White, J.) Yes. If a rule invades or frustrates an overriding policy of the labor laws, the rule may not be enforced, even by fine or expulsion, without violating § 8(b)(1). That section leaves a union free to enforce a properly adopted rule which reflects a legitimate union interest, impairs no congressional labor policy, and is reasonably enforced against union members who are free to quit the union. Here, as there was no showing of unreasonable fares or that union membership was involuntary, only the legitimacy of the union's interest in its rule need be considered. The union's interest appeared to be legitimate. The union sought to reduce competitive pressure amongst the employees. Also, the ceiling played an important role in negotiating the minimum hourly rate. It

helped to serve the economic interests of the whole. In light of this and the acceptable manner in which the rule was enforced, vindicating a legitimate union interest, the rule did not violate the Act. Affirmed.

▶ **ANALYSIS**

Note, that such a rule as that employed above cannot be enforced by the employer. It is simply a matter of internal union discipline. The NLRB is not to judge the fairness or wisdom of particular union rules, but only whether they violated an overriding policy of the labor laws. A wage ceiling does not impede collective bargaining as long as it is an issue open to collective bargaining at contract renewal time. Nor do wage ceilings comprise featherbedding (§ 8[b][6]) because all work done is paid for; pay is not given for no work in return.

■■■

## Quicknotes

**NLRA (NATIONAL LABOR RELATIONS ACT)** Guarantees employees the right to engage in collective bargaining, and regulates labor unions.

**NLRB (NATIONAL LABOR RELATIONS BOARD)** An agency established pursuant to the National Labor Relations Act for the purpose of prohibiting unfair labor practices by employers and unions.

■■■

# Pattern Makers' League of North America v. NLRB

Union (D) v. Labor Board (P)

473 U.S. 95 (1985).

**NATURE OF CASE:** Review of an NLRB order.

**FACT SUMMARY:** The NLRB (P) found that the Pattern Makers' League of North America (D) violated federal labor law by fining 10 union members who resigned in violation of a provision in the union's constitution.

🏛 **RULE OF LAW**
Federal labor law is violated when a union fines or otherwise punishes employees who resign from the union in contravention of the union's constitution.

**FACTS:** A provision in the constitution of the Pattern Makers' League of North America (League) (D) prohibited resignations during a strike or when a strike was imminent. Ten members of the League (D) resigned during a strike and returned to work, whereupon they were fined by the League (D). The NLRB (P) held that imposition of the fines violated the NLRA. The Seventh Circuit Court of Appeals enforced the NLRB's (P) order. The Supreme Court granted certiorari to resolve a conflict in the appellate courts over the validity of restrictions on union members' right to resign.

**ISSUE:** Does federal labor law prohibit a union from imposing punishment upon a member for resigning from the union when resignations are prohibited by the union's constitution?

**HOLDING AND DECISION:** (Powell, J.) Yes. The NLRA may reasonably be construed as prohibiting a union from fining or otherwise punishing members for attempting to resign from the union when resignations are prohibited by the union's constitution. While federal labor law recognizes the unions' rights to prescribe rules respecting the acquisition or retention of membership, it does not allow unions to make rules restricting the right to resign or punishing members not free to resign. The Board's (P) decision is thus entitled to deference. Affirmed.

**DISSENT:** (Blackmun, J.) A union member should have to live up to his promise not to resign.

▶ *ANALYSIS*

Section 101(a)(5) of the Landrum-Griffin Act imposes on unions the obligation of providing a "full and fair hearing" before a member can be "fined, suspended, expelled, or otherwise disciplined" by the union or its officers. In addition, § 609 prohibits taking such actions against a member for exercising any rights provided him under the Act.

*Quicknotes*

**NLRA (NATIONAL LABOR RELATIONS ACT)** Guarantees employees the right to engage in collective bargaining, and regulates labor unions.

**NLRB (NATIONAL LABOR RELATIONS BOARD)** An agency established pursuant to the National Labor Relations Act for the purpose of prohibiting unfair labor practices by employers and unions.

# Glossary

*Common Latin Words and Phrases Encountered in the Law*

**A FORTIORI:** Because one fact exists or has been proven, therefore a second fact that is related to the first fact must also exist.

**A PRIORI:** From the cause to the effect. A term of logic used to denote that when one generally accepted truth is shown to be a cause, another particular effect must necessarily follow.

**AB INITIO:** From the beginning; a condition which has existed throughout, as in a marriage which was void ab initio.

**ACTUS REUS:** The wrongful act; in criminal law, such action sufficient to trigger criminal liability.

**AD VALOREM:** According to value; an ad valorem tax is imposed upon an item located within the taxing jurisdiction calculated by the value of such item.

**AMICUS CURIAE:** Friend of the court. Its most common usage takes the form of an amicus curiae brief, filed by a person who is not a party to an action but is nonetheless allowed to offer an argument supporting his legal interests.

**ARGUENDO:** In arguing. A statement, possibly hypothetical, made for the purpose of argument, is one made arguendo.

**BILL QUIA TIMET:** A bill to quiet title (establish ownership) to real property.

**BONA FIDE:** True, honest, or genuine. May refer to a person's legal position based on good faith or lacking notice of fraud (such as a bona fide purchaser for value) or to the authenticity of a particular document (such as a bona fide last will and testament).

**CAUSA MORTIS:** With approaching death in mind. A gift causa mortis is a gift given by a party who feels certain that death is imminent.

**CAVEAT EMPTOR:** Let the buyer beware. This maxim is reflected in the rule of law that a buyer purchases at his own risk because it is his responsibility to examine, judge, test, and otherwise inspect what he is buying.

**CERTIORARI:** A writ of review. Petitions for review of a case by the United States Supreme Court are most often done by means of a writ of certiorari.

**CONTRA:** On the other hand. Opposite. Contrary to.

**CORAM NOBIS:** Before us; writs of error directed to the court that originally rendered the judgment.

**CORAM VOBIS:** Before you; writs of error directed by an appellate court to a lower court to correct a factual error.

**CORPUS DELICTI:** The body of the crime; the requisite elements of a crime amounting to objective proof that a crime has been committed.

**CUM TESTAMENTO ANNEXO, ADMINISTRATOR (ADMINISTRATOR C.T.A.):** With will annexed; an administrator c.t.a. settles an estate pursuant to a will in which he is not appointed.

**DE BONIS NON, ADMINISTRATOR (ADMINISTRATOR D.B.N.):** Of goods not administered; an administrator d.b.n. settles a partially settled estate.

**DE FACTO:** In fact; in reality; actually. Existing in fact but not officially approved or engendered.

**DE JURE:** By right; lawful. Describes a condition that is legitimate "as a matter of law," in contrast to the term "de facto," which connotes something existing in fact but not legally sanctioned or authorized. For example, de facto segregation refers to segregation brought about by housing patterns, etc., whereas de jure segregation refers to segregation created by law.

**DE MINIMIS:** Of minimal importance; insignificant; a trifle; not worth bothering about.

**DE NOVO:** Anew; a second time; afresh. A trial de novo is a new trial held at the appellate level as if the case originated there and the trial at a lower level had not taken place.

**DICTA:** Generally used as an abbreviated form of obiter dicta, a term describing those portions of a judicial opinion incidental or not necessary to resolution of the specific question before the court. Such nonessential statements and remarks are not considered to be binding precedent.

**DUCES TECUM:** Refers to a particular type of writ or subpoena requesting a party or organization to produce certain documents in their possession.

**EN BANC:** Full bench. Where a court sits with all justices present rather than the usual quorum.

**EX PARTE:** For one side or one party only. An ex parte proceeding is one undertaken for the benefit of only one party, without notice to, or an appearance by, an adverse party.

**EX POST FACTO:** After the fact. An ex post facto law is a law that retroactively changes the consequences of a prior act.

**EX REL.:** Abbreviated form of the term "ex relatione," meaning upon relation or information. When the state brings an action in which it has no interest against an individual at the instigation of one who has a private interest in the matter.

**FORUM NON CONVENIENS:** Inconvenient forum. Although a court may have jurisdiction over the case, the action should be tried in a more conveniently located court, one to which parties and witnesses may more easily travel, for example.

**GUARDIAN AD LITEM:** A guardian of an infant as to litigation, appointed to represent the infant and pursue his/her rights.

**HABEAS CORPUS:** You have the body. The modern writ of habeas corpus is a writ directing that a person (body) being detained (such as a prisoner) be brought before the court so that the legality of his detention can be judicially ascertained.

**IN CAMERA:** In private, in chambers. When a hearing is held before a judge in his chambers or when all spectators are excluded from the courtroom.

**IN FORMA PAUPERIS:** In the manner of a pauper. A party who proceeds in forma pauperis because of his poverty is one who is allowed to bring suit without liability for costs.

**INFRA:** Below, under. A word referring the reader to a later part of a book. (The opposite of supra.)

**IN LOCO PARENTIS:** In the place of a parent.

**IN PARI DELICTO:** Equally wrong; a court of equity will not grant requested relief to an applicant who is in pari delicto, or as much at fault in the transactions giving rise to the controversy as is the opponent of the applicant.

**IN PARI MATERIA:** On like subject matter or upon the same matter. Statutes relating to the same person or things are said to be in pari materia. It is a general rule of statutory construction that such statutes should be construed together, i.e., looked at as if they together constituted one law.

**IN PERSONAM:** Against the person. Jurisdiction over the person of an individual.

**IN RE:** In the matter of. Used to designate a proceeding involving an estate or other property.

**IN REM:** A term that signifies an action against the res, or thing. An action in rem is basically one that is taken directly against property, as distinguished from an action in personam, i.e., against the person.

**INTER ALIA:** Among other things. Used to show that the whole of a statement, pleading, list, statute, etc., has not been set forth in its entirety.

**INTER PARTES:** Between the parties. May refer to contracts, conveyances or other transactions having legal significance.

**INTER VIVOS:** Between the living. An inter vivos gift is a gift made by a living grantor, as distinguished from bequests contained in a will, which pass upon the death of the testator.

**IPSO FACTO:** By the mere fact itself.

**JUS:** Law or the entire body of law.

**LEX LOCI:** The law of the place; the notion that the rights of parties to a legal proceeding are governed by the law of the place where those rights arose.

**MALUM IN SE:** Evil or wrong in and of itself; inherently wrong. This term describes an act that is wrong by its very nature, as opposed to one which would not be wrong but for the fact that there is a specific legal prohibition against it (malum prohibitum).

**MALUM PROHIBITUM:** Wrong because prohibited, but not inherently evil. Used to describe something that is wrong because it is expressly forbidden by law but that is not in and of itself evil, e.g., speeding.

**MANDAMUS:** We command. A writ directing an official to take a certain action.

**MENS REA:** A guilty mind; a criminal intent. A term used to signify the mental state that accompanies a crime or other prohibited act. Some crimes require only a general mens rea (general intent to do the prohibited act), but others, like assault with intent to murder, require the existence of a specific mens rea.

**MODUS OPERANDI:** Method of operating; generally refers to the manner or style of a criminal in committing crimes, admissible in appropriate cases as evidence of the identity of a defendant.

**NEXUS:** A connection to.

**NISI PRIUS:** A court of first impression. A nisi prius court is one where issues of fact are tried before a judge or jury.

**N.O.V. (NON OBSTANTE VEREDICTO):** Notwithstanding the verdict. A judgment n.o.v. is a judgment given in favor of one party despite the fact that a verdict was returned in favor of the other party, the justification being that the verdict either had no reasonable support in fact or was contrary to law.

**NUNC PRO TUNC:** Now for then. This phrase refers to actions that may be taken and will then have full retroactive effect.

**PENDENTE LITE:** Pending the suit; pending litigation under way.

**PER CAPITA:** By head; beneficiaries of an estate, if they take in equal shares, take per capita.

**PER CURIAM:** By the court; signifies an opinion ostensibly written "by the whole court" and with no identified author.

**PER SE:** By itself, in itself; inherently.

**PER STIRPES:** By representation. Used primarily in the law of wills to describe the method of distribution where a person, generally because of death, is unable to take that which is left to him by the will of another, and therefore his heirs divide such property between them rather than take under the will individually.

**PRIMA FACIE:** On its face, at first sight. A prima facie case is one that is sufficient on its face, meaning that the evidence supporting it is adequate to establish the case until contradicted or overcome by other evidence.

**PRO TANTO:** For so much; as far as it goes. Often used in eminent domain cases when a property owner receives partial payment for his land without prejudice to his right to bring suit for the full amount he claims his land to be worth.

**QUANTUM MERUIT:** As much as he deserves. Refers to recovery based on the doctrine of unjust enrichment in those cases in which a party has rendered valuable services or furnished materials that were accepted and enjoyed by another under circumstances that would reasonably notify the recipient that the rendering party expected to be paid. In essence, the law implies a contract to pay the reasonable value of the services or materials furnished.

**QUASI:** Almost like; as if; nearly. This term is essentially used to signify that one subject or thing is almost analogous to another but that material differences between them do exist. For example, a quasi-criminal proceeding is one that is not strictly criminal but shares enough of the same characteristics to require some of the same safeguards (e.g., procedural due process must be followed in a parole hearing).

**QUID PRO QUO:** Something for something. In contract law, the consideration, something of value, passed between the parties to render the contract binding.

**RES GESTAE:** Things done; in evidence law, this principle justifies the admission of a statement that would otherwise be hearsay when it is made so closely to the event in question as to be said to be a part of it, or with such spontaneity as not to have the possibility of falsehood.

**RES IPSA LOQUITUR:** The thing speaks for itself. This doctrine gives rise to a rebuttable presumption of negligence when the instrumentality causing the injury was within the exclusive control of the defendant, and the injury was one that does not normally occur unless a person has been negligent.

**RES JUDICATA:** A matter adjudged. Doctrine which provides that once a court of competent jurisdiction has rendered a final judgment or decree on the merits, that judgment or decree is conclusive upon the parties to the case and prevents them from engaging in any other litigation on the points and issues determined therein.

**RESPONDEAT SUPERIOR:** Let the master reply. This doctrine holds the master liable for the wrongful acts of his servant (or the principal for his agent) in those cases in which the servant (or agent) was acting within the scope of his authority at the time of the injury.

**STARE DECISIS:** To stand by or adhere to that which has been decided. The common law doctrine of stare decisis attempts to give security and certainty to the law by following the policy that once a principle of law as applicable to a certain set of facts has been set forth in a decision, it forms a precedent which will subsequently be followed, even though a different decision might be made were it the first time the question had arisen. Of course, stare decisis is not an inviolable principle and is departed from in instances where there is good cause (e.g., considerations of public policy led the Supreme Court to disregard prior decisions sanctioning segregation).

**SUPRA:** Above. A word referring a reader to an earlier part of a book.

**ULTRA VIRES:** Beyond the power. This phrase is most commonly used to refer to actions taken by a corporation that are beyond the power or legal authority of the corporation.

## Addendum of French Derivatives

**IN PAIS:** Not pursuant to legal proceedings.

**CHATTEL:** Tangible personal property.

**CY PRES:** Doctrine permitting courts to apply trust funds to purposes not expressed in the trust but necessary to carry out the settlor's intent.

**PER AUTRE VIE:** For another's life; during another's life. In property law, an estate may be granted that will terminate upon the death of someone other than the grantee.

**PROFIT A PRENDRE:** A license to remove minerals or other produce from land.

**VOIR DIRE:** Process of questioning jurors as to their predispositions about the case or parties to a proceeding in order to identify those jurors displaying bias or prejudice.

# Casenote® Legal Briefs